SLEEP CHEAP
IN NEW YORK

by Lisa Mullenneaux

THE PENINGTON PRESS

Copyright © 2002 by Lisa Mullenneaux

All rights reserved. No part of this book may be reproduced or
transmitted in any form or by any means, electronic or mechanical,
including photocopying, recording, or by any information storage
and retrieval system without written permission from the author.
Send requests for permission c/o The Penington Press,
PO Box 829, NY, NY 10009-9998.

The publisher does not assume and hereby disclaims any liability
to any party for any loss or damage resulting from errors or
omissions in this publication, whether errors or omissions result from
negligence, accident, or any other cause.

"New York, New York" by Betty Comden, Adolph Green and
Leonard Bernstein © 1945 Warner Bros. Inc. (Renewed). All Rights Reserved.
Used by permission of Warner Bros. Publications U.S., Inc., Miami, FL 33014.

"The Quotable New York," William Rossa Cole, editor,
© 1992, used by permission of The Pushcart Press.

"Minor Characters" reprinted by permission of the author and
the Irene Skolnick Literary Agency. Copyright Joyce Johnson,
1983, 1994. First published by Houghton Mifflin in 1983.
Published by Penguin Books 1999.

Cover illustration by Angela C. Park
Graphic design by Angela C. Park

ISBN: 0-9704296-2-2
Library of Congress Card Number: 2001091224

TO ORDER COPIES, CALL 1 800-431-1579

CONTENTS

INTRODUCTION 1

MANHATTAN
- LOWER MANHATTAN 12
- GREENWICH VILLAGE 24
- GRAMERCY PARK 46
- CHELSEA/FLATIRON 66
- MURRAY HILL 90
- MIDTOWN WEST 108
- MIDTOWN EAST 180
- UPPER WEST SIDE 188
- UPPER EAST SIDE 226
- MORNINGSIDE HEIGHTS 232
- HARLEM 242

THE OUTER BOROUGHS
- THE BRONX 254
- BROOKLYN 257
- QUEENS 266
- STATEN ISLAND 287

B & B AND APARTMENT AGENCIES 295

HOTEL RESERVATION SERVICES 299

INDEXES
- ALPHABETICAL 304
- BY TYPE OF LODGING AND VALUE RATING 307

INTRODUCTION

> *"New York, New York, a helluva town,*
> *The Bronx is up but the Battery's down,*
> *And people ride in a hole in the ground."*
> —On the Town, *musical comedy*

New York *is* a hell of a town, consistently rated the top destination choice for millions of vacationers and conventioners. The tragedy of September 11, 2001, gives us even more reason to take advantage of the city's attractions, clean streets, and low crime. Frankly, it needs our support. New York has survived plagues, fires, blackouts, riots, and paralyzing blizzards and emerged with a civic pride more buoyant than ever. Come feel the spirit.

But come prepared. We want to spread the good word: you don't have to be a pasha to enjoy the best and brightest of New York's parade of lights. You do have to be well informed. In this case, knowledge is not only power; it's money in your pocket.

Until *Sleep Cheap in New York*, the biggest challenge to budget travelers was the high cost of hotels. Those of us who live in Manhattan have ways to find cheap lodging, those "small wonders" that get advertised by word of mouth. Residents tend to know the hotel industry's pricing patterns, an old hotel's current reputation, or a new "hot property." But that doesn't help the outlanders, whose long-awaited vacation feels like a fleecing.

Several years ago, a couple we know took their three children to the Big Apple for four days. It was a first for the kids, so their parents spared no expense and took in all the sights. Unaware of discounted theater tickets, affordable restaurants, and hotels with family suites or quads, they paid far more than they should have. The result? They won't be able to afford another such gambit for five years.

This book is designed to make lodging more affordable for tourists like our friends' family. After all, this is "the city that never sleeps." New York City offers every variety of accommodation: bed-and-breakfast inns, hostels, short- and long-term residences, and boutique hotels. (Each category is defined later in this chapter under "Lodging Categories.") The truth is many of them advertise abroad because Americans expect comforts and services that international travelers do not. If a turn-of-the-century building with small rooms and shared baths scares you, choose the more traditional chain hotels—Best Western, Howard Johnson, or Comfort Inn. Of course, you will pay more for their comforts and services. Bottom line: the more flexible you can be, the more lodging options you'll have.

Discounted rates are increasingly available on the internet, either on the hotel's own website, which offers "internet-only specials," or through a hotel reservations service, like www.quikbook.com or www.hoteldiscount.com. These companies allow you to enter your target city, arrival date, and price range and search their databases. You can then choose from a list of available rooms and book a reservation with your credit card. Your room reservation will be confirmed by email. Be sure to shop around. We found a wide variation in price for the same hotel on the same date. (So what else is new?)

Frankly, we're proud of the pavement we've pounded, down the alleys and up the avenues, the walk-ups we've scaled, the light switches that failed, the little gems we discovered in neighborhoods we thought we knew. It all adds up to a bargain-hunter's bonanza for those who want to brag to their neighbors in Peoria that they paid $99 for cheap sleeps in one of the costliest hotel cities in the world. Is there a clean, safe, and inexpensive place to lay your head in bed? Rest assured.

INTRODUCTION

FIRST, SOME GROUND RULES

TRADING UP: Always try to get the most desirable room at the best price. That means interviewing and negotiating with reservations. Do any rooms have a view? Can you get extra value, like a mini-fridge or kitchenette, at no extra cost? Would you prefer a king-sized bed to two doubles? It never hurts to ask.

GET IT IN WRITING: Ask the hotel to confirm the features and price of the room you are reserving.

PRICING: Published (or "rack") rates are almost always meaningless. All hotel managers admit that prices are adjusted daily based on supply and demand. Demand is lowest in January and February, begins to build during the summer—with a slight dip in July and August—and is greatest from fall through the end of the year. Demand is always high during holidays. Supply is also affected if large conventions or special events like the New York Marathon are happening in the city. You can usually assume that if one hotel is pricing high, they all will be. Book as far ahead as possible so you can stay at the hotel of your choice and not on a park bench.

HOTEL TAXES: Remember to include the 13.25 percent state and city taxes (plus a $2-per-night occupancy charge). It means that a $105 quoted rate is really $120.91.

PHONE CHARGES: Always ask about the hotel's telephone charge policy. Forewarned is forearmed. On average, local calls are $1 for the first three minutes and about 20 cents thereafter. Some hotels will charge you even if you call toll-free numbers or use your own calling card. Consider buying a phone card, which most hotels sell in their gift stores.

STREET NOISE: In a busy neighborhood, top floors and off-street rooms in a mid-block hotel will always be more peaceful than front rooms on lower floors of a hotel on the avenue. Newer and renovated hotels may have windows that are double-paned (or double-glazed) to shield out street noise.

CONSTRUCTION NOISE: New budget hotels are popping up all over town and older hotels are renovating. Ask about construction noise (usually a problem only during weekdays from 8 to 5). It can be disruptive, but it can also be a lever to increase your bargaining power.

ROOM INSPECTION: Check out your room before you accept it. Many of the rooms we visited did not pass the sniff test, even by minimal standards. Some smelled of cigarette smoke, some of chemicals, some of cleaning solvent, some of mold. Reserve the option of switching before you unpack and settle in.

PARKING: Most hotels in Manhattan don't own garages and will offer what they call "discounted rates" at garages nearby. But a hotel with a 24-hour rate of $25 is not doing you a favor. The average midtown parking rate is about $18. We define "parking" as a free service to hotel guests.

CONCIERGE: A staff member whose sole function is to give you information about and/or arrange city activities for you. A concierge is not front desk staff.

SECURITY GUARD: Someone hired to guard security and not the bellman doing double duty.

STREET SMARTS

Streets below Houston, especially those below Canal Street, resemble the dirt paths they were when lower Manhattan was Dutch farmland. They tend to be narrow and twisting, not north-south, east-west. But in 1807, engineer John Randal, Jr., devised a grid system for the rest of Manhattan, from Houston north to 155th Street. It's been a blessing for city navigators ever since. With the exception of Broadway, streets and avenues are laid out in a north-south, east-west pattern. Fifth Avenue is the dividing line between east-west streets, which tend to be one-way. Even-numbered streets tend to be eastbound, odd-numbered streets to be westbound. Avenues are also one-way, alternatively northbound and southbound. Major thoroughfares–Canal, Houston, 14th, 23rd, 34th, 42nd, 57th, 72nd, 79th, 86th, 96th, 110th, and 125th–are two-way.

Central Park stretches north from 59th Street to 110th Street. Everything east of the park is called the Upper East Side, west of the park the Upper West Side. Unlike midtown, which is largely commercial, the Upper East and West sides are largely residential.

LODGING CATEGORIES

BUDGET HOTEL: For the purposes of this book, a budget hotel is defined as a hotel whose lowest room rate is no more than $150. On that basis, many fine properties did not qualify, and they are listed in other guidebooks.

FULL SERVICES HOTEL: A hotel that offers several hundred guest rooms and a variety of on-site services, including restaurants, exercise equipment, conference rooms, and a concierge. This is a good choice for business travelers and groups that need meeting space.

LIMITED SERVICES HOTEL: A hotel with usually under 200 rooms and sufficient in-room amenities. Guest services are limited, and there is rarely a restaurant or bar. Private bathrooms are standard. A good choice for leisure travelers and some business travelers.

MOTEL: A limited services hotel that caters to motorists and offers free parking.

EURO-STYLE HOTEL: Typically a brownstone with less than 100 small guest rooms that share bathrooms. There are minimal in-room amenities and no guest services.

BOUTIQUE HOTEL: The hottest trend in New York's hotel market. Sixty-four percent of all new rooms in 2001 were in boutique properties. These small-scale hotels in newly renovated older buildings emphasize quirky character and modern design often at the expense of space.

BED-AND-BREAKFAST INN: An owner-operated lodging that offers several rooms. Either a full or continental breakfast is included in the rate as are taxes. A B&B can be very pricey due to its historic nature and period furnishings. Many residents offer rooms in their apartments through agencies. While "technically" B&Bs, they are listed separately under B&B Agencies.

GUEST HOUSE: A residential dwelling that offers a limited number of rooms. The proprietor usually does not live there, and a manager may be in charge. This is a good choice for independent travelers, who can fend for themselves.

BARE ESSENTIALS HOTEL: Offers about 100 rooms, often with shared bath, and emphasizes economy. A luggage room and vending machines may be its only services. A good choice for low-maintenance travelers.

HOSTEL: Rooms are usually shared, though some hostels also offer private rooms. Shared rooms (dorms) are equipped with bunk beds and can be same-sex or coed. Communal kitchens are common, but ask if towels and bedding are provided. Devotees usually carry *The Hostel Handbook* in their backpacks.

RESIDENCE: Low-cost housing for long-term guests is often run by nonprofit religious groups or charities, like the Catholic Church, Society of Friends, or the Salvation Army. Very often, they can accommodate overnight guests as well. Rent usually includes breakfast and dinner. The building may be residential, like a brownstone with patio gardens, or institutional, like the 92nd street YM-YWHA.

UNIVERSITY HOUSING: Some schools open their dormitories to visitors, especially during the summer.

INTRODUCTION

Facilities will be clean and safe, but you may have to share a bathroom.

YMCA: A nonprofit organization that offers several hundred private rooms in an institutional setting. Some rooms share baths, and there are lots of guest services.

FORMAT OF THIS BOOK

Evaluations were prepared after two visits to each hotel. The first unannounced visit allowed us to see staff interacting with their clientele and access to standard rooms that any guest would see. A second visit and tour with the hotel manager allowed us to complete a detailed checklist and ask specific questions. After site inspections, we rated each hotel on four criteria:

1-VALUE How is this property priced compared to similar properties? Hostels are compared with hostels, Euro-style hotels to other Euro-style hotels, chains to chains, and to other properties in the same neighborhood.

2-CLEANLINESS means the condition of the physical structure as well as guest rooms and public space.

3-GUEST SERVICES All such services are designed for a guest's convenience. Some are enhancements, like a fitness center or concierge. Others—like coin-operated washers and dryers, free breakfast or parking, and mini-fridges—can really save you money.

4-SECURITY Are room keys numbered or are they plastic computerized cards? Are there security guards on duty or just a bellman who doubles as a bouncer? Are there video monitors on all floors or just the lobby? Are front doors locked at night?

Each property is assigned a ranking from five stars (excellent) to one star (poor).

RATES: All rates show a range from the least-expensive to the most-expensive room. The lowest may only be available during January and February, but all rates fluctuate. Refer to the previous section "Pricing."

PLEASE NOTE: *The information listed in this book was current as of press time. Because of the changeable nature of this information, we strongly recommend that readers check with each hotel before making a reservation.*

ACKNOWLEDGMENTS

NYC & Company, the fancy name for New York's convention and visitor's bureau, was a primary inspiration for this project because of its consistent efforts to publicize information about affordable lodging in its publications and on its website, www.nycvisit.com. Staff members Arleen Kropf and Maricella Herzog were especially generous and efficient in sharing their knowledge and resources. Many hotel managers set aside time to show us rooms and describe their properties; those who did not might want to take a refresher course in Hospitality 101. Photographer Desmond Shaw used a digital camera (his first!) to showcase those properties to best advantage. Designer Angela C. Park melded his graphic images and our text with her usual wizardry. Finally, *Sleep Cheap in New York* would have, like Sleeping Beauty, remained dormant had it not been for the exhaustive leg work, unflagging enthusiasm, and perceptive writing of Nora D. Wood.

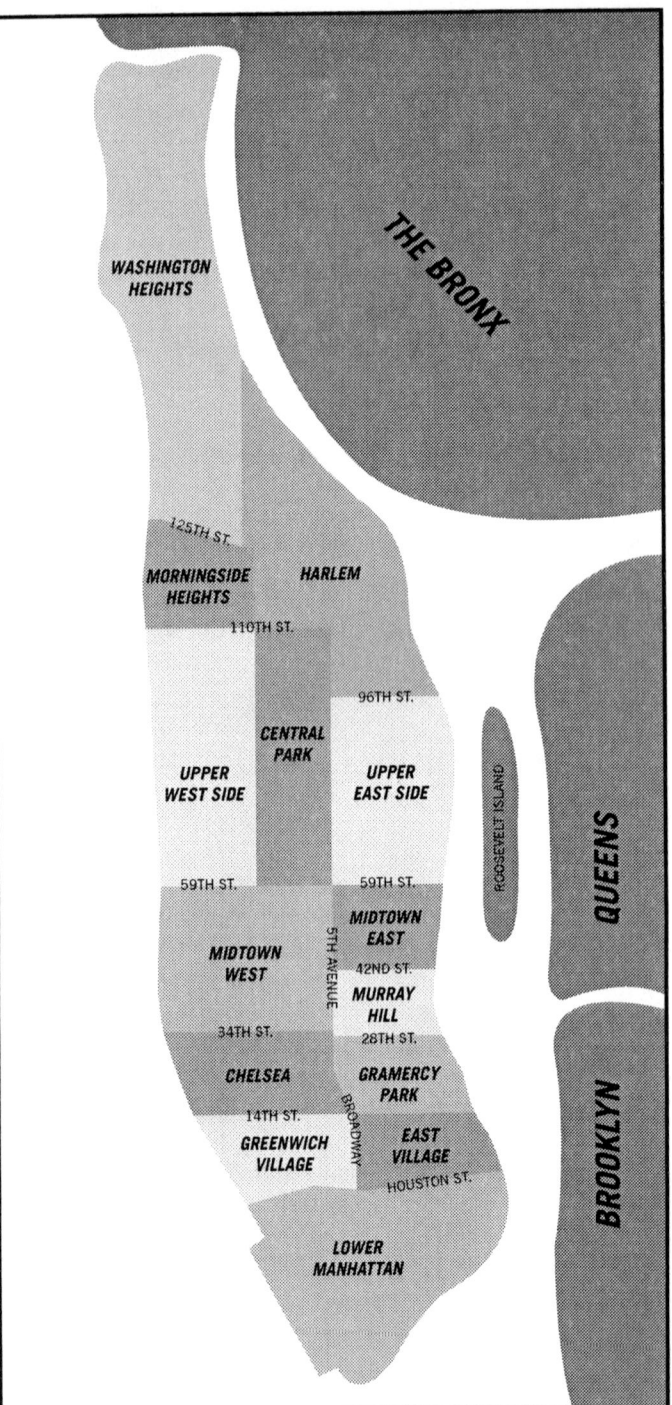

MANHATTAN

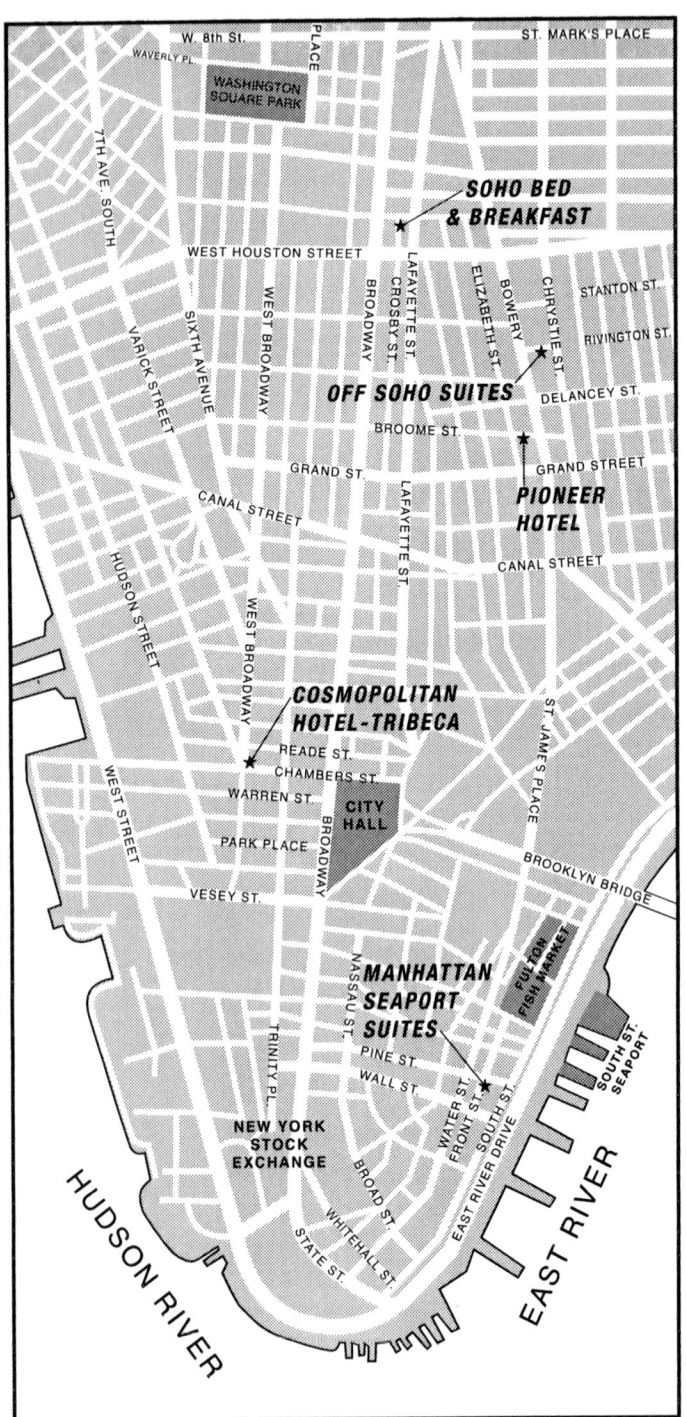

LOWER MANHATTAN

"Every now and then, seeking to rid my mind of thoughts of death and doom, I get up early and go down to Fulton Fish Market."
—Joseph Mitchell

THE NEIGHBORHOODS: Financial District, TriBeCa (Triangle Below Canal Street), Chinatown, SoHo (South of Houston Street), Little Italy, and the Lower East Side.

Manhattan grew from old New Amsterdam, at the island's southern tip, steadily northward. Today, historic sites like Fraunces Tavern (1719), St. Paul's Chapel (1686), and Trinity Church (1846) are dwarfed by the eye-catching skyscrapers of the Financial District. Wheeler-dealers on Wall Street, named for a barrier Dutch settlers built to protect themselves from the British, control the purse strings of the world. On the waterfront, South Street Seaport Museum celebrates the early days of New York Harbor with maritime films, exhibits, and tours of ships like the 1885 schooner *Pioneer*. Battery Park is the departure point for the Statue of Liberty, Ellis Island, and Staten Island.

It's difficult to find affordable hotels in the Financial District, but there are a few attractive options in SoHo, TriBeCa, Chinatown, Little Italy, and the Lower East Side, all distinctly different neighborhoods. North of Houston Street, in Greenwich Village, those options increase.

COSMOPOLITAN HOTEL-TRIBECA

95 W. Broadway
New York, NY 10007
(AT CHAMBERS ST.)

VALUE ★ ★ ★ ★

CLEANLINESS ★ ★ ★ ★

GUEST SERVICES ★

SECURITY ★ ★ ★

(★ POOR - ★ ★ ★ ★ ★ EXCELLENT)

CATEGORY	Limited Services
PHONE	(212) 566-1900
	(888) 895-9400 Reservations
FAX	(212) 566-6909
EMAIL	chnyc95@aol.com
WEBSITE	www.cosmohotel.com
RATES	$109-$159
GUEST ROOMS	113 rooms on 7 floors, all smoking
ROOM AMENITIES	AC, cable TV with HBO, phone with voice mail and dataport, binder of restaurants that deliver
RESTAURANTS	None
BARS	None
CLIENTELE	Mix of business and leisure travelers
GUEST SERVICES	Valet laundry
PARKING	None
CANCELLATION POLICY	24 hours before check-in
WHEELCHAIR ACCESS	None

Renovated in 1995, the Cosmopolitan is one of the few affordable and safe hotels left downtown. The building has been a hotel of some sort since 1850, making it one of the oldest properties in the city. Unfortunately when it was renovated, any historic charm was tossed out with the old wiring and plumbing.

Of decent size, rooms feature either full- or queen-sized beds and an armoire rather than a closet. Some of the rooms offer sofa beds as well. All the accommodations have a desk and voice mail; however, that is the extent of the hotel's business services. Guests enjoy a full array of cable channels, including free HBO, but no pay-per-view movies. The larger than expected bathrooms are one of the hotel's better assets and a welcome change from the usual tiny facilities.

Rates don't vary much on weekends, unlike other downtown properties. The cheapest rooms are minilofts, where guests climb a short flight of stairs to the bed. There are only a few of these $109 units, however, and the standard room with one bed starts at $119. Larger rooms with two beds begin at $149. Security could be improved. No bellman or security guard mans the entrance.

Within a four-block radius there are more than 35 restaurants. Each guest room features a large book of menus from nearby eateries that deliver. The hotel is right across the street from a subway station and the neighborhood is fairly safe. The Cosmopolitan isn't the prettiest hotel in Manhattan, but it's a good choice for budget travelers who insist on a private bathroom.

MANHATTAN SEAPORT SUITES

129 Front St.
New York, NY 10005
(BETWEEN WALL ST. AND MAIDEN LANE)

VALUE ★ ★ ★ ★ (WEEKENDS ONLY)
CLEANLINESS ★ ★ ★ ★
GUEST SERVICES ★ ★ ★
SECURITY ★ ★ ★ ★
(★POOR - ★★★★★EXCELLENT)

CATEGORY	Limited Services
PHONE	(212) 742-0003
	(877) 777-8483 Reservations
FAX	(212) 742-0124
EMAIL	None
WEBSITE	www.manhattanseaport.citysearch.com
	Offers special packages
RATES	Mon-Thurs: $209-$249
	Fri-Sun: $109-$149
GUEST ROOMS	56 rooms on 8 floors, about one-fourth allow smoking

ROOM AMENITIES	AC, cable TV, hair dryer, kitchenettes in suites, safe, phone
RESTAURANTS	None
BARS	None
CLIENTELE	Corporate travelers during the week and leisure crowd on weekends
GUEST SERVICES	Continental breakfast, free day-pass to New York Sports Club, valet laundry
PARKING	None
CANCELLATION POLICY	24 hours before check-in
WHEELCHAIR ACCESS	2 rooms

At the heart of Wall Street's financial action, the Manhattan Seaport Suites is a good deal on weekends and holidays, but not a bargain during the week.

Overall, guest rooms provide more space than the average Manhattan hotel, but this one lacks any charm or ambience. It's in need of sprucing up. All the rooms have light-colored hardwood floors with a throw rug here and there. Mattresses are adequately firm. Even the smallest rooms feature a good-sized bathroom with a vanity shelf and built-in hair dryer. They also offer a decent amount of closet space.

Standard and deluxe rooms come with a mini-fridge. Suites feature kitchenettes with a full-sized refrigerator, small stove, dishwasher, and plenty of plates and silverware. Larger suites can handle small meetings, and two have in-room fax machines. Voice mail is not available, despite brochures to the contrary. Two floors are set aside for smokers. Continental breakfast is served in a drab area sectioned off from the lobby by a large aquarium. A bellman doubles as the security guard.

Wall Street is deserted on weekends and holidays, but the hotel is close to downtown's main attractions, such as the ferries to the Statue of Liberty and Ellis Island. Four subway stations are within a five- to 10-minute walk.

Manhattan Seaport Suites is a real find for travelers who need to be in the city for an extended stay and can overlook tired rooms for prime location and value.

LOWER MANHATTAN

OFF SOHO SUITES

11 Rivington St.
New York, NY 10002
(BETWEEN CHRYSTIE ST. AND BOWERY)

VALUE ★ ★ ★

CLEANLINESS ★ ★ ★ ★ ★

GUEST SERVICES ★ ★ ★

SECURITY ★ ★ ★

(★ POOR - ★ ★ ★ ★ ★ EXCELLENT)

CATEGORY	Euro-style
PHONE	(212) 979-9808 (800) 633-7646 Reservations
FAX	(212) 979-9801
EMAIL	info@offsoho.com
WEBSITE	www.offsoho.com
RATES	Shared bath for 2: $98-$129 Private bath for 2-4: $179-$189
GUEST ROOMS	38 rooms on 6 floors, about one-half smoking, some shared baths
ROOM AMENITIES	AC, cable TV with movie channels, phone with voice mail and dataport, hair dryer, kitchenette, iron and ironing board, clock radio
RESTAURANTS	Yes, breakfast and lunch
BARS	No
CLIENTELE	Primarily European and Asian tourists
GUEST SERVICES	Room service in the morning, small exercise area, small coin-operated laundry
PARKING	None
CANCELLATION POLICY	24 hours before check-in
WHEELCHAIR ACCESS	5 rooms

Why be picky? The Off SoHo Suites Hotel is A-OK, as long as you understand that it's 10 minutes from SoHo proper and not an all-suite property.

Rooms advertised as a two-person suite include some shared-bath accommodations. These are small rooms with two twin beds that share one bathroom and a small kitchen area with an identical guest room. It's very much

A hall of mirrors reflects good value at Off SoHo Suites.
Credit: Desmond Shaw

like a tiny apartment with two bedrooms. Each room has its own phone, television, and key. If a group takes both rooms, this is considered a suite with a private bath.

The official suites with a private bath resemble a one-bedroom apartment and are spacious. Bedrooms offer either twin or double beds. A television, couch, kitchen, and table for four are in the outer room. The couch opens up into a bed, but it's better suited for two children than two adults. Most rooms gleam with polished hardwood floors. All provide decent-sized closets with hangers. Overall, the sparse room décor is nothing to commend or criticize.

All the kitchens supply cookware, dishes, utensils, dishwasher, stove, and a full-sized refrigerator. Average-sized bathrooms feature a built-in hair dryer and tub/shower, and some have shelves. Towels are tiny. Breakfast is not included in the room rate, but it's available served either in your room or at the downstairs café.

Clean and quiet, the Off SoHo Suites offers a fair deal for those willing to share a bathroom; but its private rooms are a bit pricey. On the other hand, with the money you'll save by cooking in your suite, you can afford to grocery shop at Balducci's.

PIONEER HOTEL

341 Broome St.
New York, NY 10013
(BETWEEN ELIZABETH ST. AND BOWERY)

VALUE ★★★

CLEANLINESS ★★

GUEST SERVICES ★

SECURITY ★★

(★POOR - ★★★★★EXCELLENT)

CATEGORY	Bare Essentials
PHONE	(212) 226-1482 (800) 737-0702 Reservations
FAX	(212) 226-3525
EMAIL	pioneer_hotel@worldnet.att.net
WEBSITE	www.pioneerhotel.com
RATES	Shared bath: $69 Private bath: $89-$100, includes taxes
GUEST ROOMS	125 rooms on 3 floors, all smoking, no elevator
ROOM AMENITIES	AC, TV without cable, sink in rooms without private bath
RESTAURANTS	None
BARS	None
CLIENTELE	Low-maintenance travelers
GUEST SERVICES	Vending machines, public phones, free coffee and tea in the lobby
PARKING	None
CANCELLATION POLICY	24 hours before check-in
WHEELCHAIR ACCESS	None

The Pioneer is about as bare bones as you can get without staying in a hostel, but if you're just looking for a cheap place to sleep and shower, you might give it a try. Its Little Italy location—with proximity to SoHo, Chinatown, and several subway lines—helps balance out its flaws.

The lobby is homey enough, and a young, cheerful staff will invite you to help yourself to coffee, watch the tube, or read the *New York Times*. Every guest gets a packet of tourist brochures. Keep your expectations low when you ascend to the guest rooms. Soundproofing is at a minimum, so be prepared for a certain amount of noise. Rooms are sparsely furnished but do the job. All provide at least a double bed, a chest of drawers, and a few hooks for your clothes. Rooms have small TVs, ceiling fans, and, during the summer, air conditioners. None offers telephones, but there are several public phones located off the lobby.

Smaller double rooms, especially those without a private bath, are only big enough for one person despite the double bed. Larger units offer more clothes storage space and a bit more furniture that usually matches. Beds in the larger rooms, especially those with private baths, are firmer and in better shape. About one-third of the rooms share hallway shower stalls and toilets, which are adequately clean as is the rest of the hotel.

For accommodations with private baths, the Pioneer Hotel is about as cheap as there is without putting yourself at risk. But if you're willing to share a bath, there are nicer inns or guest houses for about the same price.

LOWER MANHATTAN

SOHO BED & BREAKFAST

167 Crosby St.
New York, NY 10012
(JUST OFF BLEECKER ST. BETWEEN BROADWAY AND LAFAYETTE ST.)

VALUE ★ ★ ★ ★ ★
CLEANLINESS ★ ★ ★ ★
GUEST SERVICES ★ ★
SECURITY ★ ★ ★ ★
(★POOR - ★★★★★EXCELLENT)

CATEGORY	Bed & Breakfast
PHONE	(212) 925-1034
FAX	(212) 226-9081
EMAIL	crosby3@juno.com
WEBSITE	www.sohobandb.com
RATES	Singles: $125 Doubles: $150 Cash only, includes all taxes and tariffs
GUEST ROOMS	2 walk-up units with private baths, smoking, no elevator
ROOM AMENITIES	AC, cable TV, VCR, private line with answering machine (free local calls), ceiling fan, kitchen in private studio
RESTAURANTS	None
BARS	None
CLIENTELE	Primarily international crowd
GUEST SERVICES	Continental breakfast for B&B guests
PARKING	None
CANCELLATION POLICY	Refundable within reason
WHEELCHAIR ACCESS	None

The most popular fantasy of real-estate-hungry New Yorkers is an affordable, spacious loft in a trendy neighborhood. The SoHo Bed & Breakfast turns this myth into reality. You may not find this place after dark, so make sure you arrive before nightfall. While some people may find this annoying, most will feel they're discovering a hidden treasure.

The SoHo B&B offers two guest quarters. The hosted accommodation is located in the main townhouse on the third floor. With its 12-foot-high ceilings, exposed brick walls, and wood floors, it's a true artist's loft. One end of this large space features a sitting area with a full-sized sofa bed, television, and VCR. There is also a writing desk, private phone line, and exotica the owner has collected in his travels.

A kitchen takes up the other side, where a continental breakfast is served. Guests may not cook in the kitchen, which is used solely by the owner who lives downstairs. He has access to the loft space via an old-fashioned metal staircase located in the corner, so no lounging in the sitting area unclothed. In a private area, you'll find the master bedroom with a queen-sized bed and a bathroom with a soaking tub.

The unhosted accommodation is a second-story studio apartment adjacent to the townhouse. Completely private, it commands its own street entrance, with a small and fully equipped kitchen, skylights, and bright décor. For breakfast, carriage house guests fend for themselves from the refrigerator stocked with juice, bagels, jams, and fruit.

A deposit of 25 percent is required to hold reservations, and full payment is expected upon arrival. In the hosted quarters, smoking is not allowed in the bedroom. In the private studio, don't smoke in bed. "No pets, small children, or art dealers," says innkeeper Garry Rich.

The SoHo B&B offers all the enjoyable elements of a bed-and-breakfast without most of the bothersome quirks.

LOWER MANHATTAN

GREENWICH VILLAGE

"I regret profoundly that I was not an American and not born in Greenwich Village. That's where I should have been."
—John Lennon

THE NEIGHBORHOODS: East Village, West Village

At the foot of Fifth Avenue, Washington Square is the symbolic heart of Greenwich Village, a more-or-less arbitrary dividing line between its east and west halves. This area has always been a magnet for free-spirited artists, who as early as 1913 claimed it as their own kingdom. In that year, the painter Marcel Duchamp climbed to the top of the Square's famous Triumphal Arch to declare the

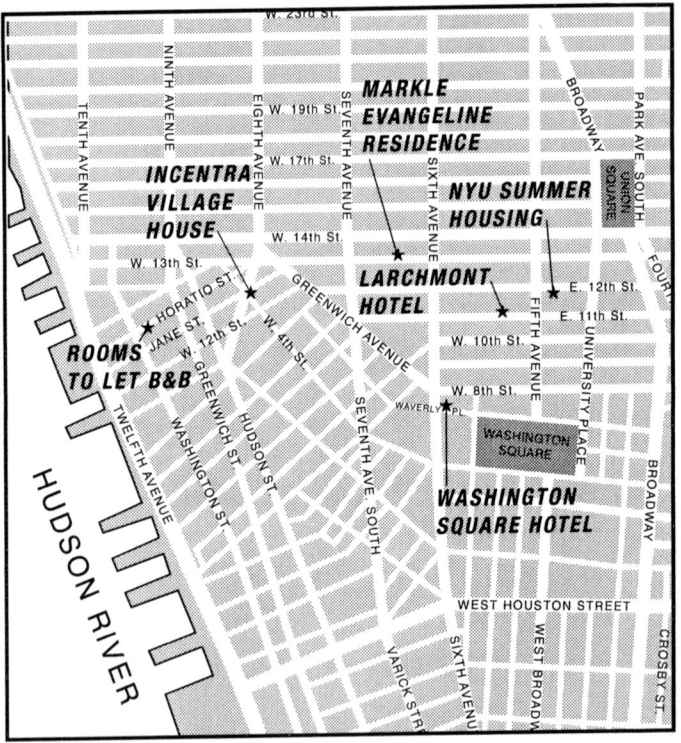

Free Republic of Greenwich Village. The term "Greenwich Village" still defines a certain bohemian lifestyle, comparable to Paris' Left Bank.

In the early 1900s, the Village was also a magnet for reformers and radicals—like John Reed, Emma Goldman, and Margaret Sanger—as well as aspiring playwrights such as Eugene O'Neill. Later, in the 1950s, Beat poets would immortalize their hangouts, like the Café Figaro, which now charge top dollar to people-watchers for croissants and cappuccino. When gentrification and escalating rents forced writers and artists out of the West Village, they moved east.

Today's East Village exudes bohemianism, if of a commercial variety, in the vintage clothing boutiques, aromatherapy shops, and punky bars clustered along streets between Astor Place and Tompkins Square Park. East of Tompkins Square, extending south to East Houston Street, Alphabet City (for avenues A-D) has been dramatically reclaimed from crime and decay in the last decade and is a hot piece of real estate.

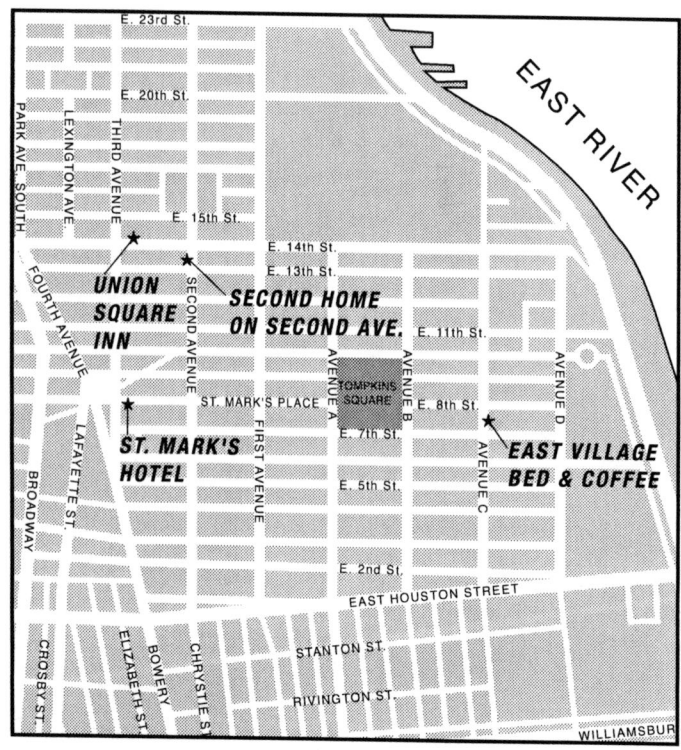

EAST VILLAGE

EAST VILLAGE BED & COFFEE

110 Avenue C
New York, NY 10009
(BETWEEN E. 7TH AND E. 8TH STREETS)

VALUE ★ ★ ★ ★

CLEANLINESS ★ ★ ★

GUEST SERVICES ★ ★ ★

SECURITY ★ ★ ★ ★

(★ POOR - ★ ★ ★ ★ ★ EXCELLENT)

CATEGORY	Guest House
PHONE/FAX	(212) 533-4175
EMAIL	EVBandC@aol.com
WEBSITE	www.bedandcoffee.com
RATES	Singles with shared bath: $60 Doubles with shared bath: $75
GUEST ROOMS	6 rooms on 2 floors, smoking in common areas, no elevator
ROOM AMENITIES	AC
RESTAURANTS	None
BARS	None
CLIENTELE	Leisure travelers, especially Europeans
GUEST SERVICES	TV, access to house answering machine, VCR and stereo in both living areas, full use of kitchen, free use of bicycles, and free local phone calls, local faxes, and internet access on house phone
PARKING	None
CANCELLATION POLICY	4 days before check-in, 2-night penalty
WHEELCHAIR ACCESS	None

One of four upstairs bedrooms at East Village Bed & Coffee.
Credit: Desmond Shaw

Don't let the graffiti-splashed front door scare you. This charming guest house was for many years the only bright spot in Alphabet City (a nickname for avenues A, B, C, and D). The area isn't as safe as the Upper West Side, but then you're not paying Upper West Side prices either. East Village Bed & Coffee doesn't provide an abundance of frills, but thoughtful touches and a warm attitude make you feel more than welcome.

Owner Carlos Delfin offers two separate living areas. Exposed brick and high ceilings dominate the cozy downstairs loft space. Two small bedrooms are located on an enclosed mezzanine, allowing for lots of common space below. These rooms share one average-sized bathroom on the main floor near a large kitchen. Closets are more of an indentation with hangers, and rooms are small, so leave the steamer trunk at home.

Upstairs, four bedrooms share a full bathroom as well

as a kitchen and living room. The space isn't as aesthetically pleasing as the loft, but the bedrooms are larger. Furthermore, this area has its own entrance and offers complete privacy for a family or small group. A shy German shepherd, misnamed Fang, roams around downstairs so those with allergies should stay above. Guests are encouraged to cook and congregate in the fully equipped kitchens. Breakfast is not served, but coffee and tea are free. Also, guests may cook and store food. Smoking is allowed in the common areas.

A serious drawback of this guest house is the lack of convenient public transportation. The closest subway is at least 15 minutes away—and not a walk we would recommend at night. Two bus routes are nearby, but the above-ground system isn't anywhere as reliable as the subway. As for taxis, they aren't as plentiful on Avenue C as they are in other parts of the city.

NEW YORK UNIVERSITY SUMMER HOUSING

7 E. 12th St., 6th Floor
New York, NY 10003
(BETWEEN FIFTH AVE. AND UNIVERSITY PL.)

VALUE ★ ★ ★ ★

CLEANLINESS ★ ★

GUEST SERVICES ★ ★

SECURITY ★ ★ ★ ★

(★POOR - ★★★★★EXCELLENT)

CATEGORY	University
PHONE	(212) 998-4621
FAX	(212) 995-4642
EMAIL	summer.web@nyu.edu
WEBSITE	www.nyu.edu/housing/summer
RATES	Dorm rooms: $110-$140 per week Apartment style: $190-$260 per week 3-week minimum stay, application required
GUEST ROOMS	Most are on or near main NYU campus, all shared baths

ROOM AMENITIES	Most have AC, a twin bed, desk, dresser; suites offer a kitchen
RESTAURANTS	Student cafeteria
BARS	None
CLIENTELE	Students and interns at least 17 years old
GUEST SERVICES	Laundry facilities, vending machines
PARKING	None
CANCELLATION POLICY	21 days before check-in
WHEELCHAIR ACCESS	Yes

Living in campus housing was bad enough the first time around, but accommodations available through New York University satisfy your basic needs. This is not the best choice for leisure travelers due to its three-week minimum stay. For summer interns, it's something to consider. The term usually runs from the end of May through the first week of August. Reservations are accepted January through March, and it's first come, first served. Last-minute cancellations do occur so it's worth a call.

The cheapest accommodations go for about $650 per month, including five meals a week. The most expensive are close to $1,050 per month. Eligibility for housing does not require college enrollment, however preference is given to NYU summer students.

The traditional dorm room houses two to four people and comes with a bed, dresser, and desk. Guests must provide their own bed linens, pillows, and towels. Bathrooms are hallway facilities. Residents in a dorm must buy a weekly meal plan, ranging from five meals for $49 to 15 meals for $89. With these extra costs, the Chelsea Hostel (see page 72) is only about $15 to $20 more per week.

The larger apartments accommodate four to eight housemates. These feature a kitchen, but residents must supply their own cooking utensils, plates, and glasses. Those with a kitchen are not required to buy meal plans.

Cameras and guards provide 24-hour security. Laundry and vending machines are available. Smokers and nonsmokers should note preferences on their application. A three-week deposit is required with the application. You can pay in full at the beginning of your stay to avoid service charges.

ST. MARK'S HOTEL

2 St. Mark's Place
New York, NY 10003
(AT THIRD AVE.)

VALUE ★ ★ ★

CLEANLINESS ★ ★ ★

GUEST SERVICES NONE

SECURITY ★ ★ ★

(★POOR - ★★★★★EXCELLENT)

CATEGORY	Bare Essentials
PHONE	(212) 674-2192
FAX	(212) 420-0854
EMAIL	None
WEBSITE	www.stmarkshotel.qpg.com
RATES	Singles: $100 Doubles: $115-$130 Cash or traveler's checks only
GUEST ROOMS	67 rooms, all smoking, no elevator
ROOM AMENITIES	AC, TV without cable, phone with voice mail
RESTAURANTS	None
BARS	None
CLIENTELE	Budget travelers, especially those under 30 years old
GUEST SERVICES	None
PHONE POLICY	Phone cards are needed and can be purchased at the front desk
PARKING	None
CANCELLATION POLICY	None
WHEELCHAIR ACCESS	None

Because this hotel offers an hourly rate, we half expected to find a flophouse. We were wrong. A perky parakeet greets guests at check-in, which is just a hallway on the other side of a large security window manned by a few burly, friendly fellows. The hotel seems to be put together in pieces, as if the proprietors expanded by buying as they needed. The alpine look and kelly green accents add a certain cheerfulness and youthful appeal.

Overall, the hotel is in good shape and clean.

A bit sparse but functional, all the rooms provide private baths, carpet, a small desk, dresser, telephone, and television. Beds are either twins or doubles. Since the St. Mark's Hotel caters to the backpack crowd, rooms come in various configurations. You'll find everything from a double with twin beds to three double beds in a room. Bathrooms are medium-sized and in good condition. Some feature black-and-white tile as well as bathroom fans, a rarity in Manhattan's budget hotels. All provide shampoo and conditioner, another shock.

At the gateway to the East Village, the hotel's greatest asset is its location. It's only a few minutes from Astor Place and about a 10- to 15-minute walk to Union Square as well as New York University. Guests are less than five minutes from two subway stations. Right on the corner, you'll find St. Mark's Ale House. Starbuck's coffee is just down the block to help you recover in the morning.

Neither a blessing nor a curse, the St. Mark's Hotel is a step above the lowest-end budget accommodation. Our biggest concern—the hourly rate—may affect the hotel's security. The hotel discourages visitors, and everyone walking in or out is accounted for by the burly desk man. But be aware, the walls are paper-thin.

SECOND HOME ON SECOND AVENUE

221 Second Ave.
New York, NY 10003
(BETWEEN E. 13TH AND E. 14TH STREETS)

VALUE ★ ★ ★ ★

CLEANLINESS ★ ★ ★ ★ ★

GUEST SERVICES ★ ★

SECURITY ★ ★ ★ ★

(★ POOR - ★ ★ ★ ★ ★ EXCELLENT)

CATEGORY	Guest House
PHONE/FAX	(212) 677-3161
EMAIL	SecondH@aol.com
WEBSITE	www.secondhome.citysearch.com
RATES	Singles with shared bath: $75-$95 Doubles with shared bath: $125 Doubles with private bath: $150-$180
GUEST ROOMS	7 rooms on 2 floors, mostly shared bath, smoking in common areas, no elevator
ROOM AMENITIES	AC, cable TV, phone with private answering machine (free local calls)
RESTAURANTS	None
BARS	None
CLIENTELE	A mixed crowd
GUEST SERVICES	Use of a fully furnished kitchen
PARKING	None
CANCELLATION POLICY	4 days before check-in, 2-night penalty
WHEELCHAIR ACCESS	None

Most people's first homes aren't as nice as the rooms at Second Home on Second Avenue. The spacious, airy design is an unusual find for such a small property. Both shared and private bath accommodations are good values and pretty to boot. Not opulent but well appointed, the rooms are decorated in Peruvian, tribal, Caribbean, and 20th-century modern themes. A wide, curving staircase connects two floors.

All the rooms have double beds. Some feature carved

wooden headboards and others use black wrought iron. Several of the rooms provide a writing desk. The larger quarters have a stereo, CD player and VCR, as well as charming coffee tables and comfy chairs and couches.

Most of the rooms share a bathroom. On the first level one room with two full beds shares hallway facilities with a smaller bedroom. Medium-sized, the bathroom is more than adequate, but tub lovers may not like the shower stall. The large suite with a private bath belongs in *Better Homes and Gardens* and can easily accommodate four people. Above, three rooms share one good-sized bathroom. The fourth bedroom has a private bath.

Guests have access to a modern kitchen on the second level. With a dishwasher, full-sized refrigerator, stove and oven, microwave, toaster, and coffeemaker, it's easy to make yourself at home. Smoking is allowed in the common areas as well as the outdoor terrace. All visitors must be buzzed in; a manager is usually on duty but not always.

Guests are three blocks from Union Square and its subway station. Also, the inn is five minutes from the famous Second Avenue Deli. In terms of noise, Second Avenue is a busy street and the Gemini Lounge, below this inn, is a hopping spot during warm summer evenings. Storm windows should help keep out most of the noise.

UNION SQUARE INN

209 E. 14th St.
New York, NY 10003
(BETWEEN SECOND AND THIRD AVENUES)

VALUE ★ ★ ★

CLEANLINESS ★ ★ ★ ★

GUEST SERVICES ★ ★

SECURITY ★ ★ ★ ★

(★POOR - ★★★★★EXCELLENT)

CATEGORY	Euro-style
PHONE	(212) 614-0500
FAX	(212) 614-0512
EMAIL	unionsquareinn@aol.com
WEBSITE	www.UnionSquareInn.com

RATES	$119–$169
GUEST ROOMS	41 rooms with private bath, third floor is nonsmoking, no elevator
ROOM AMENITIES	AC, cable TV, phone with voice mail and dataport
RESTAURANTS	None
BARS	None
CLIENTELE	New York University parents and business travelers
GUEST SERVICES	Continental breakfast, fax and copy services for a charge
PARKING	None
CANCELLATION POLICY	48 hours before check-in
WHEELCHAIR ACCESS	None

This attractive new hotel joins its siblings—the Murray Hill Inn and Amsterdam Inn—under management by Inns of New York. Just hope the bellman isn't on his lunch break when you arrive: there are five floors and no elevator.

Guest rooms are pint-sized with a rack to hang up your clothes and a small dresser. Avoid booking the front rooms because of noise from commercial 14th Street. You'll find firm mattresses, air conditioners, phones with voice mail and a dataport to plug in a laptop computer, cable television, and small bathrooms with stall showers. There are a few rooms with tub baths, so if you want one, ask for it. Ditto hair dryers and irons. As of press time, there are no surveillance cameras and the bellman doubles as a security guard.

The Union Square Inn is a popular choice for parents of New York University students because of its proximity to the campus and to Greenwich Village. Otherwise, its location on noisy East 14th Street may be a handicap. The crosstown L subway, just steps from the hotel, connects to uptown and downtown trains.

WEST VILLAGE

INCENTRA VILLAGE HOUSE
32 Eighth Ave.
New York, NY 10014
(BETWEEN W. 12TH AND JANE STREETS)

VALUE ★ ★ ★ ★

CLEANLINESS ★ ★ ★ ★ ★

GUEST SERVICES ★ ★

SECURITY ★ ★ ★

(★POOR - ★★★★★EXCELLENT)

CATEGORY	Guest House
PHONE	(212) 206-0007
FAX	(212) 604-0625
EMAIL	None
WEBSITE	None
RATES	Singles: $119-$149 Doubles: $169-$199 No children under 10 years old
GUEST ROOMS	10 studios and 2 suites on 3 floors, all smoking, no elevator
ROOM AMENITIES	AC, cable TV, phone with dataport, kitchenette with coffeemaker, some rooms have microwaves, most have working fireplaces
RESTAURANTS	None
BARS	None
CLIENTELE	Strong gay and lesbian following
GUEST SERVICES	Newspapers, piano
PARKING	None
CANCELLATION POLICY	3 days before check-in
WHEELCHAIR ACCESS	None

If you hate overpriced, impersonal hotels with staff who treat you like an intruder, you'll love the Incentra Village House. Easy to miss, only a small sign above the doorbell indicates that the attractive drawing room visible from the street is part of a guest house. And cozy it is with two fireplaces, a piano, and the daily papers. The Incentra Village House encompasses two red brick townhouses dating to 1841. In fact, most of the surrounding area is landmarked for historic preservation, making the neighborhood a favorite among history and architecture buffs.

Each guest room features a private bath and kitchenette as well as its own doorbell at the main entrance. Most of them contain a double bed with a few offering twin beds or pull-out couches. All the mattresses are firm and in good shape. The larger suites and studios can accommodate up to four guests. Several rooms provide VCRs.

Each guest room is uniquely decorated and named for something important in the life of founder Gaylord Hoftiezer. For instance, guests in the Garden Suite enjoy

Cozy Victorian drawing room at the Incentra Village House.
Credit: Incentra Village House

exclusive access to their own little Eden. The Maine Room has a four-poster bed from a farm in that state.

The Incentra Village House doesn't offer any meals. All the kitchenettes are in good shape, if small, and the suites have a microwave. Also, the rooms don't have voice mail or answering machines, so guests rely on the house manager for phone messages.

Guests are welcome to lounge in the downstairs parlor as well as borrow newspapers, magazines, and books. Smoking is permitted throughout the house. If you enjoy playing the piano, the 1930s baby grand is always in tune. Public transportation is a cinch with two subway stations within a five-minute walk.

On average, expect to book four to eight weeks in advance, especially for weekends. Also, prices increase approximately $20 during holidays. Considering price, location, and the guest rooms themselves, this was our favorite property in Greenwich Village.

LARCHMONT HOTEL

27 W. 11th St.
New York, NY 10011
(BETWEEN FIFTH AND SIXTH AVENUES)

VALUE ★ ★ ★ ★ ★

CLEANLINESS ★ ★ ★ ★

GUEST SERVICES ★ ★ ★

SECURITY ★ ★ ★

(★POOR - ★★★★★EXCELLENT)

CATEGORY	Euro-style
PHONE	(212) 989-9333
FAX	(212) 989-9496
EMAIL	None
WEBSITE	www.larchmonthotel.com
RATES	Singles: $70-$95 Doubles: $90-$125
GUEST ROOMS	58 rooms on 6 floors, all shared baths, all smoking
ROOM AMENITIES	AC, TV without cable, phone with voice mail, clock radio, robes, slippers

RESTAURANTS	None
BARS	None
CLIENTELE	Primarily Europeans
GUEST SERVICES	Continental breakfast, kitchenettes on every floor, luggage storage
PARKING	None
CANCELLATION POLICY	48 hours before check-in
WHEELCHAIR ACCESS	None

This Beaux Arts brownstone with geranium window boxes and lanterns blends smoothly with its neighbors on West 11th Street. Location is part of its popularity. On the eastern border of Greenwich Village, the hotel is about five blocks from both Washington Square Park and Union Square. Some of Fifth Avenue's most impressive and historic mansions are in this neighborhood. Six subway stations are within a 10- to 15-minute walk.

The Larchmont is one of the city's best residential-style lodgings, but if shared bathrooms are a phobia, skip it. Each floor has two toilets and two shower stalls, all clean and in good condition. The no-frills guest rooms are bright and homey with rattan furniture, ceiling fans, a sink, a desk, and books.

The Larchmont offers every bed size from twin to king, a nice and unexpected perk for a smaller hotel. Mattresses are firm, but not hard. Staff pay attention to small details and offer as many amenities as possible, such as short robes and slippers as well as extra pillows and blankets in every room. Smoking is allowed throughout the property, but the hotel doesn't smell like an ash can.

Despite its small size, the Larchmont provides a bellman, free luggage storage and kitchenettes on each floor. A small continental breakfast of fresh pastries, juice, coffee, and tea is available daily in the lobby. During peak season, expect to book reservations six to eight weeks in advance.

The all-shared bath situation is a turn-off for many people, but rest assured the Larchmont Hotel ranks among the top properties of its kind in Manhattan.

GREENWICH VILLAGE

MARKLE EVANGELINE RESIDENCE

123 W. 13th St.
New York, NY 10011
(BETWEEN SIXTH AND SEVENTH AVENUES)

VALUE ★ ★ ★ ★ ★

CLEANLINESS ★ ★ ★

GUEST SERVICES ★ ★ ★ ★ ★

SECURITY ★ ★ ★

(★POOR - ★★★★★EXCELLENT)

CATEGORY	Residence
PHONE	(212) 242-2400
FAX	(212) 229-2801
EMAIL	None
WEBSITE	None
RATES	Under 31 days: single rooms cost $80 nightly, $436 weekly; doubles cost $110 nightly and $634 weekly
	Over 30 days, weekly rates per person are: singles $235, doubles $164-$185, triples $158, quads $143
	Rates include breakfast and dinner. One-month security deposit for long-term stays, $100 deposit for short-term stays
GUEST ROOMS	200 nonsmoking rooms with private baths
ROOM AMENITIES	Phone, bedding, and towels
RESTAURANTS	Cafeteria
BARS	None
CLIENTELE	Women professionals, students, and seniors
GUEST SERVICES	Maid service, self-service laundry, beauty salon, roof garden, TV lounge, kitchen
PARKING	None
CANCELLATION POLICY	48 hours prior to arrival
WHEELCHAIR ACCESS	None

The Salvation Army established this residence in 1930 for young women who are either working, studying, or both and for senior women over 60 years old. There is no maximum stay and about a three-to-six-month wait for a permanent room.

Those rooms are average-sized with private baths, phones (50 cents a call plus long-distance charges), small desks, large closets, and good-sized dressers. If you install your own AC unit, you'll pay $25 a month to cover electricity. Two daily meals are included in your rent, though lunch isn't served on weekends. There's no curfew, but there is a dining room dress code. (This is the Salvation Army, after all.) In between meals, you can prepare a snack in a kitchen on the fourth floor. Among the public areas, the roof garden is popular in summer, the TV lounge at night.

Its location on a quiet street within walking distance of New York University at Washington Square and the retail and subway nexus at Union Square is a huge drawing card for the Markle. Friendly staff and a comfortable setting help maintain this intergenerational community.

ROOMS TO LET B&B

83 Horatio St.
New York, NY 10014
(BETWEEN WASHINGTON AND GREENWICH STREETS)

VALUE ★ ★ ★

CLEANLINESS ★ ★ ★ ★

GUEST SERVICES ★

SECURITY ★ ★ ★ ★ ★

(★POOR - ★ ★ ★ ★ ★ EXCELLENT)

CATEGORY	Bed & Breakfast
PHONE	(212) 675-5481
FAX	(212) 675-9432
EMAIL	margecolt@aol.com
WEBSITE	www.roomstolet.net
RATES	Singles: $95 Doubles: $150-$190 Cash and traveler's checks only, 4-night minimum stay with advance reservations

GUEST ROOMS	2 singles, 2 doubles, 1 suite with private bath, 1 apartment, no smoking, no elevator
ROOM AMENITIES	AC, doubles have private telephone (free local calls)
RESTAURANTS	None
BARS	None
CLIENTELE	Primarily European
GUEST SERVICES	Continental breakfast
PARKING	None
CANCELLATION POLICY	10 days before check-in
WHEELCHAIR ACCESS	None

Rooms to Let belies the silly notion that New York isn't a B&B-friendly town. The parlor and guest rooms are filled with antiques and personal touches that make you feel you've walked through the door of your own home.

Three rooms are located on the second floor. Two double rooms—one with a queen bed, the other with two twins—as well as a single share one bathroom. The bathroom is as well decorated as the rest of the house, but there is only one on the second floor. That means you could pay $150 to share a bathroom with a stranger.

On the third level, one single shares a bathroom with the proprietor. Above, the attic houses a queen-sized bed and its own bath area. The space is large enough for two people, but the toilet and bathtub are merely curtained off so privacy is minimal. Double rooms have their own phones, and guests in the single units may use the house phone for local calls. A furnished apartment rents for $3,700 monthly or about $124 nightly.

Guests help themselves to the continental breakfast, and are welcome to enjoy the private garden behind this historic home. Security is reassuring; all guests must be buzzed in. A minimum of four nights is required with advance reservations, but shorter stays are often possible. A 25 percent deposit is necessary. Payment in full is expected upon arrival. Infants and young children are not welcomed. If you suffer from allergies, be aware that a dog and a couple of cats have the run of the house.

Rooms to Let offers a nice change of pace from the typical New York hotel. But its price seems high for a shared bathroom and cold cereal in the morning.

SLEEP CHEAP IN NEW YORK

WASHINGTON SQUARE HOTEL

103 Waverly Place
New York, NY 10011
(BETWEEN MACDOUGAL ST. AND SIXTH AVE.)

VALUE ★ ★ ★ ★

CLEANLINESS ★ ★ ★ ★

GUEST SERVICES ★ ★ ★ ★

SECURITY ★ ★ ★

(★POOR - ★★★★★EXCELLENT)

CATEGORY	Limited Services
PHONE	(212) 777-9515 (800) 222-0418 Reservations
FAX	(212) 979-8373
EMAIL	reservations@wshotel.com
WEBSITE	www.washingtonsquarehotel.com
RATES	Singles: $126-$148 Doubles: $148-$181
GUEST ROOMS	165 rooms on 9 floors, all smoking
ROOM AMENITIES	AC, cable TV with HBO, safe, phone with voice mail
RESTAURANTS	C3 Restaurant serves lunch, dinner, weekend brunch, and afternoon tea
BARS	C3 Lounge offers drinks and a full dinner menu
CLIENTELE	European travelers, primarily, but it's popular with parents of NYU students
GUEST SERVICES	Continental breakfast, small workout room, luggage storage
PARKING	None
CANCELLATION POLICY	48 hours before check-in
WHEELCHAIR ACCESS	None

The Washington Square Hotel would be considered an attractive property in any part of the city, but its Greenwich Village location at the northwest corner of Washington Square Park makes it a winner. This 1900 landmark hotel boasts an Art Deco lobby with characteristic green-and-white checkered floor, green marble fixtures, and brass front doors.

The century-old Washington Square Hotel boasts a newly renovated Art Deco lobby. Credit: Washington Square Hotel

The C3 Restaurant & Lounge is an unusual find in a relatively affordable hotel. The dinner menu departs from the ordinary with dishes like lobster and asparagus salad and a slow-smoked venison loin. Separate from the restaurant, the C3 Lounge hosts a popular Sunday jazz brunch. It can be used for small meetings or events during the day or reserved for parties at night.

Guest rooms neither entice nor repulse, and were being refurbished at press time. A bright blue-and-green décor helps cheer up the otherwise nondescript rooms. The largest beds are queen-sized. Most of the bathrooms are at least medium-sized and all have a tub/shower. Closets are a welcome change from the usual, with even the smallest offering a couple of shelves. Be aware, some rooms don't have a window.

For business travelers, the biggest drawback is the lack of a desk. All the rooms have voice mail, but no dataport phones. The small workout room features cardiovascular equipment and weight machines, but it is a very small space with no room for stretching. The hotel does not have a security guard or bellman, but it does use electronic key cards.

It's a brisk five-minute walk from the Washington Square Hotel to the New York University campus. Another five minutes will get you to SoHo. Also the hotel is very close to one of the larger subway stations offering both local and express train service.

We were surprised this hotel fit our budget parameters, but it was definitely a pleasant surprise. At press time, it was offering a 20 percent slice off bookings made Sunday through Wednesday.

GREENWICH VILLAGE

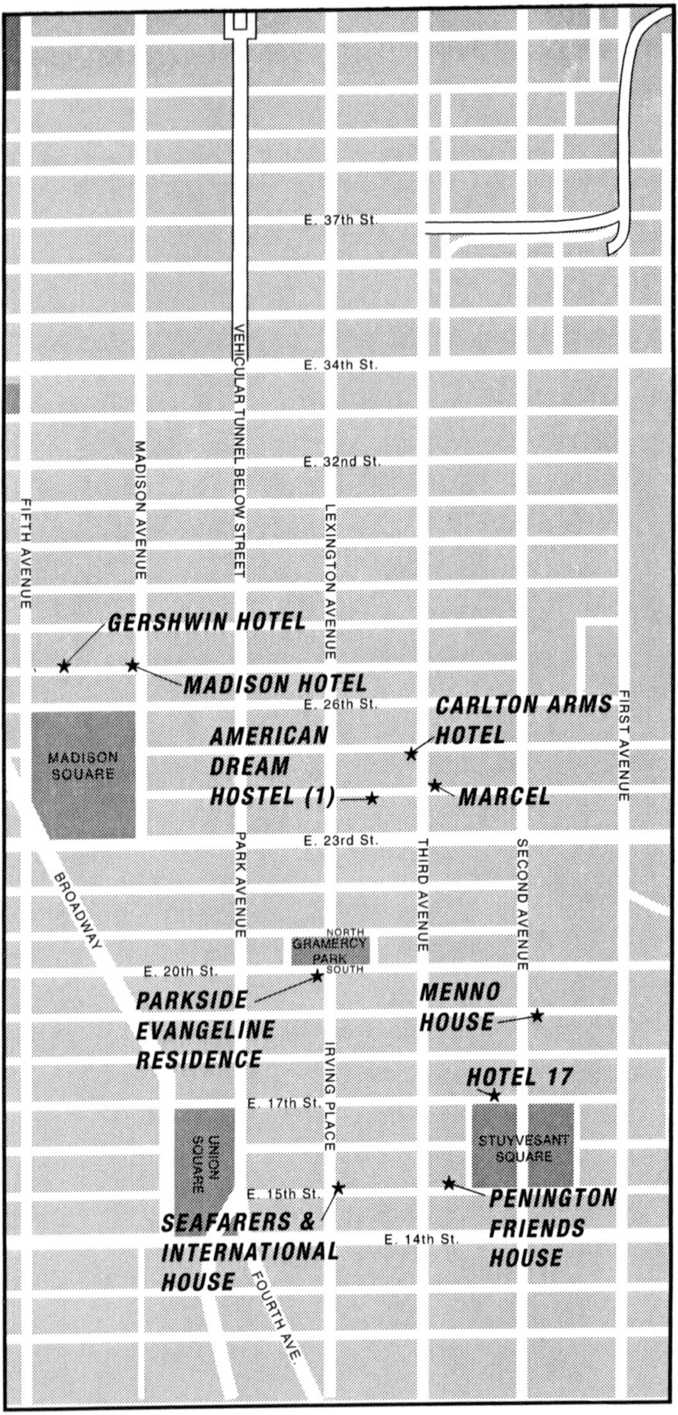
E. 37th St.
E. 34th St.
E. 32nd St.
VEHICULAR TUNNEL BELOW STREET
MADISON AVENUE
FIFTH AVENUE
LEXINGTON AVENUE
GERSHWIN HOTEL
MADISON HOTEL
E. 26th St.
CARLTON ARMS
HOTEL
FIRST AVENUE
AMERICAN
DREAM
HOSTEL (1)
MARCEL
MADISON
SQUARE
E. 23rd St.
BROADWAY
PARK AVENUE
THIRD AVENUE
SECOND AVENUE
NORTH
GRAMERCY
PARK
SOUTH
E. 20th St.
PARKSIDE
EVANGELINE
RESIDENCE
MENNO
HOUSE
HOTEL 17
E. 17th St.
IRVING PLACE
UNION
SQUARE
STUYVESANT
SQUARE
E. 15th St.
PENINGTON
FRIENDS
HOUSE
SEAFARERS &
INTERNATIONAL
HOUSE
E. 14th St.
FOURTH AVE.

GRAMERCY PARK

> "Fourth Avenue—born and bred in the Bowery—
> staggers northward full of good resolutions.
> Where it crosses Fourteenth Street it struts for
> a brief moment proudly in the glare of the
> museums and cheap theatres....It passes Union
> Square; and here the hoofs of the dray horses
> seem to thunder in unison, recalling the tread
> of marching hosts—Hooray!"
>
> —O. Henry

The center of this neighborhood is a tranquil and mostly empty spot of greenery. Gramercy Park is the city's last remaining private park, and only those lucky enough to live in the historic buildings that border the park get a key. The actor Edwin Booth, who founded The Players at 16 Gramercy Park South, and philanthropist Joseph Pulitzer were among the park's famous residents. Next door to The Players is the equally patrician National Arts Club and at 52 Gramercy Park North, the 1920s Gramercy Park Hotel

Bustling Union Square was so named because it was the "union" of two main roads. Today farmers, fishermen, and bakers travel those roads and more to sell their produce and baked goods at the green market. Surrounded by superstores like Barnes & Noble, Circuit City, and Toys 'R' Us; popular eateries such as the Union Square Café and Zen Palate; and the ubiquitous Starbuck's Coffee, the square is lively and colorful, especially during the summer. Perhaps the most consistent draw in this neighborhood, though, is not a newcomer: it's Pete's Tavern on 18th Street, where legend has it O. Henry wrote *The Gift of the Magi*.

AMERICAN DREAM HOSTEL (1)

168 E. 24th St.
New York, NY 10016
(BETWEEN LEXINGTON AND THIRD AVENUES)

VALUE ★ ★ ★
CLEANLINESS ★ ★ ★
GUEST SERVICES ★ ★ ★
SECURITY ★ ★ ★ ★
(★POOR - ★★★★★EXCELLENT)

CATEGORY	Hostel
PHONE	(212) 260-9779
FAX	(212) 260-9944
EMAIL	americandream24@aol.com
WEBSITE	www.americandreamhostel.com
RATES	Dorm rooms: $40, $250/week ($29 for students) Single private rooms: $60, $375/week Double private rooms: $80, $500/week Only cash and traveler's checks Rates include taxes
GUEST ROOMS	27 rooms on 3 floors, all shared baths, no elevator
ROOM AMENITIES	TV without cable in private rooms, towels, linens
RESTAURANTS	None
BARS	None
CLIENTELE	95 percent foreign students and teachers
GUEST SERVICES	Internet access, fax service, continental breakfast served in a common kitchen where guests can use the refrigerator but not cook
PARKING	None
CANCELLATION POLICY	7 days before check-in
WHEELCHAIR ACCESS	None

Lou Barreto, a ringer for Father Guido Sarducci, is your host at this bare-bones hostel, "dedicated to the youth and teachers from overseas." We arrived as three German fräulein were off to see the sights, carrying their pillows with them. Barreto doesn't bother marketing to Americans because his international traffic is steady and sure. Wherever they hail from, happy wanderers find this small hostel's laid-back staff, price, and location agreeable. A buzz-in security system leads up one flight to a tiny lobby and two more floors. Be prepared to carry your luggage; there is no elevator.

Private rooms can accommodate one, two, or three guests, who sleep in bunk beds. There is a rack to hang your clothes, but no closets. Dorm rooms sleep four or six people, and towels and linens are provided. All rooms share hallway bathrooms, consisting of a toilet and separate tub/shower.

The same company owns another American Dream Hostel 10 blocks uptown (see page 92). The uptown version is more attractive, offers more amenities and, because prices are nearly identical, would be our preference.

CARLTON ARMS HOTEL

160 E. 25th St.
New York, NY 10010
(AT THIRD AVE.)

VALUE ★ ★ ★

CLEANLINESS ★ ★

GUEST SERVICES None

SECURITY ★ ★ ★ ★ ★

(★POOR - ★★★★★EXCELLENT)

CATEGORY	Bare Essentials
PHONE	(212) 684-8337
	(212) 679-0680 Reservations
FAX	None
EMAIL	None
WEBSITE	www.carltonarms.com
	Offers an excellent virtual tour
RATES	Singles shared bath: $60
	Singles private bath: $75
	Doubles shared bath: $80
	Doubles private bath: $95
GUEST ROOMS	54 rooms, 20 with private bath, all allow smoking

ROOM AMENITIES	Dixie cups, soap, towels
RESTAURANTS	None
BARS	None
CLIENTELE	Students and international tourists
GUEST SERVICES	None
PARKING	None
CANCELLATION POLICY	No penalty, but prefers advance notice
WHEELCHAIR ACCESS	None

Ya gotta love this place, but you won't necessarily love staying here. Happy campers tend to be young, free-spirited, and artistic. Creativity is the hallmark of the Carlton Arms, announced by a handpainted billboard at the entrance that insists "We ain't no Holiday Inn." In the upstairs parlor, two cats and a cat-sized Pomeranian named Kashew hold court on blue-cushioned chairs. Goldfish swim behind the screen of an Admiral TV set. Walk down the first floor hallway under twinkling

A hand-painted billboard welcomes guests at The Carlton Arms Hotel. Credit: Desmond Shaw

Christmas lights, and you might see bottles of Bud cooling on the fire escape alongside plates of cat food.

Artists from around the world have left legacies in all the rooms and hallways. The Egyptian-themed D floor, for example (floors are lettered, not numbered), boasts a life-size bas relief of Isis in resplendent gold paint. One room looks like Monet's garden, another like a Buddhist temple. The Versailles Room is a mélange of trompe l'oeil trellises and classical urns. Graffiti are both whimsical and stark. One lists the phone number for methadone maintenance, another a Bob Dylan lyric.

Get a room with a bath at a slightly higher rate because shared baths are tiny. All rooms have sinks, however, as well as fans, soap, double-paned windows (for noise relief), and towels. Half of them have showers, half offer tubs.

Fun and funky, the hotel has a nurturing quality and weekly rentals are common. It's a touch of la vie Bohème in genteel Gramercy Park.

GERSHWIN HOTEL

7 E. 27th St.
New York, NY 10016
(BETWEEN FIFTH AND MADISON AVENUES)

VALUE ★ ★ ★ ★

CLEANLINESS ★ ★ ★ ★ ★

GUEST SERVICES ★ ★ ★ ★

SECURITY ★ ★ ★ ★

(★POOR - ★★★★★EXCELLENT)

CATEGORY	Boutique
PHONE	(212) 545-8000
FAX	(212) 684-5546
EMAIL	gershwinhotel@pobox.com
WEBSITE	www.gershwinhotel.com Offers special packages
RATES	Private rooms: $99-$295 Dorm beds: $29.99-$59.99
GUEST ROOMS	120 nonsmoking rooms on 13 floors, 13 suites, 66 dorm beds
ROOM AMENITIES	AC, cable TV, phone with voice mail and dataport, hair dryer

RESTAURANTS	Café serves a continental and American breakfast buffet
BARS	The Red Room Bar is open 7 p.m. to 2 a.m.
CLIENTELE	60 percent Europeans, 20 percent Americans, 20 percent other nationalities
GUEST SERVICES	Valet laundry, internet kiosks, gift shop, meeting rooms, live entertainment, art gallery
PARKING	None
CANCELLATION POLICY	48 hours before check-in
WHEELCHAIR ACCESS	None

It's hard to miss Stefan Lindfors' fiberglass "flame" sculptures that project from the entrance to this hip hotel just off Fifth Avenue. Andy Warhol's Campbell's Soup can and Roy Lichtenstein's "As I Open Fire" identify the lobby as a haven of Pop Art.

At the front desk, a youthful, multinational staff makes you feel like your "little town shoes" are already melting away. Maybe you'd like to have a beer at the bar off the lobby or admire the city lights from the astroturfed rooftop. (One caveat: two tiny elevators are s-l-o-w, so it may take a while to ascend.) You'll never feel too far from home because two internet kiosks in the café let you read your email with a swipe of a credit card.

Each room type—economy, standard, and superior—is unique in size and amenities. All feature original artwork as do the hallways on each floor. Fifty rooms have been renovated with modern bathrooms and wooden floors. (You might want to ask for one.) Each room provides an iron, new AC, cable TV, a phone with voice mail, a walk-in closet or armoire, and a small tiled bathroom with toiletries and hair dryer. Suites are comfortably spacious with a living room, coffeemaker, mini-fridge, wine, and fresh flowers; some have kitchenettes. There are dormitory rooms, which will eventually be phased out.

The Gershwin is flashy, and owner Urs Jakob keeps adding new features, like a cabaret, the Modern Culture at the Gershwin art gallery, and piano music in the lobby. It all makes for a lively scene. But if you chat with guests, as we did, you'll find few happy campers. Management and maintenance problems have plagued this hotel almost from its opening. Its largest client base are Europeans, who, perhaps, can adjust to inconveniences like lack of hot water, lost reservations, and inadequate lighting better than Americans.

We're hoping this original venue gets its behind-the-scenes act together.

Digital mural by pop artist Brad Howe captures the Gershwin Hotel's youthful spirit. Credit: Desmond Shaw

SLEEP CHEAP IN NEW YORK

HOTEL 17
225 E. 17th St.
New York, NY 10003
(BETWEEN SECOND AND THIRD AVENUES)

VALUE ★ ★ ★ ★
CLEANLINESS ★ ★ ★ ★
GUEST SERVICES ★ ★
SECURITY ★ ★ ★ ★ ★
(★POOR - ★★★★★EXCELLENT)

CATEGORY	Euro-style
PHONE	(212) 475-2845
FAX	(212) 677-8178
EMAIL	hotel17@worldnet.att.net
WEBSITE	www.hotel17.citysearch.com
RATES	Singles shared bath: $55-$65 Doubles shared bath: $60-$85 Doubles private bath: $95-$110 Cash and traveler's checks only. No credit card reservations
GUEST ROOMS	100 rooms on 8 floors, 15 with private bath, half are nonsmoking
ROOM AMENITIES	AC, cable TV, no phones
RESTAURANTS	None
BARS	None
CLIENTELE	Young artists, 30 percent German, 40 percent American, the rest Asian, no children under 17
GUEST SERVICES	Self-service laundry, concierge
PARKING	None
CANCELLATION POLICY	Prefers 48 hours before check-in
WHEELCHAIR ACCESS	None

According to manager Jamie Young, this hotel is popular with filmmakers and photographers. (He claims he gets a phone call a week.) Woody Allen shot *Manhattan Murder Mystery* here. Madonna posed for the camera as have many other actresses and fashion models. It's easy to understand the appeal: the neighborhood is quietly residential and the handsome 19th-century brownstone is carefully maintained. Still, its single-file hallways with linoleum floors and creaky elevator remind you that this is an older building.

Singles, doubles, and triples are immaculate and attractively decorated. Amenities are sparse, but each room has AC and a tiny TV with cable; doubles also provide hair dryers and clock radios. All rooms have small sinks, but only 15 doubles offer private baths. Shared bathrooms and toilets are in the hallways. Triples tend to be spacious with wooden-shuttered windows, fireplaces, and other period touches. Still, if you want to make a phone call, you must use a pay phone in the lobby.

Security is reassuring. All guests must show their room key every time they enter and the lobby is equipped with surveillance cameras. No hotel guests are allowed to enter after 10 p.m. For those who want peace and privacy, this is a good choice. The in-room rating card suggests that management wants your feedback. Always a good sign.

MADISON HOTEL

21 E. 27th St.
New York, NY 10016
(AT MADISON AVE.)

VALUE ★ ★

CLEANLINESS ★ ★

GUEST SERVICES ★ ★

SECURITY ★

(★POOR - ★★★★★EXCELLENT)

CATEGORY	Bare Essentials
PHONE	(212) 532-7373
	(800) 962-3476 Reservations
FAX	(212) 686-0092
EMAIL	madihotel@aol.com
WEBSITE	www.madison-hotel.com
RATES	$99-$145; offers seasonal discounts
GUEST ROOMS	74 rooms on 12 floors, all smoking
ROOM AMENITIES	AC, cable TV, phone
RESTAURANTS	None
BARS	None

CLIENTELE	Primarily European and Asian tourists, about 4 percent Americans
GUEST SERVICES	Voucher for continental breakfast at coffee shop, luggage room
PARKING	None
CANCELLATION POLICY	48 hours before check-in
WHEELCHAIR ACCESS	None

You could die of old age waiting for the tiny elevator here and never need a room at all. When it arrives, the elevator deposits you into a narrow hallway with stained, frayed carpet and paint that's seen better days. All of which points to a poorly maintained property.

Double rooms are larger than singles and those with two double beds are the largest. The ancient air conditioning may be unreliable, and mattresses are chosen for economy, not comfort. Tiled bathrooms have tub/showers and no amenities.

Though a brochure describes staff as "courteous," they were shouting at each other when we visited.

THE MARCEL

201 E. 24th St.
New York, NY 10010
(AT THIRD AVE.)

VALUE ★ ★ ★ ★ ★
CLEANLINESS ★ ★ ★ ★ ★
GUEST SERVICES ★ ★ ★ ★
SECURITY ★ ★ ★ ★ ★
(★POOR - ★★★★★EXCELLENT)

CATEGORY	Boutique
PHONE	(212) 696-3800 (888) 664-6835 Reservations
FAX	(212) 696-0077
EMAIL	None
WEBSITE	www.nychotels.com Offers internet specials
RATES	$109-$269

GUEST ROOMS	100 rooms on 7 floors, 1 floor reserved for smokers
ROOM AMENITIES	AC, cable TV with pay games and movies, phone with voice mail and dataport, Belgian linens, CD player, iron and ironing board, hair dryer
RESTAURANTS	Spread serves dinner
BARS	Yes
CLIENTELE	Half leisure and half corporate travelers, with many guests doing business with Silicon Alley companies and modeling agencies
GUEST SERVICES	Continental breakfast, room service 5 p.m.-2 a.m., valet laundry, turn-down service, 24-hour coffee and tea in lounge, meeting room/library
PARKING	None
CANCELLATION POLICY	24 hours before check-in
WHEELCHAIR ACCESS	None

Goodman Charlton couches and a well-stocked library invite Marcel guests to unwind. Credit: Desmond Shaw

When the bellman sweeps you through the glass doors of this stylish hotel, opened by Amsterdam Hospitality Group in 1997, you might well think you are about to part with a big chunk of change. Classical music, white lilies in a tall silver vase, soft lighting, teak-paneled walls, and leather upholstery suggest a classy pad for classy tastes. Front desk staff, never less than two, are as attentive as the bellman. The Marcel has the same elegant appeal of much higher-priced properties on the East Side, but, at least for now, gives excellent value.

Cool tones of robin's egg blue, browns, and cream accented by contemporary art and custom furniture decorate the lobby and guest rooms. Accommodations are small, but adequate, with climate control, a desk, TV with all the extras, a tiny closet with an iron, and built-in shelves in the fancy headboards. Large picture windows bring light and city views into the interior space. Bathrooms are cream-colored marble with a glass-enclosed tub/shower, phone, hair dryer, and toiletries. Rooms are priced the same regardless of bed size, and those sizes include a king, queen, double, or double/double. The hotel is adding rooms on the eighth and ninth floors.

Why the name "Marcel"? You'll find the answer in works by famous Marcels—Duchamp and Proust—throughout the hotel. (It had to be called something besides "the no-name hotel.") Help yourself to herbal tea or espresso in the small lounge off the lobby or to a book in the library, which also serves as meeting space. Flick off the TV if you want to talk.

Take advantage of this gem, especially its occasional website discounts, before they raise their rates. It's a well-kept secret that should be the talk of the town.

THE MENNO HOUSE

314 E. 19th St.
New York, NY 10003
(BETWEEN FIRST AND SECOND AVENUES)

VALUE ★ ★ ★ ★

CLEANLINESS ★ ★ ★

GUEST SERVICES ★ ★ ★

SECURITY ★ ★ ★

(★POOR - ★★★★★EXCELLENT)

CATEGORY	Residence
PHONE	(212) 677-1611
FAX	(212) 673-7970
EMAIL	manager@mennohouse.com
WEBSITE	www.mennohouse.com
RATES	$370-$570 monthly. Overnight: $45 per person, $70 for two people, $20 extra person
GUEST ROOMS	10 for permanent residents, 3 for overnight guests are all nonsmoking, shared bath
ROOM AMENITIES	Bedding and towels, clock radio
RESTAURANTS	None
BARS	None
CLIENTELE	Half the permanent residents are students; overnight guests include missionaries and tourists
GUEST SERVICES	TV lounge, library, coin-operated washer and dryer, fully equipped kitchen, free local calls on public phone, iron, patio garden with barbeque grill
PARKING	None
CANCELLATION POLICY	Nonrefundable deposit of one-night's stay
WHEELCHAIR ACCESS	None

Menno House is a ministry of hospitality of the Manhattan Mennonite Fellowship established in the 1950s as housing for conscientious objectors. The small brownstone within walking distance of Union Square offers three rooms to overnight guests, who have full use of a large kitchen, TV lounge, and laundry but also compete with permanent residents to use the public toilet and stall shower. There's ample refrigerator space to store food and an outdoor grill in the patio to cook it, weather permitting. Rooms are very basic and can sleep from three to five people. All rooms have lofts for extra space. Room #2 is the only one with a sink; the largest room, #3, overlooks the garden and has a desk.

This is a very youthful residence with friendly tenants and staff. If you need an East Side location, the rate for singles is unbeatable. Leo House, on the West Side, offers more for couples or groups.

THE PARKSIDE EVANGELINE RESIDENCE

18 Gramercy Park South
New York, NY 10003
(BETWEEN PARK AVENUE SOUTH AND IRVING PLACE)

VALUE ★ ★ ★ ★ ★

CLEANLINESS ★ ★ ★ ★

GUEST SERVICES ★ ★ ★ ★

SECURITY ★ ★ ★ ★ ★

(★POOR - ★★★★★EXCELLENT)

CATEGORY	Residence
PHONE	(212) 677-6200
FAX	(212) 677-0640
EMAIL	None
WEBSITE	None
RATES	Singles: $203-$223 weekly, Doubles: $198 weekly, per person. Includes breakfast and dinner. Three-month minimum stay

GUEST ROOMS	292 nonsmoking rooms on 17 floors, some shared baths
ROOM AMENITIES	Phone
RESTAURANTS	Cafeteria
BARS	None
CLIENTELE	Women, mainly ages 18-35
GUEST SERVICES	Maid service, TV lounges, fax and photocopy machines, self-service laundry, piano, irons and vacuum cleaners, sundeck, exercise equipment, access to (private) Gramercy Park
PARKING	None
CANCELLATION POLICY	4 weeks before arrival
WHEELCHAIR ACCESS	None

Rooms at the Parkside Evangeline overlook Gramercy Park.
Credit: Salvation Army

Most New Yorkers would kill for a room facing, and key to, Gramercy Park. Guests at the Parkside pay as little as $30 a night for both. Its location, low rates, and clublike atmosphere make it a top choice for young collegiate and career women. Rooms are generally small and vary in shape. Both singles and doubles are available with either private or shared bath, but no more than three rooms on a floor share a bathroom. There's a sink, phone, desk, and dresser, but permanent residents supply their own TVs, air conditioners, bedding, towels, soap, and toilet tissue. There's a $10 a week charge for the AC unit and a $10 installation fee.

No male guests are allowed in guest rooms, but you can entertain them in all the public areas. A pretty dining room off the lobby serves breakfast, lunch, and dinner; breakfast and dinner are included in your rent. There's a nonrefundable $25 application fee and refundable deposits for (long-term) security, phone service, and keys. If you are lucky enough to snag space here, you'll get a prime location at unbeatable rates.

PENINGTON FRIENDS HOUSE

215 E. 15th St.
New York, NY 10003
(BETWEEN SECOND AND THIRD AVENUES)

VALUE ★ ★ ★ ★

CLEANLINESS ★ ★ ★ ★

GUEST SERVICES ★ ★ ★ ★

SECURITY ★ ★ ★

(★POOR - ★★★★★EXCELLENT)

CATEGORY	Residence
PHONE	(212) 673-1730
FAX	None
EMAIL	None
WEBSITE	None
RATES	Long-term: $719-$1122 monthly, depends on room size and location. Sublets occasionally available. Overnight guests: $80 for one, $115

	for two, $135 for three, $150 for four. Rates include breakfast and dinner, except Saturday
GUEST ROOMS	24 rooms for permanent residents on 4 floors, 2 rooms for overnight guests, all nonsmoking, all shared bath
ROOM AMENITIES	Bedding and towels for overnight guests
RESTAURANTS	Dining room in basement
BARS	None
CLIENTELE	All nationalities, all ages
GUEST SERVICES	TV and VCR, kitchen, roof sundeck, patio garden, sidedeck, piano, coin-operated washer and dryer, *New York Times*
PARKING	None
CANCELLATION POLICY	10 days before arrival
WHEELCHAIR ACCESS	None

This Quaker community is truly a "little peace of Manhattan." You don't have to be a member of the Society of Friends, but all 24 residents are encouraged to practice Quaker principles of harmony and community service. The large brownstone forms part of a Quaker complex that includes the huge Quaker meeting house facing Stuyvesant Square and a private school on 16th Street.

Rooms on four floors vary in size, configuration, and furnishings. Some have lofts, some built-in book shelves, sinks, and desks; all have radiator heat. There is an extra charge for AC if you install a unit. At breakfast and dinner, residents and guests gather around trestle tables in the basement for meals that are the Penington's best-kept secret. Two chefs prepare a variety of vegetarian and meat dishes that are both flavorful and nutritious (They co-wrote a cookbook entitled *Meeting and Eating*.) Not surprisingly, there's little temptation to dine out; in fact, there's little temptation to leave. If you want a residence here, your best bet is a sublet, which puts you in line for a permanent room when one becomes available. Three months' rent (first, last, plus a security deposit) is required for permanent residence.

The Edith Darlington Room, decorated in Early American style and furnished with a small desk, two full-sized beds, and a sink, can accommodate overnight guests, who are advised to book a month in advance. Talented chefs; a relaxed, liberal atmosphere; and spacious public areas are Penington's perks as is its proximity to Union Square and New York University.

SEAFARERS AND INTERNATIONAL HOUSE

123 E. 15th St.
New York, NY 10003
(AT IRVING PLACE)

VALUE ★ ★ ★
CLEANLINESS ★ ★ ★ ★
GUEST SERVICES ★ ★ ★
SECURITY ★ ★ ★

(★POOR - ★★★★★EXCELLENT)

CATEGORY	Bare Essentials
PHONE	(212) 677-4800
FAX	(212) 353-0526
EMAIL	res@sihnyc.org
WEBSITE	www.sihnyc.org
RATES	Singles shared bath: $70
Singles private bath: $100
Doubles shared bath: $90
Doubles private bath: $120
Sailors get a discount.
21-day maximum stay
GUEST ROOMS	84 rooms on 9 floors, 50 allow smoking, only 17 have private baths
ROOM AMENITIES	AC, cable TV, phone with voice mail, hair dryer and iron on request
RESTAURANTS	None
BARS	None
CLIENTELE	Sailors and international travelers

GUEST SERVICES	Self-service laundry, 2 lounges, library, vending machines
PARKING	None
CANCELLATION POLICY	4 weeks before arrival
WHEELCHAIR ACCESS	None

Established in 1873 by the Lutheran Church to minister to immigrants and seafarers, this low-maintenance hotel now offers a port in the storm to budget travelers as well. A plaque reads: "Help us sustain our care to the brave and lonely worker of the sea and the forlorn traveler." A chapel off the lobby features modernistic stained-glass windows and an organ.

All rooms were refurbished in early 2001. The clean but shabby public areas are due for a makeover next, hopefully by early 2002. A spacious, quiet TV lounge and library on the second floor offers tables to work at, sofas, and a large desk. In the basement you'll find a smoking lounge, vending machines, a microwave, coin-operated laundry, and lockers.

The smallest room is clean and comfortable with a small desk and three-drawer armoire, central heat and air, a wall phone with voice mail, cable TV, and extra bedding. Doubles with private bath are roomy with the same furniture. Rooms without private baths have a sink. There are no closets. Bathrooms have a stall shower and soap, but no shampoo.

The advantage of SIH is its quiet location one block from Union Square with its subway connections and attractions. Management also gets points for its commitment to recycling and a guest survey. But if you need a room with private bath, SIH's rate can be improved and the facility itself lacks any trace of charm.

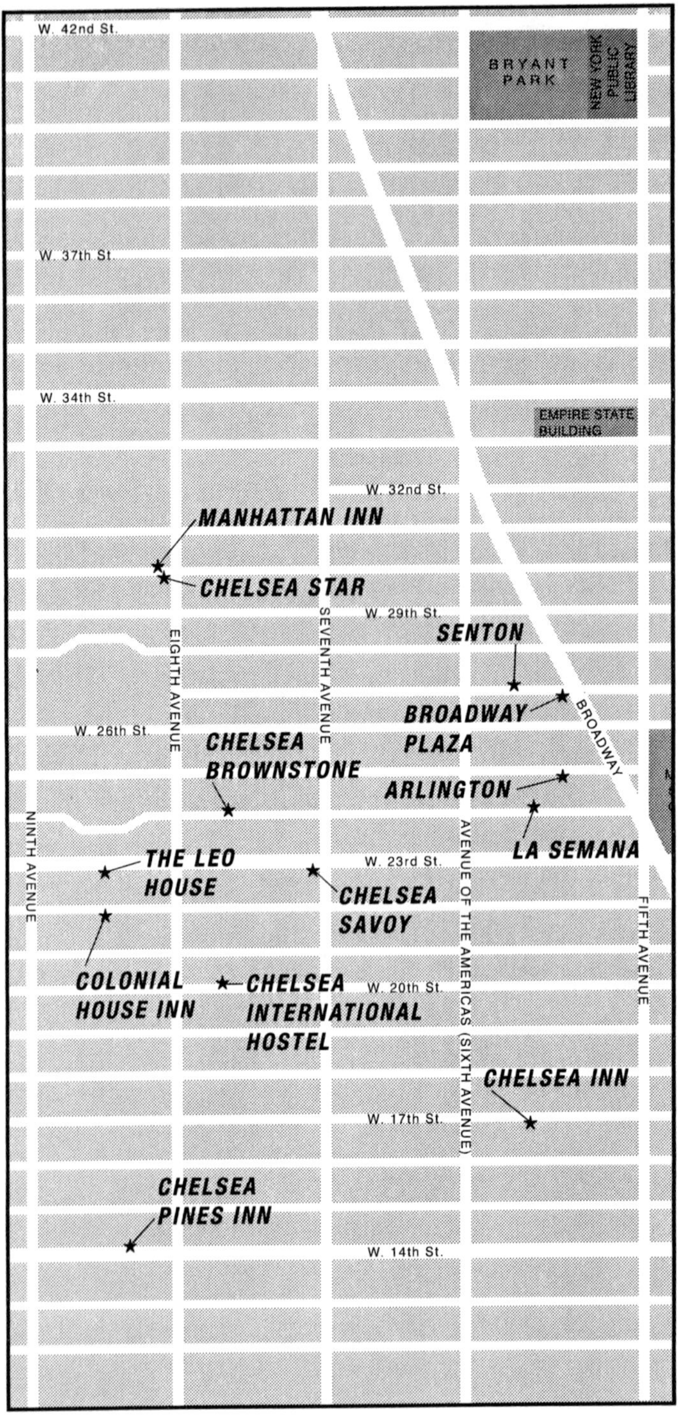
W. 42nd St.
BRYANT PARK
NEW YORK PUBLIC LIBRARY
W. 37th St.
W. 34th St.
EMPIRE STATE BUILDING
W. 32nd St.
MANHATTAN INN
CHELSEA STAR
W. 29th St.
SENTON
EIGHTH AVENUE
SEVENTH AVENUE
BROADWAY PLAZA
BROADWAY
W. 26th St.
CHELSEA BROWNSTONE
ARLINGTON
NINTH AVENUE
LA SEMANA
AVENUE OF THE AMERICAS (SIXTH AVENUE)
THE LEO HOUSE
W. 23rd St.
CHELSEA SAVOY
FIFTH AVENUE
COLONIAL HOUSE INN
CHELSEA INTERNATIONAL HOSTEL
W. 20th St.
CHELSEA INN
W. 17th St.
CHELSEA PINES INN
W. 14th St.

CHELSEA/FLATIRON

> *"From Eighth Street down, the men are earning it.*
> *From Eighth Street up, the women are spurning it.*
> *That's the way of this great town,*
> *From Eighth Street up and Eighth Street down!"*
> —19th-century reference to the Ladies
> Mile shopping district

THE NEIGHBORHOODS: Chelsea, the Flatiron District

Streets in Chelsea are largely residential, turn-of-the-century townhouses and apartment buildings; its avenues are commercial. Galleries representing some of America's best contemporary artists fill the converted warehouses from 10th to 12th avenues. The Flatiron District is named for the architectural oddity that stands where Broadway crosses Fifth Avenue at 23rd Street. This area was called the "Ladies Mile" in the late 19th century for its elegant department stores and has once again become a retail hub with superstores like Barnes & Noble and Bed Bath & Beyond.

   The resurgence of Chelsea as a vibrant neighborhood began in the 1980s with the arrival of a large gay community, joined in the 1990s by the art community, each group seeking alternatives to soaring rents in SoHo and Greenwich Village. More recently, the sports and entertainment complex along the Hudson River called Chelsea Piers has revitalized the waterfront. It offers everything from rock climbing to ice skating.

ARLINGTON HOTEL

18 W. 25th St.
New York, NY 10010
(BETWEEN BROADWAY AND SIXTH AVE.)

VALUE ★ ★ ★

CLEANLINESS ★ ★ ★ ★

GUEST SERVICES ★ ★ ★

SECURITY ★ ★ ★ ★

(★ POOR - ★ ★ ★ ★ ★ EXCELLENT)

CATEGORY	Bare Essentials
PHONE	(212) 645-3990
FAX	(212) 633-8952
EMAIL	brookew@hotelarlington.com
WEBSITE	www.hotelarlington.com
RATES	$109-$159; 2-night minimum on weekends. 10 percent discount to International Student Identity members, corporate guests, and travel agents
GUEST ROOMS	120 rooms, all smoking
ROOM AMENITIES	AC, cable TV, phone with voice mail, safe, mini-fridge
RESTAURANTS	None
BARS	None
CLIENTELE	Primarily European tourists with some Asians and Americans
GUEST SERVICES	Gift shop, tour desk, ATM in lobby, meeting room, vending machines
PARKING	None
CANCELLATION POLICY	48 hours before check-in
WHEELCHAIR ACCESS	None

A turn-of-the-century hotel with turn-of-the-century electrical wiring may be a poor choice for guests who crave in-room comforts. The good news is that all rooms have recently been refurbished and appear clean and attractive. But they are short on amenities. Televisions lack cable, and there are no hair dryers, toiletries, nor irons in sight. Telephones have voice mail but no dataports. On the plus side, all rooms have a safe, mini-fridge, and air conditioning, and most rooms have a closet and desk.

Technically, the Arlington is situated in a narrow slice of midtown known as the Flatiron District, for the curiously shaped building at the intersection of Broadway and Fifth Avenue at 23rd Street. It offers convenient access to Fifth Avenue shopping and tourist attractions, such as the Empire State Building. It also offers a discount to students with the ISI card, business clients, and travel agents. Tour desk staff help visitors take advantage of the city's brightest lights.

CHELSEA BROWNSTONE

241 W. 24th St.
New York, NY 10011
(BETWEEN SEVENTH AND EIGHTH AVENUES)

VALUE ★ ★ ★ ★

CLEANLINESS ★ ★ ★ ★

GUEST SERVICES NONE

SECURITY ★ ★

(★POOR - ★★★★★EXCELLENT)

CATEGORY	Guest House
PHONE	(212) 206-9237
FAX	(212) 388-9954
EMAIL	None
WEBSITE	www.chelsea-apts.com
RATES	Studio: $130-$150 1-bedroom: $150-$180 Cash and traveler's checks only 3-night minimum
GUEST ROOMS	8 units on 4 floors, all nonsmoking
ROOM AMENITIES	AC, cable TV, phone (free local calls), kitchenette
RESTAURANTS	None
BARS	None
CLIENTELE	Mix of European and extended-stay Americans
GUEST SERVICES	None

PARKING	None
CANCELLATION POLICY	7 days before check-in
WHEELCHAIR ACCESS	None

Chelsea Brownstone is both the official name and description of this semi-hosted lodging. Don't bother looking for a sign. In fact, nothing about this building distinguishes it as a hotel. The guest units look and feel just like a Manhattan apartment—except they are cleaner, bigger, and everything works.

Both studios and one-bedrooms feature exposed brick walls and hardwood floors. The décor is by no means opulent, but definitely comfortable. Most of the furniture was recently refurbished, even though it wasn't in disrepair. (Harken, midtown hotels.) Also, all the televisions will be replaced and answering machines added by the end of 2001. Two studios have a loft bed with a second bed below. All the others feature one queen bed. Several of the rooms also offer sofa beds.

Kitchenettes come equipped with a dishwasher, microwave, coffeemaker, stove, refrigerator, and all utensils. Tiny bathrooms are the only real drawback here, but they're clean and in good condition.

Payment is expected upon arrival. Pets and smoking are not allowed. The two rooms with a private terrace and outdoor garden accommodate smokers. There's no daily maid service, rather rooms are cleaned once a week and whenever guests leave. There isn't a hotel desk or staff on site 24 hours, but usually someone is around during the day, and the owners are accessible. All visitors must be buzzed in.

If you like being independent and truly feeling part of a Manhattan neighborhood, you'll enjoy the Chelsea Brownstone.

CHELSEA/FLATIRON

CHELSEA INN

46 W. 17th St.
New York, NY 10011
(BETWEEN FIFTH AND SIXTH AVENUES)

VALUE ★ ★ ★
CLEANLINESS ★ ★ ★ ★
GUEST SERVICES NONE
SECURITY ★ ★ ★
(★POOR - ★ ★ ★ ★ ★ EXCELLENT)

CATEGORY	Euro-style
PHONE	(212) 645-8989
	(800) 640-6469 Reservations
FAX	(212) 645-1903
EMAIL	reservations@chelseainn.com
WEBSITE	www.chelseainn.com. Offers special rates during January, February, and July
RATES	Shared bath: $109-$149
	Private bath: $149-$269
GUEST ROOMS	26 rooms on 5 floors, all smoking, no elevator
ROOM AMENITIES	AC, cable TV, phone with voice mail, mini-fridge, coffeemaker, safe, hot plate
RESTAURANTS	None
BARS	None
CLIENTELE	A mixed crowd
GUEST SERVICES	None
PARKING	None
CANCELLATION POLICY	48 hours before check-in
WHEELCHAIR ACCESS	None

Geography is the best thing the Chelsea Inn has going for it. Just off Fifth Avenue on the eastern border of Chelsea, this small hotel is an easy 10 minutes to both Union Square and the Flatiron District. New York University and the heart of Greenwich Village are no more than 20 minutes on foot.

That's the good news; now for the rest. The rooms are in fair repair but on the small side. With little natural lighting, the muted décor comes off as tired and a bit depressing rather than subtle. An odd, yet functional collection of furniture fills the rooms. Knitted coverlets may remind you of childhood visits to your grandparents.

Most rooms have double beds, and all feature at least a small desk. Mattresses are firm, but some of them are lower to the floor than one would like. Surprisingly, many of the rooms offer good-sized closets with hangers and shelves. The average kitchenette is really more of a tiny closet equipped with a mini-refrigerator, coffeemaker and an ancient hot plate we'd be wary of using. Utensils and dishes are available upon request. Kitchen areas in the three studios are larger.

Bathrooms make a respectable showing, both in size and décor. Some have black-and-white tile with rather cool fixtures as well as a full-length mirror. However, no vanity shelf plus the bathroom's dim lighting ensure you'll be applying your makeup near the window. Baths are shared by two rooms, so you're not using hallway facilities. The studios and one-room suites have a private bath and small living-room area. Two-room suites are just two average guest rooms that share one bathroom.

Overall, there's nothing seriously wrong with the Chelsea Inn. However, there's nothing notably right about it either.

CHELSEA INTERNATIONAL HOSTEL

251 W. 20th St.
New York, NY 10011
(BETWEEN SEVENTH AND EIGHTH AVENUES)

VALUE ★ ★ ★ ★

CLEANLINESS ★ ★ ★

GUEST SERVICES ★ ★ ★ ★

SECURITY ★ ★ ★

(★POOR - ★★★★★EXCELLENT)

CATEGORY	Hostel
PHONE	(212) 647-0010
	(800) 720-5086 Reservations
FAX	(212) 727-7289
EMAIL	Chelsea_International_Hostel@msn.com
WEBSITE	www.chelseahostel.com

RATES	Dorm rooms: $25 Double private rooms: $60 Prices include taxes and tariffs
GUEST ROOMS	Accommodations for 320 guests primarily in bunk beds, all shared baths, smoking throughout, no elevator
ROOM AMENITIES	AC, sink, locker, no towels
RESTAURANTS	None
BARS	None
CLIENTELE	Budget travelers at least 18 years old, unless accompanied by an adult
GUEST SERVICES	Communal kitchens, vending machines, internet kiosks, free coffee and tea, coin-operated washers and dryers, TV lounge
PARKING	None
CANCELLATION POLICY	None
WHEELCHAIR ACCESS	None

We didn't believe it either, but there is a hostel in one of the coolest and safest neighborhoods in Manhattan. The buildings and guest accommodations at the Chelsea International Hostel are about as bare bones as you can get. Unless you're in a private room, men and women are assigned separate quarters. Rooms feature bunk beds, except for some of the private accommodations, which have double beds. Most of the rooms sleep four to six people. Wall hooks and lockers are the only storage space. Remember to bring your own padlock.

Each room features one sink and a small mirror. Bathrooms are adequate—not terrifying but not a pleasant surprise. Four to six rooms share one bathroom with multiple shower stalls and toilets. Note: The hostel provides all bed linens but no towels.

What the hostel lacks in aesthetics, it makes up for in guest services. Every Wednesday is free pizza night. There are two communal kitchens and dining areas, open until midnight. Most people hang out in the outdoor courtyard, TV lounge, or internet kiosk area. The coin-operated laundry machines are a great perk, but the facilities close at 8 p.m.

Expect to make reservations at least six weeks in advance for June through October visits, as well as for

Spring Break. A credit card is necessary to hold a room. No deposit is required, but full payment is expected upon arrival. For security purposes, guests need a valid passport, including Canadian and U.S. travelers. The hostel is right across the street from a police station, plus it has its own 24-hour security. But when it gets hectic around the main entrance and check-in desk, it's easy for a nonguest to slip by.

The biggest drawback to this place is that it looks like a hostel. Its strongest selling point is location. New Yorkers pay top dollar to live in Chelsea.

CHELSEA PINES INN

317 W. 14th St.
New York, NY 10014
(BETWEEN EIGHTH AND NINTH AVENUES)

VALUE ★ ★ ★ ★

CLEANLINESS ★ ★ ★ ★

GUEST SERVICES ★ ★

SECURITY ★ ★ ★ ★

(★POOR - ★★★★★EXCELLENT)

CATEGORY	Bed & Breakfast
PHONE	(212) 929-1023
FAX	(212) 620-5646
EMAIL	cpiny@aol.com
WEBSITE	www.chelseapinesinn.com Offers last-minute specials
RATES	Shared bath: $89-$159 Private bath: $119-$189
GUEST ROOMS	24 rooms on 5 floors, some shared toilets, smoking throughout, no elevator
ROOM AMENITIES	AC, cable TV with HBO, phone with answering machine, clock radio, mini-fridge, hair dryer, iron and ironing board, shampoo
RESTAURANTS	None
BARS	None
CLIENTELE	Strong gay and lesbian following

GUEST SERVICES	Continental breakfast, free coffee, tea and cookies all day, soda and bottled water for sale
PARKING	None
CANCELLATION POLICY	$50 or 1-night penalty if cancelled within 7 days of check-in
WHEELCHAIR ACCESS	None

The Chelsea Pines Inn has two defining characteristics: its connection to the gay and lesbian community and an amazing collection of vintage movie posters. Each room is named for a movie star—Paul Newman, Sophia Loren, and Deborah Kerr—and features posters of their films. Naturally, these collectibles are bolted to the walls lest temptation overcome star-gazing guests. Rooms are attractive, but not opulent, and the owners pay special attention to small details and homey touches.

Of the shared-bath accommodations, all have a sink and shower, but rely on hallway toilets. Usually no more than two units per floor share a toilet. Some of the rooms with a private bath also have a breakfast area and microwave oven. One drawback: closets tend to be small.

A continental breakfast is served in a café sitting area, which also offers newspapers and magazines. Guests are welcome to gather here all day and help themselves to coffee and tea or buy soda and bottled water. An outdoor garden is popular when warm weather permits. The owners really want you to indulge your sweet tooth: you'll enjoy chocolate mints on your pillow at night, chocolate kisses at the front desk, and Krispy Kreme donuts for breakfast.

Most weekends require a three-night minimum stay. Plan to book six to eight weeks in advance, but special last-minute and seasonal rates are offered online. Full payment is required upon arrival. A tight security system is reassuring. All visitors must be buzzed in and guest rooms open with an electronic key card rather than a key.

On the border between Chelsea and the West Village, the Chelsea Pines Inn is both fun and affordable.

SLEEP CHEAP IN NEW YORK

CHELSEA SAVOY HOTEL

204 W. 23rd St.
New York, NY 10011
(AT SEVENTH AVE.)

VALUE ★ ★ ★
CLEANLINESS ★ ★ ★ ★ ★
GUEST SERVICES ★ ★ ★
SECURITY ★ ★ ★

(★ POOR - ★ ★ ★ ★ ★ EXCELLENT)

CATEGORY	Limited Services
PHONE	(212) 929-9353
FAX	(212) 741-6309
EMAIL	None
WEBSITE	www.citysearch.com/nyc/chelseasavoy
RATES	Singles: $99-$115 Doubles: $135-$165 Quads: $145-$195
GUEST ROOMS	90 rooms on 5 floors, 3 smoking floors
ROOM AMENITIES	AC, cable TV, phone with voice mail and dataport, Gilchrist & Soames bath products, hair dryer, iron and ironing board
RESTAURANTS	Yes
BARS	None
CLIENTELE	A mixed crowd
GUEST SERVICES	Continental breakfast, *USA Today* delivered weekdays, vending machines on every floor
PARKING	None
CANCELLATION POLICY	24 hours before check-in
WHEELCHAIR ACCESS	Yes

Unveiled about four years ago, this very affordable hotel offers many of the amenities seen in more expensive and larger properties. From the magnetic-lock system to the Gilchrist & Soames bath products to the goose down pillows, the Chelsea Savoy is a good value.

Rooms are average, both in size and décor. All the beds are doubles or queens. The solid, wood furniture certainly isn't trendy, but what it may lack in style it makes up for in substance. You won't find any lumpy mattresses or broken furniture in this hotel. Generous closets and large writing desks are a welcome surprise. All the bathrooms offer plenty of space and feature a built-in hair dryer and vanity shelf. During the week, *USA Today* is delivered to each room.

A new restaurant just off the hotel lobby opened in Fall 2001. If you're in the mood for donuts, walk a block to Krispy Kreme. A visit to New York isn't complete without a sugar headache from too many Krispy Kreme donuts. Every five to 10 minutes, hot donuts come off the conveyer belt and they are worth the wait. Also, this shop keeps late hours so it's the perfect last stop after a night on the town.

A subway station next door to the hotel puts you in easy reach of Macy's Department Store, Penn Station, Madison Square Garden, Times Square, Central Park, and a ferry

The Savoy offers value and comfort at a convenient location.
Credit: Chelsea Savoy Hotel

to the Statue of Liberty. While its location is great in terms of getting around, 23rd Street as well as Seventh Avenue are noisy, busy thoroughfares. They are not the streets for a relaxing Sunday stroll. Double-paned windows keep out some of the hubbub, but if you're a light sleeper make sure your room is on the top floor.

CHELSEA STAR HOTEL

300 W. 30th St.
New York, NY 10001
(AT EIGHTH AVE.)

VALUE ★ ★ ★

CLEANLINESS ★ ★ ★

GUEST SERVICES ★ ★ ★

SECURITY ★ ★ ★ ★

(★POOR - ★★★★★EXCELLENT)

CATEGORY	Euro-style
PHONE	(212) 244-7827 (877) 827-6969 Reservations
FAX	(212) 279-9018
EMAIL	reservations@starhotelny.com
WEBSITE	www.chelseastar.com
RATES	Dorms: $25-$35 Private rooms: $82-$148 Suites: $129-$250, $920 per week, and $3,000 per month. Rates include taxes
GUEST ROOMS	All nonsmoking, 2 coed dorms sleep 4 to 8, 20 private rooms share baths, 4 one-room suites have private baths
ROOM AMENITIES	AC, cable TV
RESTAURANTS	None
BARS	None
CLIENTELE	Europeans of all ages
GUEST SERVICES	Lunch voucher, valet laundry, internet kiosk, terrace, fax for a charge
PARKING	None
CANCELLATION POLICY	48 hours before check-in
WHEELCHAIR ACCESS	None

This theme hotel is like a tidy Carlton Arms. But unlike its East Side counterpart, which displays work by many international artists, rooms here have been designed by one artist, Rob Graf, and they are tame by comparison.

The Cher Room boasts leopard-print painted walls, carpet, and lamp. The Shakespeare Room displays a faux canopy bed and the Bard's immortal poetry on the wall. Add to these the Star Trek Room, the Madame Butterfly Room, the Cleopatra Room, and the room Madonna lived in when she was a struggling artist, and you've got a bizarre cultural grab bag.

All private rooms are just large enough to fit a double bed. Two dorm rooms are coed, and all rooms share attractive black-tiled bathrooms with spacious stall showers. Suites can sleep up to five people on double, fold-out, and roll-away beds. They offer a fully equipped kitchen, sitting room, and separate bedroom. Hallways are brightly painted and feature the Chelsea's logo—a neon star. Retaining the metal fire doors to each room is another quirky, pleasing touch. Security here is tight, with a buzz-in system, numberless keys, and front desk staff on duty 24 hours.

This lodging especially appeals to the young, who can shift for themselves, need cheap sleeps, and don't miss amenities—though it's not clear why sleeping in the Cher Room makes one "historically cool," which is how the hotel describes its niche. Suites are also not a bad deal, rented at $920 a week, including taxes.

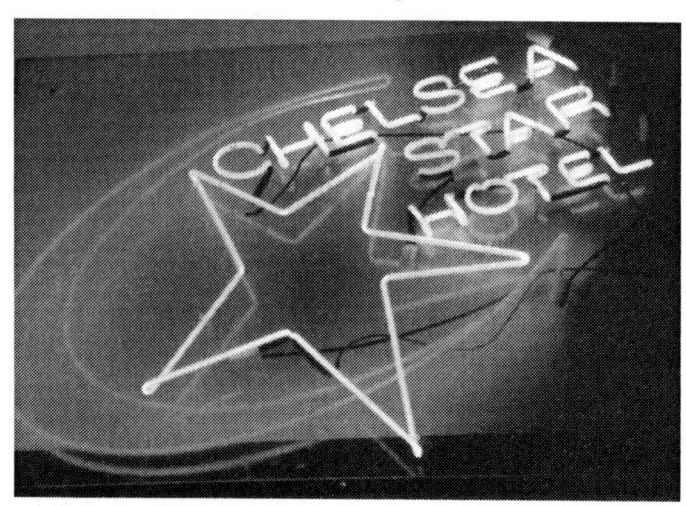

Credit: Chelsea Star Hotel

SLEEP CHEAP IN NEW YORK

COLONIAL HOUSE INN

318 W. 22nd St.
New York, NY 10011
(BETWEEN EIGHTH AND NINTH AVENUES)

VALUE ★ ★ ★
CLEANLINESS ★ ★ ★ ★ ★
GUEST SERVICES ★ ★ ★
SECURITY ★ ★ ★ ★
(★POOR - ★ ★ ★ ★ ★ EXCELLENT)

CATEGORY	Bed & Breakfast
PHONE	(212) 243-9669
FAX	(212) 633-1612
EMAIL	houseinn@aol.com
WEBSITE	www.colonialhouseinn.com Offers seasonal and weekday discounts
RATES	Shared bath: $80-$125 Private bath: $125-$140
GUEST ROOMS	20 rooms on 4 floors, about one-half shared bath, smoking throughout, no elevator
ROOM AMENITIES	AC, cable TV, phone, sink in shared bath units, mini-fridge in larger rooms
RESTAURANTS	None
BARS	None
CLIENTELE	A strong gay and lesbian following
GUEST SERVICES	Continental breakfast, internet kiosk, sundeck, newspapers
PARKING	None
CANCELLATION POLICY	14 days before check-in, 2-night penalty
WHEELCHAIR ACCESS	None

This 1850 brownstone on a quiet residential block caters to a largely gay and lesbian crowd, but welcomes everyone equally. It's aesthetically pleasing—an art collection brightens public areas—and staff don't balk if you pester them with questions or requests.

Cheaper units have a full-sized bed, and the larger rooms offer a queen-sized bed and a bit more furniture.

Closets are usually little more than an indentation in the wall with wooden hangers, so be advised to pack light. Unfortunately, the rooms don't have answering machines or voice mail, so you have to rely on the desk staff. About half of the 20 accommodations feature private bathrooms. So on each floor, two to three rooms share one bathroom. Carefully decorated and sparkling clean, each provides a hair dryer and vanity shelf.

A well-maintained, gently curving staircase connects all four floors. Guests enjoy access to the rooftop sundeck, which has a clothing optional area. Also, rates include a continental breakfast served on the first floor in a separate area from the small lobby. Good news for sleepy heads: breakfast is served until noon. An internet kiosk in the lobby allows you to check your email. Weekends are more expensive than weekdays. A two-night deposit is required and full payment is expected upon arrival. All reservations for seven or more days receive a 5 percent discount. Security is well maintained. The main desk is staffed 24 hours, and everyone must be buzzed in—whether it's 2 p.m. or 2 a.m.

Rooms are small and shared baths can be inconvenient, but this is a welcoming environment with excellent facilities.

SLEEP CHEAP IN NEW YORK

HOTEL BROADWAY PLAZA

1155 Broadway
New York, NY 10001
(AT 27TH ST.)

VALUE ★ ★ ★ ★
CLEANLINESS ★ ★ ★ ★ ★
GUEST SERVICES ★ ★ ★ ★
SECURITY ★ ★ ★ ★ ★
(★POOR - ★★★★★EXCELLENT)

CATEGORY	Boutique
PHONE	(212) 679-7665
	(877)-50HOTEL Reservations
FAX	(212) 679-7694
EMAIL	broadwayplaza@aol.com
WEBSITE	www.broadwayplazahotel.com
	Offers packages from $109
RATES	$149-$309
	Corporate and government discounts
GUEST ROOMS	69 rooms on 12 floors, some nonsmoking floors
ROOM AMENITIES	AC, cable TV with pay movies, 2-line phone with voice mail and dataport, hair dryer, iron and ironing board, mini-fridge
RESTAURANTS	None
BARS	None
CLIENTELE	64 percent are business travelers, mostly tourists on weekends
GUEST SERVICES	Continental breakfast, coffee and tea available on 4th floor, 24-hour room service from neighborhood restaurants, valet laundry
PARKING	None
CANCELLATION POLICY	48 hours before check-in
WHEELCHAIR ACCESS	Yes

On bustling Broadway in the wholesale shopping district, a narrow marbled entrance leads to one of the city's most intriguing new hotels. Guest rooms in this former office building vary in shape, though their décor is identical: a palette of soft pastels. Rooms are bright, fresh, and spacious. The smallest and least expensive offers a double bed, the next step up is a queen-sized bed, then a king, and the suites are as large as condos.

Standard amenities include phones with voice mail and dataports, irons, cable TV with pay movies, mini-fridges, and a thermostat that lets you control the amount of heat and air. Mattresses are nice and firm. There's no trace of smoke in the rooms that allow smoking (a tribute to an efficient cleaning staff).

As with room configurations, no two bathrooms are alike, and they all offer ample toiletries and a hair dryer. The trapezoidal corner rooms on upper floors face the Empire State Building, hence their popularity. Extra services—24-hour room service, overnight dry cleaning, and free tea and coffee—add to your comfort and convenience. (Sleepy heads beware: breakfast is first come, first served.)

General Manager Peter Jaques and staff operate in overdrive to please their guests. "We have the advantage over our competition," says Jaques, "in that we're modern and offer lots of space and light." The space alone makes this squeaky clean lodging an excellent and (by New York standards) unusual find.

A palette of soft pastels brightens guest quarters.
Credit: Hotel Broadway Plaza

SLEEP CHEAP IN NEW YORK

LA SEMANA HOTEL

25 W. 24th St.
New York, NY 10010
(BETWEEN BROADWAY AND SIXTH AVE.)

VALUE ★ ★ ★

CLEANLINESS ★ ★ ★

GUEST SERVICES ★

SECURITY ★ ★ ★ ★

(★POOR - ★★★★★EXCELLENT)

CATEGORY	Euro-style
PHONE	(212) 255-5944
FAX	(212) 675-3830
EMAIL	None
WEBSITE	www.citysearch.com/nyc/lasemana
RATES	$119-$269
GUEST ROOMS	44 rooms on 5 floors, 31 with shared bath, 1 suite, all smoking
ROOM AMENITIES	AC, cable TV, mini-fridge, Jacuzzis in 10 rooms
RESTAURANTS	None
BARS	None
CLIENTELE	Primarily Korean, Hispanic, and African-American
GUEST SERVICES	Continental breakfast
PARKING	None
CANCELLATION POLICY	48 hours before check-in
WHEELCHAIR ACCESS	None

"New York's premier boutique Jacuzzi hotel" caters to those who want more than a bed for sleeping. Guests who take advantage of its three-hour "freshen-up special," for example, won't be wasting precious time on ZZZs.

The rooms with shared bath are the least desirable, and they don't include those relaxing whirlpool tubs. (In one that we visited, the air conditioning unit and windows were 15 feet high, inaccessible to anyone but an NBA player.) Jacuzzi rooms that get the hotel's star billing are equipped with huge ceiling and wall mirrors, large-screen TVs, and a splashy décor—like zebra-patterned carpets and leopard-

CHELSEA/FLATIRON

skin bedspreads—that would keep anyone wide awake. Mini-fridges are nearby to chill your favorite bottle of bubbly. The Jacuzzi suite has a steam room and a walk-in closet, but most rooms offer only a few shelves, hardly conducive to long stays. Tiny bathrooms with stall showers provide hair dryers so you can return to work looking tidy.

For players whose idea of excitement is indoor sports, La Semana is probably just the ticket. But family entertainment it's not.

THE LEO HOUSE

332 W. 23rd St.
New York, NY 10011
(BETWEEN EIGHTH AND NINTH AVENUES)

VALUE ★ ★ ★ ★ ★
CLEANLINESS ★ ★ ★ ★
GUEST SERVICES ★ ★ ★ ★ ★
SECURITY ★ ★ ★ ★ ★
(★POOR - ★ ★ ★ ★ ★ EXCELLENT)

CATEGORY	Guest House
PHONE	(212) 929-1010
FAX	(212) 366-6801
EMAIL	None
WEBSITE	None
RATES	Singles: $62-$72 Doubles: $70-$78 Family rooms (up to 6): $140 Discounts to clergy and hospital visitors Minimum stay: 3 nights Maximum stay: 2 weeks
GUEST ROOMS	60 nonsmoking rooms, some shared baths
ROOM AMENITIES	TV, phone, some rooms have AC June-September for an extra $2 a night; safe, hair dryer, and iron available on request
RESTAURANTS	Cafeteria serves breakfast
BARS	None
CLIENTELE	Families and couples

GUEST SERVICES	Maid service, TV lounge, vending machines, self-service laundry, meeting room and library, wake-up calls, continental breakfast on Sunday
PARKING	None
CANCELLATION POLICY	5 days before arrival
WHEELCHAIR ACCESS	None

Formerly a residence that dates to 1889, this Catholic nonprofit now caters to overnight guests. All rooms are clean but well-worn. Even the singles and doubles that share a tub shower in the hallway have a sink and toilet in the room; the savings is $10. Family rooms can sleep up to six people and have private baths. About one-third of the rooms are equipped with air conditioners and the extra $2 charge is a blessing when New York sidewalks are sizzling. Each room has a TV with limited channels, a desk, a walk-in closet, and a phone. Ask for a hair dryer, iron, or safe, if you need one.

Two second floor rooms are dedicated to reading and meeting space with two conference tables, a copy machine, and audio visual equipment. The dining room serves a hot and cold breakfast for $6. Free continental breakfast is served Sundays. You may want to eat it in the pleasant patio garden. Security is exemplary: guests are buzzed in, the front desk is staffed 24 hours, and a security guard is always on duty. Don't expect to entertain guests in your room; they are confined to public areas. And no burning incense in your room either. It may set off the smoke alarm.

The Leo House is a remarkable find in bustling Chelsea. This peaceful retreat with a Christian consciousness offers plenty of services at very reasonable rates.

CHELSEA/FLATIRON

MANHATTAN INN

303 W. 30th St.
New York, NY 10001
(BETWEEN EIGHTH AND NINTH AVENUES)

VALUE ★ ★ ★ ★

CLEANLINESS ★ ★ ★

GUEST SERVICES ★ ★ ★

SECURITY ★ ★ ★ ★

(★POOR - ★★★★★EXCELLENT)

CATEGORY	Bare Essentials
PHONE	(212) 629-9612
FAX	(212) 629-9613
EMAIL	reservations@manhattaninn.com
WEBSITE	www.manhattaninn.com
RATES	Singles: $69-$89 Doubles: $89-$120
GUEST ROOMS	33 rooms on 4 floors, all smoking, no elevator
ROOM AMENITIES	AC, phone, cable TV, VCR
RESTAURANTS	None
BARS	None
CLIENTELE	Leisure travelers, especially European and Japanese
GUEST SERVICES	Continental breakfast, video rentals, valet laundry
PARKING	None
CANCELLATION POLICY	48 hours before check-in
WHEELCHAIR ACCESS	None

This is a tourist-class lodging that really knows how to cater to tourists. Friendly, casual front-desk staff set a welcoming tone.

Guest rooms are not Martha Stewart-approved; their décor and amenities are sparse. But the small accommodations are adequately clean and smell fresh despite a "smoking permitted" policy. Closets range from hooks on the wall to a small area with hangers. The larger rooms have better closets, and all have a chest of drawers. The hotel doesn't offer voice mail, but does provide a video library at $2 per movie. Most bathrooms have tub/showers, and generally they're in fair condition. Bathrooms in the smaller rooms are tiny. How tiny? You have to kneel on the toilet to shut the door.

Full payment is required upon arrival. A minimal continental breakfast is included in your rate. Luckily, the hotel is right next to a small 24-hour grocery. Valet laundry is available for washables, no dry cleaning. The same-day service is $4 per load. Security is acceptable: all guests are required to leave their room key at the front desk, and everyone must be buzzed in. The front desk is staffed 24 hours a day.

The Manhattan Inn is across the street from the Chelsea Star Hostel, if part of your group needs cheaper accommodations. Penn Station and Madison Square Garden are within a few blocks. The Jacob Javits Convention Center is a brisk 15-minute walk away.

You wouldn't book a room at the Manhattan Inn to bask in its services and amenities. But for a clean room with a private bath, it offers excellent value.

SENTON HOTEL

39-41 W. 27th St.
New York, NY 10001
(BETWEEN BROADWAY AND SIXTH AVE.)

VALUE ★

CLEANLINESS ★ ★

GUEST SERVICES NONE

SECURITY ★ ★

(★POOR - ★★★★★EXCELLENT)

CATEGORY	Bare Essentials
PHONE	(212) 684-5800
FAX	(212) 545-1690
EMAIL	None
WEBSITE	www.sentonhotel.com
RATES	$60-$100
GUEST ROOMS	70 rooms on 7 floors, some shared baths, all smoking

ROOM AMENITIES	AC, cable TV, phone, mini-fridge
RESTAURANTS	None
BARS	None
CLIENTELE	Mostly foreign tourists
GUEST SERVICES	None
PARKING	None
CANCELLATION POLICY	24 hours before check-in
WHEELCHAIR ACCESS	None

The half-lit blue neon sign that identifies the Senton Hotel is your first clue that this lodging may be half-serious. It's definitely at the low-end of the budget hotel spectrum.

Double/doubles are large with a mini-fridge, phone, ancient AC, radiator heat, and TV with limited cable channels. A single with double bed is much smaller, with the same equipment. Suites can sleep up to eight in two rooms, each with two double beds. They have a full-sized refrigerator, microwave, large desk, and a vanity dresser.

Electric radiators in all rooms may indicate drafty rooms and/or inadequate heat in winter. Why management has placed a wall mirror only high enough to show your knee caps or a TV 20 feet off the floor is one of the Senton's little mysteries. One of the shared toilets was so poorly designed the door wouldn't fully open. Bathrooms are equipped with stall showers, towels, soap, and plastic cups. They don't want to pamper you too much.

Though rates are attractive, the Senton comes close to the proverbial roach motel. We took their advice and followed a sign that read "This Way Out." The rate card quotes Woody Guthrie, but we promise you won't be bound for glory if you stay here. Seek elsewhere if you want to be in this neighborhood.

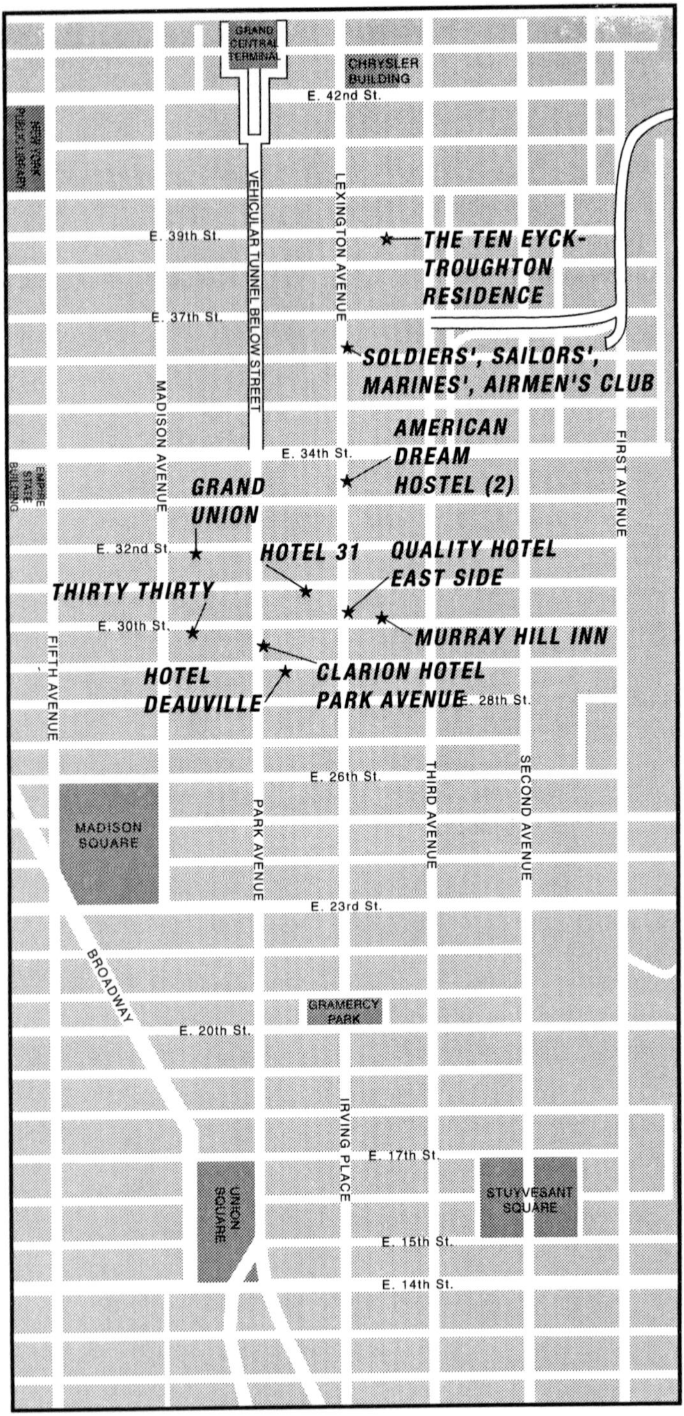
GRAND CENTRAL TERMINAL
CHRYSLER BUILDING
E. 42nd St.
NEW YORK PUBLIC LIBRARY
VEHICULAR TUNNEL BELOW STREET
LEXINGTON AVENUE
E. 39th St.
THE TEN EYCK-TROUGHTON RESIDENCE
E. 37th St.
SOLDIERS', SAILORS', MARINES', AIRMEN'S CLUB
MADISON AVENUE
AMERICAN DREAM HOSTEL (2)
E. 34th St.
FIRST AVENUE
EMPIRE STATE BUILDING
GRAND UNION
E. 32nd St.
HOTEL 31
QUALITY HOTEL EAST SIDE
THIRTY THIRTY
E. 30th St.
MURRAY HILL INN
FIFTH AVENUE
HOTEL DEAUVILLE
CLARION HOTEL PARK AVENUE
E. 28th St.
E. 26th St.
THIRD AVENUE
SECOND AVENUE
MADISON SQUARE
PARK AVENUE
E. 23rd St.
BROADWAY
GRAMERCY PARK
E. 20th St.
IRVING PLACE
E. 17th St.
UNION SQUARE
STUYVESANT SQUARE
E. 15th St.
E. 14th St.

MURRAY HILL

> "I practically lived in Grand Central Terminal at one period (it has all the conveniences and I had no other place to stay) and the great hall seemed to me one of the more inspiring interiors in New York...."
>
> —E.B. White

Lined with brownstones and condominiums from E. 28th Street north to E. 42nd Street, this neighborhood is a respite from the din and commotion of midtown. Of course, it also lacks the excitement of midtown with the only visitor attractions being the sedate Morgan Library and high-tech Science, Industry, and Business Library in the former B. Altman Building. If you include Grand Central Terminal on 42nd Street, the excitement factor jumps. This Beaux Arts gem with its sky ceiling depicting the constellations, gold- and nickel-plated chandeliers, and marble corridors has been recently renovated, and the result is a triumph. Stop in, even if you're not catching a train, or take the Municipal Art Society's free tour.

SLEEP CHEAP IN NEW YORK

AMERICAN DREAM HOSTEL (2)

227 Lexington Ave.
New York, NY 10016
(BETWEEN E. 33RD AND E. 34TH STREETS)

VALUE ★ ★ ★ ★

CLEANLINESS ★ ★ ★ ★

GUEST SERVICES ★ ★

SECURITY ★ ★ ★ ★

(★POOR - ★★★★★EXCELLENT)

CATEGORY	Bed & Breakfast
PHONE	(212) 779-3974
FAX	(212) 481-0417
EMAIL	Amdreltd1@aol.com
WEBSITE	www.hostels.com/americandream
RATES	Dorms: $40, $250/week Private rooms: $80, $500/week Only cash and traveler's checks Rates include taxes
GUEST ROOMS	Coed dorm rooms sleep 6 in bunk beds, 4 private rooms share a bathroom, all nonsmoking
ROOM AMENITIES	AC, TV without cable
RESTAURANTS	None
BARS	None
CLIENTELE	Europeans who usually book for a week or more
GUEST SERVICES	Common kitchen where guests help themselves to breakfast foods, living-room with a phone and cable TV
PARKING	None
CANCELLATION POLICY	48 hours before check-in
WHEELCHAIR ACCESS	None

The misnamed "American Dream Hostel" is truly a bed and breakfast, and a small street sign on Lexington Avenue announces just that. Manager Brenda Barreto will buzz you in to a second floor walk-up and invite you to help yourself to tea or coffee after you unpack. She and husband Lou don't live on the premises, but Lou often stays over if the place is crowded. Guests are given a key to the front door as well as to their room.

Open two years, they have a loyal following of European singles and families, who usually stay a week. And who can blame them? The place is clean, homey, and though there are no cooking privileges, the refrigerator allows you to store food and save your money for serious pleasures.

One private room sleeps four, another three, and two rooms sleep two people. While there are two toilets and separate baths, it does get crowded at rush hour. Guests usually gather in the evenings around a TV in the common room because, unlike room TVs, it offers a variety of cable channels. This B&B offers good value and the comforts of home in a central location.

CLARION HOTEL PARK AVENUE

429 Park Ave. South
New York, NY 10016
(BETWEEN E. 29TH AND E. 30TH STREETS)

VALUE ★ ★ ★ ★ ★

CLEANLINESS ★ ★ ★ ★

GUEST SERVICES ★ ★ ★

SECURITY ★ ★ ★ ★ ★

(★POOR - ★★★★★EXCELLENT)

CATEGORY	Limited Services
PHONE	(212) 532-4860
	(800) 258-4290 Reservations
FAX	(212) 545-9727
EMAIL	clarionhotelpark@hotmail.com
WEBSITE	www.bestnyhotels.com
RATES	$89-$299
	10 percent discount to AAA and AARP members
GUEST ROOMS	60 rooms on 7 floors, 2 smoking floors
ROOM AMENITIES	AC, cable TV with HBO, 2 phones with voice mail and dataport, coffeemaker, hair dryer, safe
RESTAURANTS	None
BARS	None

CLIENTELE	Popular with business travelers, except in summer; about one-third international travelers
GUEST SERVICES	Valet laundry, continental breakfast served in Café au Lait, $15 daily rate at the New York Sports Club
PARKING	None
CANCELLATION POLICY	24 hours before check-in
WHEELCHAIR ACCESS	None

A new name and makeover has raised this former Hojo to the top echelon of budget properties. Its handsome lobby features blonde wood paneling, fresh flowers, recessed lighting, and an elegantly appointed sitting room that's very handy if you want to relax after checking in or out. Breakfast is served in a café off the lobby.

One tiny elevator and narrow hallways are not designed for guests with oversized luggage. A standard double is compact and the bathroom has a doll-sized sink and tub, hair dryer, and toiletries. Mattresses are firm and all furnishings brand new. Suites aren't huge, but the extra room gives you more space. Since they rent for as low as $169, they are a pretty good deal.

Front desk staff greet new arrivals in the Clarion's newly renovated lobby. Credit: Desmond Shaw

MURRAY HILL

GRAND UNION HOTEL

34 E. 32nd St.
New York, NY 10016
(BETWEEN MADISON AND PARK AVENUES)

VALUE ★ ★ ★ ★ ★

CLEANLINESS ★ ★ ★ ★

GUEST SERVICES ★ ★

SECURITY ★ ★ ★

(★POOR - ★★★★★EXCELLENT)

CATEGORY	Limited Services
PHONE	(212) 683-5890
FAX	(212) 689-7397
EMAIL	grandunionhotel@aol.com
WEBSITE	www.hotelgrandunion.com
RATES	Doubles: $116 Triples: $132 Quads: $158 10 percent discount to ISI members and travel industry personnel
GUEST ROOMS	96 rooms on 10 floors, all smoking
ROOM AMENITIES	AC, cable TV with HBO, phone with voice mail and dataport, mini-fridge
RESTAURANTS	None
BARS	None
CLIENTELE	Mix of business guests, families, and students
GUEST SERVICES	Paperback library, luggage room, fax service for a fee
PARKING	None
CANCELLATION POLICY	24 hours before check-in
WHEELCHAIR ACCESS	None

Well situated and well priced, the Grand Union is a bargain for families or small groups who can rent a quad room for $158. Each quad has one double and two single beds in spacious surroundings. Standard doubles and triples are also roomy and come equipped with mini-fridges, cable TV, and phones with voice mail and a dataport for a computer. Hair dryers are available on request. Bathrooms have a tub/shower plus toiletries. A paperback book library is handy as is fax service and a spacious, private room off the lobby where you can greet guests, read the newspaper, or wait for an airport shuttle.

Last renovated in 1998, the Grand Union offers value and a location convenient to the Empire State Building and Fifth Avenue. Ask for a top floor room to ensure maximum quiet.

HOTEL DEAUVILLE

103 E. 29th St.
New York, NY 10016
(BETWEEN PARK AND LEXINGTON AVENUES)

VALUE ★ ★ ★

CLEANLINESS ★ ★ ★ ★

GUEST SERVICES NONE

SECURITY ★ ★ ★

(★POOR - ★★★★★EXCELLENT)

CATEGORY	Euro-style
PHONE	(212) 683-0990
	800) 333-8843 Reservations
FAX	(212) 689-5921
EMAIL	On the website
WEBSITE	www.c-i-h.com
RATES	Singles: $68-$100
	Doubles: $121
	Suites: $157
GUEST ROOMS	58 rooms on 7 floors include 5 suites and 6 rooms that share a bath; some are nonsmoking rooms
ROOM AMENITIES	AC, cable TV, phone
RESTAURANTS	None
BARS	None
CLIENTELE	German tourists and other Europeans
GUEST SERVICES	None
PARKING	None
CANCELLATION POLICY	48 hours before check-in
WHEELCHAIR ACCESS	None

Despite its name, this relic has nothing in common with the swank French resort, and as most rooms are booked by a German tour company, you won't hear many *bon mots* spoken in the hallways.

All rooms are clean with stall showers and shampoo in the private bathrooms. Shared baths have stall showers, also, and tiny sinks. Singles are small, doubles average size, and the suites are roomy, but so bare-bones you wouldn't want to pay the extra freight. Hair dryers and irons are available at the front desk. Air and heat are centrally controlled, which can mean overheated rooms in winter, glacial rooms in summer. There is basic cable TV and basic phone service.

This hotel's most memorable feature: its lavender bathrooms. Too bad the hotel itself lacks panache, and while location is an asset, it's flatly outranked by neighboring properties.

HOTEL 31

120 E. 31st St.
New York, NY 10016
(BETWEEN PARK AND LEXINGTON AVENUES)

VALUE ★ ★ ★ ★

CLEANLINESS ★ ★ ★ ★

GUEST SERVICES NONE

SECURITY ★ ★ ★ ★ ★

(★POOR - ★★★★★EXCELLENT)

CATEGORY	Euro-style
PHONE	(212) 685-3060
FAX	(212) 532-1232
EMAIL	hotel31@worldnet.att.net
WEBSITE	www.hotel31.com
RATES	January-March: $75-$110 April-July: $85-$120 August-December: $120-$160
GUEST ROOMS	110 rooms on 8 floors, some shared bath, all smoking
ROOM AMENITIES	AC, cable TV, phone with voice mail, hair dryers, VCR
RESTAURANTS	None

BARS	None
CLIENTELE	25 percent Americans, 50 percent British, 25 percent Europeans
GUEST SERVICES	None
PARKING	None
CANCELLATION POLICY	24 hours before check-in
WHEELCHAIR ACCESS	None

Like its downtown sister, Hotel 17, this lodging has lots to recommend it: a quiet residential setting, a landmark building renovated in 1999, an efficient helpful staff, and bargain rates.

Rooms with private baths are larger than those with shared baths, and both stock amenities like hair dryers and shampoo. Bathrooms, however, are tiny with child-sized tubs. The AC is new, windows are double-paned to filter out street noise, and some have a view of the Empire State Building. If you're a nonsmoker, give the room a nose test before accepting it. Some rooms smell heavily of cigarettes.

Security is tight ("We don't let people in unless we know them," front desk staff assured us). Local phone calls cost 75 cents and you need to pay for all calls in cash, not with credit cards. ("We're pretty liberal, though, unless a guest is abusive.")

"Small is beautiful" might be the Hotel 31's motto. Not surprisingly, they have many return guests.

MURRAY HILL INN

143 E. 30th St.
New York, NY 10016
(BETWEEN LEXINGTON AND THIRD AVENUES)

VALUE ★ ★ ★ ★

CLEANLINESS ★ ★ ★

GUEST SERVICES ★

SECURITY ★ ★ ★ ★ ★

(★POOR - ★★★★★EXCELLENT)

CATEGORY	Euro-style
PHONE	(212) 683-6900
FAX	(212) 545-0103
EMAIL	murrhillinn@aol.com
WEBSITE	www.murrayhillinn.com
RATES	$75-$125
GUEST ROOMS	50 rooms, 11 with private bath, all nonsmoking
ROOM AMENITIES	AC, cable TV, phone (local calls are 50 cents and there is a deposit required for long distance calls)
RESTAURANTS	None
BARS	None
CLIENTELE	30 percent American to 70 percent foreign tourists
GUEST SERVICES	ATM, vending machines
PARKING	None
CANCELLATION POLICY	Call at least 2 days before arrival to confirm or the reservation is automatically cancelled
WHEELCHAIR ACCESS	None

Friendly staff welcome you in the small lobby of this Euro-style lodging—which, in this case, means no elevator, scant amenities, and some shared baths.

If you arrive before 6 p.m., a bellman will schlep your luggage. You're on your own after that. Rooms without a private bath range from closet-sized singles to moderate-sized doubles. Shared baths have tub/showers; private baths have stall showers. All rooms offer AC and cable

TV and not much else. Management is continually refurbishing rooms and adding private bathrooms. Security is reassuring: all guests are buzzed in.

This hotel's location in residential Murray Hill makes it a peaceful retreat with convenient access to the United Nations, Macy's, and the Empire State Building.

QUALITY HOTEL EAST SIDE

161 Lexington Ave.
New York, NY 10016
(AT E. 30TH ST.)

VALUE ★ ★ ★ ★ ★

CLEANLINESS ★ ★ ★ ★

GUEST SERVICES ★ ★ ★ ★

SECURITY ★ ★ ★ ★

(★POOR - ★★★★★EXCELLENT)

CATEGORY	Limited Services
PHONE	(212) 545-1800
	(800) 567-7720 Reservations
FAX	(212) 481-7270
	(212) 790-2760 Reservations
EMAIL	reservations@applecorehotels.com
WEBSITE	www.applecorehotels.com
RATES	$79-$329
	10 percent discount to AAA and AARP members for rooms above $109
GUEST ROOMS	95 rooms on 12 floors, half are nonsmoking
ROOM AMENITIES	AC, cable TV with pay Nintendo games, internet access and movies, 2-line phone with voice mail and data-port (local calls are free), coffeemaker, iron and ironing board, hair dryer
RESTAURANTS	Coffee shop
BARS	None
CLIENTELE	40 percent business to 60 percent tourists, about half from abroad
GUEST SERVICES	Continental breakfast, business center, fitness center
PARKING	None

CANCELLATION POLICY   24 hours before check-in
WHEELCHAIR ACCESS   8 rooms

As part of its plan to reinvigorate languishing properties in desirable neighborhoods, Apple Core Hotels purchased the Rutledge in 1995. The Rutledge, built about 1905, was one of the first hotels to offer rooms to working women. It advertised a daily rate of $2.50 for a private room with meals; the weekly rate was $15. Many hotels in the early 1900s catered to bachelors, but only the Rutledge and the Martha Washington, two blocks away, catered to bachelorettes.

Apple Core converted all shared baths to private baths and decorated guest rooms in Early American themes. It also added services like a fitness center, business "nook," and breakfast room. It transformed the lobby by adding a flagstone floor, walls in brick and hunter green, and bookshelves in dark wood. A trifle cold, perhaps, but

Quality Hotel East Side began life as the women-only Rutledge Hotel. Credit: Apple Core Hotels

distinctive for a budget hotel. Front desk staff are friendly and competent; you feel you are in good hands.

Especially during the low season, rooms here are a true bargain. The standard double gives you plenty of elbow room, a marble bath with a tub/shower combination, a desk, a large walk-in closet, and conveniences like a coffeemaker. The TV is your home entertainment center, providing internet access, Nintendo games, pay movies, and endless cable channels. Phones offer voice mail and a dataport for your laptop. Although this Murray Hill neighborhood is serene, windows are double-paned to block street noise. At press time, the hotel was completing a total renovation.

All and all, this is a mighty tasty Apple Core.

SOLDIERS', SAILORS', MARINES', AND AIRMEN'S CLUB

238 Lexington Ave.
New York, NY 10016
(BETWEEN 36TH AND 37TH STREETS)

VALUE ★ ★ ★ ★

CLEANLINESS ★ ★

GUEST SERVICES ★ ★ ★ ★

SECURITY ★ ★

(★POOR - ★★★★★EXCELLENT)

CATEGORY	Bare Essentials
PHONE	(212) 683-4353
	(800) 678-8443 Reservations
FAX	(212) 683-4374
EMAIL	ssmaclub@ix.netcom.com
WEBSITE	www.ssmaclub.org
RATES	$25-$45 depending on military rank
	21-day maximum stay
GUEST ROOMS	29 rooms on 5 floors sleep from
	2-6 people in a room, all shared bath,
	1 smoking floor, no elevator
ROOM AMENITIES	TV in the larger rooms, bedding
	and towels

RESTAURANTS	None
BARS	None
CLIENTELE	Mostly single men and women, some couples and families
GUEST SERVICES	Continental breakfast on Sunday, TV lounge, copy machine, vending machines, phone cards for sale, piano, kitchen, library, meeting rooms
PARKING	None
CANCELLATION POLICY	7 days before check-in
WHEELCHAIR ACCESS	None

The SSMAC offers "no frills accommodations to the military family, past and present." Think barracks and keep your expectations low. Because the Club rents beds not rooms, single guests may be asked to share a room with guests of the same gender. The narrow cotlike beds have firm mattresses; bedding and towels are supplied. There are separate shared bathrooms for men and women. Each room has a metal armoire, desk, chairs, and lamps. Four- and six-bed rooms also have a TV. You can receive incoming phone calls on the hall phones and make outgoing calls with a phone card that's on sale at the front desk.

A spacious living room with oriental carpets and a grand piano contrasts sharply with the bare-bones private quarters. Walls are decorated with portraits of military heroes, like Eisenhower and George Washington. Unfortunately, these public areas are often rented for parties that can get mighty raucous. Most single guests hang out in the canteen over cups of coffee; a microwave, refrigerator, and stove allow them to heat up a meal instead of eating out.

You can't beat these rates if you're active or retired military, and this is a great East Side location. Many servicemen and women who would never be able to afford New York prices camp here and enjoy the camaraderie.

SLEEP CHEAP IN NEW YORK

THE TEN EYCK-TROUGHTON RESIDENCE FOR BUSINESS WOMEN

145 E. 39th St.
New York, NY 10016
(BETWEEN THIRD AND LEXINGTON AVENUES)

VALUE ★ ★ ★ ★ ★
CLEANLINESS ★ ★ ★
GUEST SERVICES ★ ★ ★ ★ ★
SECURITY ★ ★ ★ ★
(★ POOR - ★ ★ ★ ★ ★ EXCELLENT)

CATEGORY	Residence
PHONE	(212) 490-5990
FAX	(212) 697-2934
EMAIL	None
WEBSITE	None
RATES	$814-$835 monthly, includes breakfast and dinner
GUEST ROOMS	333 on 13 floors are all smoking, 4 with private bath, 27 with toilet and sink; otherwise, shared bath
ROOM AMENITIES	Bedding, phone
RESTAURANTS	Dining room in basement
BARS	None
CLIENTELE	Women 18 and older, who are working and/or studying
GUEST SERVICES	Maid service, common kitchen, sewing and hobby room, coin-operated laundry, TV lounge, library, typing room, music studios, roof garden, solarium, exercise equipment
PARKING	None
CANCELLATION POLICY	2 weeks
WHEELCHAIR ACCESS	None

This is one of four residences run by the Salvation Army, and typically its public areas are showcases, its private areas are drab. All rooms have a sink, and some have an additional toilet; otherwise tenants share hallway bathrooms. Shared bathrooms feature a tub and two stall showers; they badly need renovating. Hallways are carpeted, which helps reduce noise. Rooms are small with linoleum floors, a small desk, good-sized dresser, good-sized closet, twin bed, phone, and lamps. They are wired for a TV cable connection. The residence will install an AC unit for an extra $7 a month.

The lounge/library with a piano on lobby level is immaculate. It's used to show movies on Friday nights. A solarium and roof garden on the 17th floor are stunning in design and furnishings and offer panoramic city views. Meals are served cafeteria-style in a nondescript basement setting. Breakfast and dinner are included in the rent and lunch costs $2. Washers and dryers are located on even-numbered floors; an iron, ironing board, and wash basin on odd-numbered floors. There's a kitchenette, exercise room, and TV lounge on the second floor.

"Up on the roof" Ten Eyck-Troughton guests enjoy city views in a relaxing setting. Credit: Salvation Army

Family members can stay in a tenant's room on a cot for $35 or in a separate room for $50. Male visitors are restricted to public areas.

One month's rent and a $680 security deposit are required up front as is verification of employment or college enrollment. A character reference and credit check are also required. The $10 application fee is nonrefundable, the $10 key deposit is refundable.

THIRTYTHIRTY

(FORMERLY THE MARTHA WASHINGTON)
30 E. 30th St.
New York, NY 10016
(BETWEEN MADISON AND PARK AVENUES)

VALUE ★ ★ ★ ★

CLEANLINESS ★ ★ ★ ★ ★

GUEST SERVICES ★ ★

SECURITY ★ ★ ★ ★

(★POOR - ★★★★★EXCELLENT)

CATEGORY	Limited Services
PHONE	(212) 689-1900
	(800) 497-6028 Reservations
FAX	(212) 689-0023
EMAIL	On the website
WEBSITE	www.thirtythirty-nyc.com
RATES	$99-$185
GUEST ROOMS	280 rooms on 12 floors, some nonsmoking
ROOM AMENITIES	AC, cable TV, phone with voice mail and dataport; hair dryer, mini-fridge, and iron available on request
RESTAURANTS	Coming in 2002
BARS	None
CLIENTELE	A mix of foreign and domestic guests of all ages
GUEST SERVICES	Valet laundry, photocopying and faxing for a fee, internet kiosk
PARKING	None
CANCELLATION POLICY	24 hours before check-in
WHEELCHAIR ACCESS	Yes

Citylife Hotel Group has transformed the old Martha Washington women-only residence hotel into the hip ThirtyThirty with an infusion of $15 million. About 75 permanent residents still occupy the hotel.

Singles are small, but doubles (with either twin beds or a queen bed) are good-sized. Ask for one with kitchen facilities, at no extra cost. Some rooms have stall showers only; if you need a tub bath, ask for one. Hair dryers, mini-fridges, and irons are available on request. Décor is attractive and unvarying. Some rooms have closets, some armoires; all have thermostats to control the air and heat.

Unfortunately, because of their newness, some rooms smell of *eau de formaldehyde*. But this hotel is still an excellent choice for tourists and business travelers because of its spotlessness and convenient location. Time will no doubt smooth the rough edges.

A sparkling new lobby and a new name for the former Martha Washington residence. Credit: Desmond Shaw

MIDTOWN WEST

*"When you're away from old Broadway,
you're only camping out."*
—*George M. Cohan*

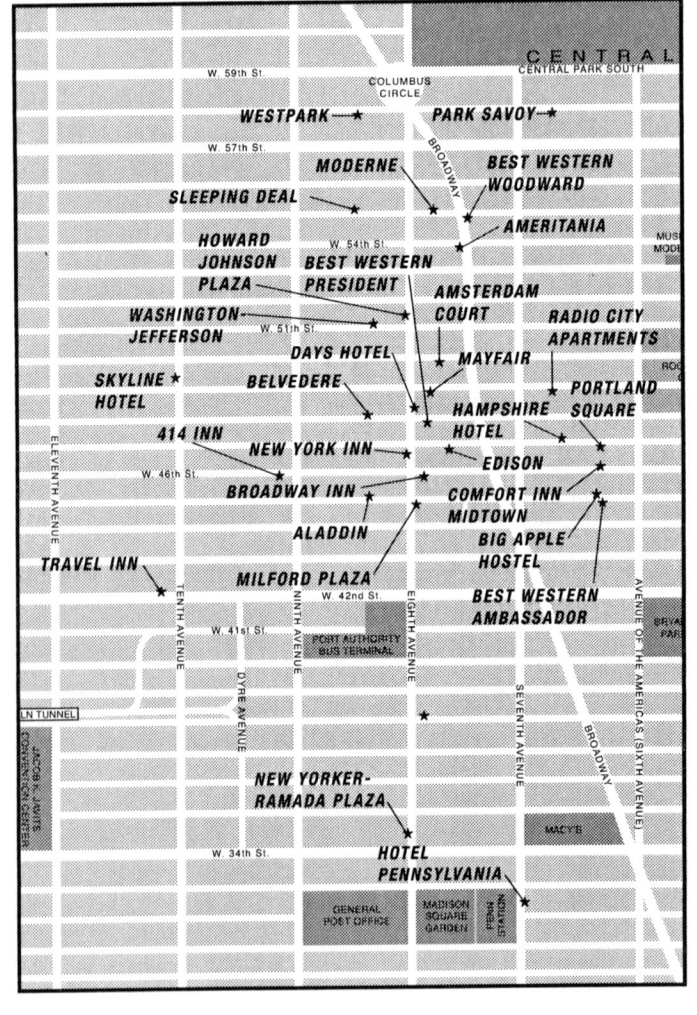

A majority of the hotels in this book are concentrated in this neighborhood, convenient to Times Square, Penn Station, the Garment District, Madison Square Garden, and the Jacob Javits Convention Center. Tourist attractions are endless, but some of the most popular include the Empire State Building, Museum of Modern Art, Rockefeller Center, and Radio City Music Hall. Among several success stories here is the cleanup of Times Square as well as the restoration of Bryant Park, where you can dine al fresco and watch free movies in summer. Disney gets credit for restoring the New Amsterdam and New Victory theaters, just two of the great palaces that make Broadway glitter. Its other luminary claim to fame—neon lights—was originally created to advertise stage shows and spawned the term "the Great White Way."

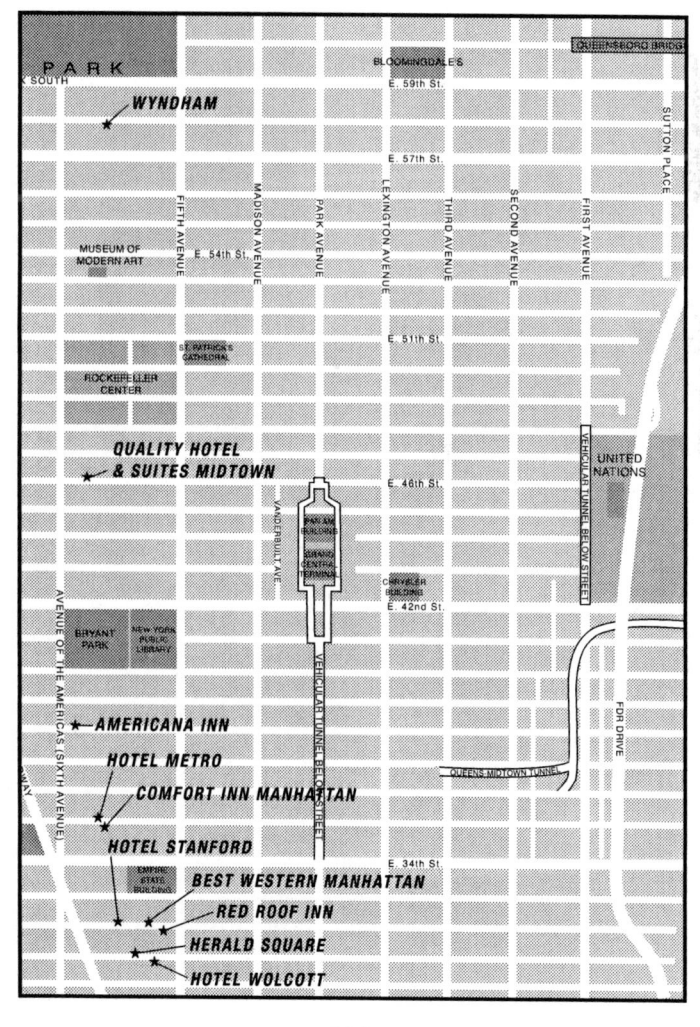

ALADDIN HOTEL

317 W. 45th St.
New York, NY 10036
(BETWEEN EIGHTH AND NINTH AVENUES)

VALUE ★★

CLEANLINESS ★

GUEST SERVICES ★★★

SECURITY ★★

(★POOR - ★★★★★EXCELLENT)

CATEGORY	Hostel
PHONE	(212) 246-8580
FAX	(212) 246-6036
EMAIL	aladdinhotl@aol.com
WEBSITE	www.aladdinhotl.com
RATES	Dorm beds: $21-$43 Private rooms: $70-$110
GUEST ROOMS	137 rooms on 9 floors, all nonsmoking, all shared bath
ROOM AMENITIES	Towels provided in private rooms
RESTAURANTS	None
BARS	None
CLIENTELE	The young and the restless
GUEST SERVICES	Self-service laundry, vending machines, lockers, internet kiosk, TV lounge, rooftop terrace, pool table
PARKING	None
CANCELLATION POLICY	24 hours before check-in
WHEELCHAIR ACCESS	None

The hostel-like Aladdin draws mostly young Europeans because of its central location and cheap prices. But the only bargain here—and it's very basic—are dorm rooms that are rented per bed. Otherwise, the Aladdin lacks the value of other hostels and hotels with comparable rates and more attractive accommodations.

Both the building and rooms are the worse for wear. There are no amenities in sight. All guests share the bathrooms, and towels are only provided in private rooms that range from singles to double/doubles. Some twins that rent for $80-$90 have bunk beds, some side-by-side beds. Each floor has a soda machine, and the lobby offers more vending choices as well as other conveniences, like internet access.

Despite its spot in the heart of the theater district, even the Phantom would get nervous haunting this place.

AMERICANA INN

69 W. 38th St.
New York, NY 10018
(BETWEEN FIFTH AND SIXTH AVENUES)

VALUE ★ ★ ★

CLEANLINESS ★ ★ ★

GUEST SERVICES ★

SECURITY ★ ★ ★ ★ ★

(★POOR - ★★★★★EXCELLENT)

CATEGORY	Bare Essentials
PHONE	(212) 840-6700 (888) 468-3558 Reservations
FAX	(212) 840-1830
EMAIL	None
WEBSITE	www.newyorkhotel.com Offers special packages
RATES	Singles: $65-$85 Doubles: $75-$105
GUEST ROOMS	48 rooms with shared bath, some nonsmoking
ROOM AMENITIES	AC, cable TV, phone
RESTAURANTS	None
BARS	None
CLIENTELE	A mix
GUEST SERVICES	Common kitchens on each floor
PARKING	None
CANCELLATION POLICY	24 hours before check-in
WHEELCHAIR ACCESS	None

In the heart of the Fashion District, there's nothing fashionable about the Americana's very basic accommodations. Singles and doubles feature twin beds, a small dresser, cable TV, a small sink and a vanity, a walk-in closet, and linoleum floors. The shared bathrooms we poked our nose into smelled bad, but more worrisome than the smell is the lack of individual temperature controls in guest rooms. The room we visited in January was uncomfortably hot. On each floor, guests can use a kitchenette the size of a closet that has a mini-fridge, microwave, and two-burner range, but no cooking utensils, pots, or pans.

Security is not an issue: all guest are buzzed in at the entrance on 38th Street and walk up stairs to the second-floor office. Front desk personnel take phone messages and can provide a hair dryer and iron if you need them.

The Americana might do for a short stay. It has value only during low season when a double rents for as low as $75.

AMERITANIA HOTEL

230 W. 54th St.
New York, NY 10019
(BETWEEN BROADWAY AND EIGHTH AVE.)

VALUE ★ ★ ★ ★

CLEANLINESS ★ ★ ★ ★ ★

GUEST SERVICES ★ ★ ★ ★ ★

SECURITY ★ ★ ★ ★

(★POOR - ★★★★★EXCELLENT)

CATEGORY	Boutique
PHONE	(212) 247-5000
	(888) 66-HOTEL Reservations
FAX	(212) 247-3313
	(212) 813-8002 Reservations
EMAIL	None
WEBSITE	www.nychotels.com
	Offers seasonal promotions
RATES	$115-$425
GUEST ROOMS	197 rooms and 12 suites on 12 floors, the top 5 floors are nonsmoking

ROOM AMENITIES	AC, cable TV with movies and games, phone with voice mail and dataport, CD player, clock radio, iron and ironing board, hair dryer
RESTAURANTS	Bar 54 serves dinner
BARS	Twist Lounge, Bar 54
CLIENTELE	Mix of business and leisure travelers
GUEST SERVICES	Continental breakfast, valet laundry, concierge, $15 passes to health club, room service until 2 a.m.
PARKING	None
CANCELLATION POLICY	24 hours before check-in
WHEELCHAIR ACCESS	None

Minimalistic lines of the '60s-inspired Twist Lounge.
Credit: Amsterdam Hospitality Group

The Ameritania strives to look hip, and, overall, it succeeds. A color scheme of browns and creams, oversized furniture, and giant silver-leaf chandeliers follow stark lines (as in the French designer Philippe Starck). In the '60s-inspired Twist Lounge, you can sip your Cosmopolitan in a suede armchair, settle back and admire the wood-panelled fireplace and mahogany bar.

Room perks include pay-per-view movies and games, a CD clock radio, and a full-length mirror. Most of the accommodations have a desk, but it's more for aesthetics than a comfortable spot to work. Mattresses are firm, and windows are double-paned, which is a necessity in this busy neighborhood. While room size is average to large, closets and bathrooms are small. The armoire with drawers helps make up for the wee closet. Unfortunately, you're stuck with the small bathroom.

The hotel doesn't offer a business center, but there is a Kinko's across the street. In terms of parking, a special rate for hotel guests, at press time $15 for 24 hours, is available at a garage nearby. However, it is not affiliated with the Ameritania, so you're on your own. Also, a health club a few doors down offers Ameritania guests a daily rate of $15.

Bar 54 serves pub food and will deliver to your room from 3 p.m. to 2 a.m. But there are countless restaurants within a few blocks. Central Park is only five minutes away, and guests are no more than 10 minutes from Times Square and Carnegie Hall. The hotel is right around the corner from the Ed Sullivan Theater, where *Late Show with David Letterman* is taped.

The Ameritania's $115 rate for a queen-sized bed is a good deal, but it's only available seasonally. Otherwise, you may have to rely on special promotions and sheer luck, making it just another expensive midtown hotel.

MIDTOWN WEST

AMSTERDAM COURT HOTEL

226 W. 50th St.
New York, NY 10019
(BETWEEN BROADWAY AND EIGHTH AVE.)

VALUE ★ ★ ★ ★
CLEANLINESS ★ ★ ★ ★
GUEST SERVICES ★ ★ ★
SECURITY ★ ★ ★ ★
(★POOR - ★★★★★EXCELLENT)

CATEGORY	Boutique
PHONE	(212) 459-1000
FAX	(212) 265-5070
EMAIL	On the website
WEBSITE	www.nychotels.com
RATES	$109-$325
GUEST ROOMS	120 rooms on 7 floors, mostly nonsmoking
ROOM AMENITIES	AC, cable TV with pay movies and games, CD player, 2-line phone with voice mail and dataport, hair dryer, Belgian linens, iron and ironing board
RESTAURANTS	Coming in 2002
BARS	Coming in 2002
CLIENTELE	A mix of business and leisure travelers
GUEST SERVICES	Continental breakfast, valet laundry, coffee and tea all day
PARKING	None
CANCELLATION POLICY	24 hours before check-in
WHEELCHAIR ACCESS	None

It's hard to imagine why the Amsterdam Hospitality Group would create a sleek, mod hotel and then not put a sign outside so guests (and hotel inspectors like ourselves) can find it. If you do find it, you'll be greeted by an eager bellman and cheerful, multilingual front desk staff, who really throw out the welcome mat.

Like its sibling, the Moderne, five blocks uptown, the Amsterdam Court gives a stylish gloss to an older building that's been renovated on the cheap. There's plenty of

Help yourself to java and the news in The Amsterdam Court's comfy library. Credit: Amsterdam Hospitality Group

opportunity for a good time—especially at 4 p.m. when wine and cheese are served—if you can ignore the chipped paint, frayed carpet, and grimy windows in hallways and guest rooms. (Maybe that's why lighting is so minimal.) Doubles vary from small to average size with small marble baths, tall mirrors, and fancy headboards on beds that are nicely swathed in Belgian linens. You'll have use of a small TV with cable channels, pay movies, and games; a phone with voice mail and dataport; and a CD player.

The deluxe king room was our favorite. It's spacious with a marble bath you won't bump your elbows in; a large desk, if you need to work; built-in wooden cabinets for the TV and your clothes; and multiple windows. It usually sells for $175. Smack in the heart of the Theater District, this hotel is making all the right changes and with the addition of a new restaurant and bar will offer even more value.

BELVEDERE HOTEL

319 W. 48th St.
New York, NY 10036
(BETWEEN EIGHTH AND NINTH AVENUES)

VALUE ★ ★ ★ ★ ★
CLEANLINESS ★ ★ ★ ★ ★
GUEST SERVICES ★ ★ ★ ★ ★
SECURITY ★ ★ ★ ★ ★
(★POOR - ★★★★★EXCELLENT)

CATEGORY	Limited Services
PHONE	(212) 245-7000
	(888) 468-3558 Reservations
FAX	(212) 265-7778
	(212) 245-4455 Reservations
EMAIL	belvedere@newyorkhotel.com
WEBSITE	www.newyorkhotel.com
	Offers special packages
RATES	$140-$280
	15 percent discount to AAA members
	10 percent to AARP members
GUEST ROOMS	400 rooms on 17 floors includes 2 suites, 5 nonsmoking floors
ROOM AMENITIES	AC; cable TV with internet access, pay movies, and games; phone with voice mail and dataport; hair dryer; kitchenette; iron and ironing board, safe
RESTAURANTS	Belvedere Café serves breakfast
BARS	None
CLIENTELE	Half tourists, half business

GUEST SERVICES	Concierge, self-service laundry, dry cleaning, gift shop, lockers, business center, fax machine at front desk
PARKING	None
CANCELLATION POLICY	24 hours before check-in
WHEELCHAIR ACCESS	Yes

The Belvedere began life in 1926 when a double room cost $6. Its contemporary deco themes are particularly striking in the multicolored terrazzo marble floor that covers its sweeping lobby and in an equally spacious breakfast room. Four new elevators repeat the deco motifs. Next to the elevators, look for a bronze letter box: it's connected to an original mail chute that lets guests on all floors deposit their mail. Everything in the public areas is either custom-made or handpicked by the Domb family, who owns the hotel.

Rooms are smartly decorated in burgundy and gold and furnished with dark wooden desks, armoires, and massive dressers (lots of space for those of you who overpack).

Deco terrazzo floor and columns add flair to The Belvedere's lobby.
Credit: Desmond Shaw

Double/doubles, queen-, and king-sized beds are available, all at the same daily rate. Each room is average-sized with a tiny kitchenette; small bath with a tub/shower, phone, hair dryer, and Gilchrist and Soames toiletries; and a walk-in closet with a safe and iron. Hallways are clean, bright, and fresh-smelling.

The hotel offers a variety of services, which include a coin-operated washer and dryer; business center; $12 all-you-can-eat breakfast in a gorgeous space on lobby level; concierge to arrange entertainment and airport transport; and a locker and dressing room, so that you can check out and still have the afternoon to explore the city before saying "adios." The Brazilian steakhouse next door has a loyal following of both New York natives and South American visitors.

As it continues to add improvements, such as a conference room with street access, the Belvedere is a good example of the thoughtful, careful renovation of a historic hotel. Add extra amenities, comfortable ambience, and competent staff and you've got a keeper.

BEST WESTERN AMBASSADOR

132 W. 45th St.
New York, NY 10036
(BETWEEN SIXTH AND SEVENTH AVENUES)

VALUE ★ ★ ★

CLEANLINESS ★ ★ ★

GUEST SERVICES ★ ★ ★

SECURITY ★ ★ ★ ★

(★POOR - ★★★★★EXCELLENT)

CATEGORY	Limited Services
PHONE	(212) 921-7600
	(800) 242-8935 Reservations
FAX	(212) 719-0171
EMAIL	bwambassadorhotel@hotmail.com
WEBSITE	www.bestnyhotels.com
RATES	$109-$499
	10 percent discount to AAA and AARP members

GUEST ROOMS	70 rooms on 8 floors, 3 floors are nonsmoking
ROOM AMENITIES	AC, cable TV, phone with voice mail and dataport, coffeemaker, hair dryer, mini-fridge available on request
RESTAURANTS	None
BARS	None
CLIENTELE	More business than leisure travelers
GUEST SERVICES	Valet laundry, continental breakfast, business center
PARKING	$10 a day
CANCELLATION POLICY	24 hours before check-in
WHEELCHAIR ACCESS	None

Let's do a reality check. The brochure and website for this Hampshire Hotels and Resorts property reads: "Once you have entered the Best Western Ambassador hotel, a wonderful feeling comes over you. It feels like you are in a small English Cottage at a very close friend's house." Reality: the cramped lobby needs new paint, carpet, and furniture.

"Our staff is well trained and responsive to your every need." Reality: It took four visits to convince front desk staff to show us a few rooms. They charged one guest a $50 penalty for early departure, though he had given prior notice to a different staff person and the message got lost.

"Spacious newly renovated rooms in the English Georgian tradition with all the modern amenities you've come to expect: in-room coffeemakers, hair dryers, two-line phones with dataport...." Reality: Rooms aren't renovated or spacious and as for tradition, well, King George has nothing to do with it. Telephones are one-line, not two.

With sprucing up this hotel would certainly increase its rating because amenities are copious and rooms are reasonably quiet. It's the only Best Western we know of that serves breakfast, and it places guests within steps of Fortune 500 offices on Sixth Avenue, Times Square, and the Best of Broadway.

Location, location, location.

MIDTOWN WEST

BEST WESTERN MANHATTAN

17 W. 32nd St.
New York, NY 10001
(BETWEEN FIFTH AVE. AND BROADWAY)

VALUE ★ ★ ★ ★
CLEANLINESS ★ ★ ★ ★
GUEST SERVICES ★ ★ ★ ★ ★
SECURITY ★ ★ ★ ★
(★POOR - ★★★★★EXCELLENT)

CATEGORY	Limited Services
PHONE	(212) 736-1600
	(800) 567-7720 Reservations
FAX	(212) 563-4007
EMAIL	reservations@applecore.com
WEBSITE	www.applecorehotels.com
RATES	$89-$399
	10 percent discount to AAA and AARP members on rates above $109
GUEST ROOMS	178 rooms on 11 floors, half are nonsmoking rooms
ROOM AMENITIES	AC; cable TV with pay movies, games, and internet access; 2-line phone with voice mail and dataport; hair dryer; iron and ironing board; coffeemaker
RESTAURANTS	Rooftop Sky Bar serves dinner
BARS	Rooftop Sky Bar
CLIENTELE	Budget-conscious tourists and business travelers
GUEST SERVICES	Continental breakfast, valet laundry, gift shop, exercise room, business center, room service 4-11 p.m.
PARKING	None
CANCELLATION POLICY	24 hours before check-in
WHEELCHAIR ACCESS	None

With its Beaux Arts façade and contemporary lobby, this Apple Core Hotels property wins your respect at first glance. It certainly has a winning pedigree. Originally the Aberdeen Hotel, designed by architect Harry B. Mulliken, it has been described by historian John Tauranac as "arguably one of the most excessive and wonderful manifestations of the *fin de siècle* fascination that American architects had with Parisian architecture at the turn of the century."

Rooms, however, are very basic and tend towards traditional American bland. Renovations are ongoing and, as of press time, six floors had been completed. Since price and amenities are the same for all floors, ask for a refurbished room: you'll appreciate the new furniture and fabrics, walk-in closets, and fresh smell. Rooms vary in size from a cramped single to a very spacious double/double. Bathrooms, old and new, have marble vanities, a large mirror, and built-in hair dryers.

In-room amenities are convenient as are the hotel's many extra services, but *caveat emptor*. The unstaffed business center is not run by the hotel. Photocopying, word processing, and internet access can be very pricey. Those minutes charged to your credit card add up fast. The small exercise room could use some bodies, and it's unlocked, which is a security risk. Breakfast is served in a bright and cheerful room at the back of the lobby; it's more than continental fare, and there's a microwave if you want to heat up your Egg McMuffin.

Perhaps the hotel's best feature is its Rooftop Sky Bar, open during warm weather, where you can nurse a cool one and admire the building where King Kong battled the biplanes.

MIDTOWN WEST

BEST WESTERN PRESIDENT

234 W. 48th St.
New York, NY 10036
(BETWEEN EIGHTH AVE. AND BROADWAY)

VALUE ★ ★ ★ ★

CLEANLINESS ★ ★ ★ ★ ★

GUEST SERVICES ★ ★ ★

SECURITY ★ ★ ★

(★POOR - ★★★★★EXCELLENT)

CATEGORY	Limited Services
PHONE	(212) 246-8800
	(800) 826-4667 Reservations
FAX	(212) 974-3922
	(212) 265-6727 Reservations
EMAIL	reshhr@aol.com
WEBSITE	www.bestnyhotels.com
	Offers a virtual tour
RATES	$89-$479
	Discount to AAA and AARP members
GUEST ROOMS	334 rooms on 16 floors, 46 suites, 3 smoking floors
ROOM AMENITIES	AC, cable TV, phone with voice mail and dataport, iron and ironing board, hair dryer, safe; mini-fridge available on request
RESTAURANTS	La Primavera and the Waterfall Café
BARS	Ziegfield's Lounge
CLIENTELE	Mix of international and American travelers
GUEST SERVICES	Valet laundry, gift shop, luggage room, 20–percent discount at La Primavera, fax and photocopying for a charge
PARKING	None
CANCELLATION POLICY	24 hours before check-in
WHEELCHAIR ACCESS	Yes

The lullaby of Broadway sounds much sweeter in the lap of this hotel's high standards of quality and service. Best Western renovated the place when it took over in 1992 and the makeover works.

The Waterfall Cafe adds a touch of class to the BW President.
Credit: Best Western President Hotel

Hallways are brightly lit, but not garish. Guest rooms are comfortable and attractively decorated in a traditional style with burgundy carpets and mahogany furniture offset by cream-colored walls and ceiling. All bed sizes are available from one twin to double/doubles, and they are priced accordingly. Small walk-in closets house an iron and ironing board. Bathrooms are tiny, but they provide hair dryers, a clothes line, a second phone, and toiletries. Overhead lights are on dimmers. Mattresses are firm, windows double-paned (for quiet), and phones have both a voice message system and a dataport for your laptop.

Executive Suites are geared to corporate clients, who will find the large desks, daily newspaper delivery, and two-line phones useful perks. Some suites have whirlpool baths, some steam showers. They provide a separate parlor for meeting clients or entertaining guests. Two deluxe penthouses offer the ultimate pampering, but not at budget prices.

The Waterfall Café off the main lobby serves breakfast, lunch, and dinner. It's also perfect for a restorative mid-afternoon cappuccino and croissant. White linen tablecloths and fresh flowers add a European flavor. A piano bar and La Primavera restaurant are also level with the lobby. The restaurant serves affordable lunch and dinner entrees and gives hotel guests a 20 percent discount.

You can enjoy all the razzmatazz of the theater district knowing you're in good hands.

BEST WESTERN WOODWARD

210 W. 55th St.
New York, NY 10019
(BETWEEN BROADWAY AND SEVENTH AVE.)

VALUE ★ ★ ★
CLEANLINESS ★ ★ ★ ★
GUEST SERVICES ★ ★ ★ ★
SECURITY ★ ★ ★ ★
(★POOR - ★★★★★EXCELLENT)

CATEGORY	Limited Services
PHONE	(212) 247-2000
	(800) 336-4110 Reservations
FAX	(212) 581-2248
EMAIL	On its website
WEBSITE	www.bestwestern.com/woodward
RATES	$99-$400
	10 percent discount to AAA and AARP members
GUEST ROOMS	196 rooms on 14 floors include 5 suites, some nonsmoking
ROOM AMENITIES	AC, cable TV with pay games and movies, phone with voice mail and dataport, coffeemaker, hair dryer, iron and ironing board, safe
RESTAURANTS	None
BARS	None
CLIENTELE	A mix of American and international tourists, groups on weekends

GUEST SERVICES	Valet laundry, meeting room, room service from the Carnegie Deli, free use of Prescriptive Fitness health club
PARKING	None
CANCELLATION POLICY	24 hours before check-in
WHEELCHAIR ACCESS	None

The Woodward's ongoing renovation requires your patience, and signs throughout the hotel ask guests to "Pardon our appearance while we make improvements." Thankfully, those improvements include a new and expanded lobby and a third elevator. The architect's renderings of this new space are posted in the lobby.

Two tiny elevators, slow and inadequate for this hotel's weekend traffic, deliver you into narrow hallways that are the worse for construction. As of press time, most of the guest rooms had been refurbished in a traditional décor that is unremarkable. Standard doubles are average-sized with small walk-in closets, a writing desk, and an armoire with three drawers. Lights are on dimmers, a nice touch.

There are plenty of amenities, such as a TV with cable channels as well as pay games and movies in four languages, a coffeemaker, iron, and phone with voice mail and a dataport. Tiny bathrooms are equipped with either a stall shower or tub/shower, a second phone, and toiletries. A thermostat allows you to regulate heat and air. Older rooms are well past their prime and best to avoid. Your best bet is to ask for a renewed room with a king-sized bed that is inside (to avoid street noise).

When its architect's vision of the future is fulfilled, the Woodward will be a great homebase and one of the best value plays on Broadway.

MIDTOWN WEST

BIG APPLE HOSTEL

119 W. 45th St.
New York, NY 10036
(BETWEEN SIXTH AND SEVENTH AVENUES)

VALUE ★★★
CLEANLINESS ★★★
GUEST SERVICES ★★★★
SECURITY ★★★★
(★POOR - ★★★★★EXCELLENT)

CATEGORY	Hostel
PHONE	(212) 302-2603
FAX	(212) 302-2605
EMAIL	bigapple@concentric.net
WEBSITE	www.bigapplehostel.com plays a mean version of "New York, New York"
RATES	4-bed dorms: $28.26 Double private rooms: $77.70
GUEST ROOMS	24 rooms on 6 floors include 11 private rooms and 116 dorm beds (coed and same-sex rooms are available); all nonsmoking
ROOM AMENITIES	Phone (free local calls), clock radio, fan, cable TV
RESTAURANTS	None
BARS	None
CLIENTELE	International students and backpackers
GUEST SERVICES	Self-service laundry, internet kiosk, kitchen and barbeque, safety deposit box, vending machines, front desk can arrange tours
PARKING	None
CANCELLATION POLICY	48 hours before check-in
WHEELCHAIR ACCESS	None

Where else can you sleep in Times Square for $28.26, except in a doorway? The building is ancient, but management has remodeled some bathrooms. There are two types of accommodations: private rooms with a double or single bed, and dormitories for four people, who sleep in two bunk beds. All rooms, including the shared baths, are clean. Mattresses in the private rooms are surprisingly firm, but be aware that the small fan is no substitute for air conditioning. No tubs; the shared bathrooms have stall showers.

There's someone at the front desk 24 hours and no curfew. Unlike at higher-priced venues, local phone calls are on the house. Guests can use the elevator to move luggage in and out, but otherwise, you climb. (It's better than StairMaster.) A communal kitchen is well equipped, and there's an outside deck popular in warm weather. Inside, there are tables and chairs to eat at and an internet kiosk nearby to check email. If you fancy a hostel in this neighborhood, the Big Apple has an edge on the Aladdin several blocks away.

BROADWAY INN

264 W. 46th St.
New York, NY 10036
(BETWEEN BROADWAY AND EIGHTH AVE.)

VALUE ★ ★ ★ ★ ★

CLEANLINESS ★ ★ ★ ★ ★

GUEST SERVICES ★ ★ ★

SECURITY ★ ★ ★ ★ ★

(★POOR - ★★★★★EXCELLENT)

CATEGORY	Bed & Breakfast
PHONE	(212) 997-9200 (800) 826-6300 Reservations
FAX	(212) 768-2807
EMAIL	broadwayinn@att.net
WEBSITE	www.broadwayinn.com Offers specials
RATES	$99-$250
GUEST ROOMS	41 rooms on 3 floors, all with private bath, allow smoking; 10 suites are nonsmoking
ROOM AMENITIES	AC, cable TV, phone, hair dryer
RESTAURANTS	Guests get a 20 percent discount at the Playwright Act II
BARS	None

CLIENTELE	65 percent Americans, 35 percent international
GUEST SERVICES	Continental breakfast, daily newspapers, library
PARKING	None
CANCELLATION POLICY	24 hours before check-in
WHEELCHAIR ACCESS	None

As you enter the second-floor lobby of this charming bed-and-breakfast inn, fresh flowers brighten the café tables, where breakfast is served each morning and the daily papers are always close at hand. The dark burnished wood of the front desk and stairs is accented by exposed brick walls and café curtains. Bookcases are well stocked in case you forgot to bring bedtime reading material.

This inn certainly adds a touch of glamour to drab Eighth Avenue, and it wins raves from its far-flung clientele, if the guestbook doesn't lie. Perhaps its only handicap is that there's no elevator. Brian the bellman calls that handicap "job security."

Exposed brick walls and café tables create a comfortable lobby at the Broadway Inn. Credit: Desmond Shaw

Rooms vary in size, and are stylish and spotless. Doubles offer a pleasing contemporary décor of black lacquered furniture, tables with black director's chairs, and walls and textiles in gray-green and rust. There's plenty of space, firm mattresses, and good lighting. Bathrooms have either a stall shower or a tub/shower. Families of four will be comfortable in the suites, which have two double beds and a pullout day bed; kitchenettes; walk-in closets; and medium-sized, fully equipped bathrooms. Double-paned windows help block street noise, but a back room is preferable.

The Broadway Inn with its enthusiastic, competent staff and personal touches scores high on all counts. Manager Mohammad Butt says, "We will gladly upgrade guests to better rooms at the same rate when we can." This bed-and-breakfast proves that it isn't necessary to sacrifice style and comfort for affordability. Reserve as far in advance as possible, especially for holidays and summer months.

COMFORT INN MANHATTAN

42 W. 35th St.
New York, NY 10001
(BETWEEN FIFTH AND SIXTH AVENUES)

VALUE ★★★
CLEANLINESS ★★★★
GUEST SERVICES ★★★
SECURITY ★★★★
(★POOR - ★★★★★EXCELLENT)

CATEGORY	Limited Services
PHONE	(212) 947-0200
	(800) 228-5150 Reservations
FAX	(212) 594-3047
EMAIL	mur75a@aol.com
WEBSITE	www.comfortinnmanhattan.com
RATES	$129-$229
	Discounts to seniors, AAA members, and government and corporate employees; children under 18 stay free
GUEST ROOMS	131 rooms, half nonsmoking

ROOM AMENITIES	AC, cable TV with pay movies, phone with voice mail and dataport, safe, iron and ironing board, hair dryer, some with microwaves and mini-fridges
RESTAURANTS	Coming in 2002
BARS	Coming in 2002
CLIENTELE	European tourists, primarily
GUEST SERVICES	Continental breakfast, *USA Today* weekdays, valet laundry, 24-hour coffee and tea in lobby
PARKING	None
CANCELLATION POLICY	24 hours before check-in
WHEELCHAIR ACCESS	None

This chain hotel occupies an older building that cries out for TLC. Elevators are tiny, and the narrow hallways show the usual scuff marks, cracks, and crumbling plaster. Improvements move at a snail's pace, but carpets in the lobby and hallways are new.

Now the good news: as in older buildings, rooms are larger than average. Ceilings are high and closets are roomy, which is great if you're staying more than a few nights. Standard doubles come with either a king, queen, or two double beds; sofa; desk; safe; iron; and a six-drawer dresser. Bathrooms are small with a tub/shower. If you can't get a room with a mini-fridge, you can rent one for an extra $25 a night.

A terrific asset for out-of-town visitors is a friendly front desk staff, for whom no question is too dumb and no demand too taxing. Their patience (no doubt the result of good training) seems Buddha-like. The inn is also within an easy walk to midtown attractions, the Theater District, Garment District, Fifth Avenue shopping, and even the Jacob Javits Convention Center—a blessing for business as well as leisure travelers.

COMFORT INN MIDTOWN

129 W. 46th St.
New York, NY 10036
(BETWEEN SIXTH AVE. AND BROADWAY)

VALUE ★ ★ ★ ★ ★
CLEANLINESS ★ ★ ★ ★
GUEST SERVICES ★ ★ ★
SECURITY ★ ★ ★
(★POOR - ★★★★★EXCELLENT)

CATEGORY	Limited Services
PHONE	(212) 221-2600
	(800) 567-7720 Reservations
FAX	(212) 764-7481
	(212) 790-2760 Reservations
EMAIL	None
WEBSITE	www.applecorehotels.com
RATES	$89-$329
	Discounts for AAA and AARP members on rates above $109
GUEST ROOMS	80 rooms on 8 floors are all nonsmoking
ROOM AMENITIES	AC; cable TV with pay games, movies, and internet access; phone with voice mail and dataport; hair dryer; coffeemaker; iron and ironing board; safe
RESTAURANTS	None
BARS	None
CLIENTELE	A mix of business and leisure travelers
GUEST SERVICES	Continental breakfast, valet laundry, fitness equipment, business center, meeting room, *USA Today*
PARKING	None
CANCELLATION POLICY	24 hours before check-in
WHEELCHAIR ACCESS	None

This Comfort Inn was upgraded by Apple Core Hotels in 1998, and its attractive guest rooms and public spaces still appear new, fragrant, and clean. A cheerful lobby with cheerful staff is managed by Rajni Rikh, who says, "We are a small-scale hotel and try to create a homey atmosphere for our guests." Simply put: they succeed, and it's a welcome oasis in busy Times Square.

Standard doubles are average-sized with large bathrooms. Amenities include large-screen TVs with all the extras, large walk-in closets with an iron and safe, and a coffeemaker so you can drink your java in bed. Even the AC units look brand new. All rooms have the same Early American décor. Ask for the largest possible room on an upper floor for maximum comfort and quiet.

The elegant lobby at the Comfort Inn Midtown is a far cry from the standard chain hotel. Credit: Apple Core Hotels

DAYS HOTEL

790 Eighth Ave.
New York, NY 10019
(AT W. 48TH ST.)

VALUE ★★★★
CLEANLINESS ★★★
GUEST SERVICES ★★★
SECURITY ★★★★

(★POOR - ★★★★★EXCELLENT)

CATEGORY	Limited Services
PHONE	(212) 581-7000
	(800) 572-6232 Reservations
FAX	(212) 974-0291
EMAIL	None
WEBSITE	www.daysinn.com
RATES	$99-$499
	Discounts to AAA and AARP members
GUEST ROOMS	367 rooms on 15 floors; nonsmoking rooms on floors 3-7, 11, and 12
ROOM AMENITIES	AC, cable TV with pay movies, phone with voice mail, safe, hair dryer, iron and ironing board
RESTAURANTS	Yes
BARS	Yes
CLIENTELE	Mix of business and leisure travelers
GUEST SERVICES	Valet laundry, concierge, gift shop
PARKING	None
CANCELLATION POLICY	24 hours before check-in
WHEELCHAIR ACCESS	Yes

Guest rooms are oversized whether they offer double/double, queen-, or king-sized beds. It's been five years since they received attention, and it shows. Telltale signs of neglect include chipped paint, stale smells, and moldy bathroom grouting. The drab, dark hallways particularly need sprucing up.

Bathrooms with tub and shower are fully equipped and closets house an iron and safe. You'll have a sofa and chair, desk, armoire holding a large-screen TV, and a phone with voice mail. Windows are double-paned, but unless you ask for an inside room, you'll hear the traffic symphony from Eighth Avenue. Executive rooms on the 11th floor offer some extras—a microwave, coffeemaker, and dataport.

Affordable rates, a pleasant lobby, and affable front desk staff add value; but Hampshire Hotels and Resorts, which owns both this property and the nearby Howard Johnson Plaza, needs to clean up its act here.

EDISON HOTEL

228 W. 47th St.
New York, NY 10036
(BETWEEN BROADWAY AND EIGHTH AVE.)

VALUE ★ ★ ★ ★

CLEANLINESS ★ ★ ★ ★

GUEST SERVICES ★ ★ ★ ★

SECURITY ★ ★ ★ ★

(★POOR - ★★★★★EXCELLENT)

CATEGORY	Limited Services
PHONE	(212) 840-5000
	(800) 637-7070 Reservations
FAX	(212) 596-6858
	(212) 596-6860 Reservations
EMAIL	info@edisonhotelnyc.com
WEBSITE	www.edisonhotelnyc.com
RATES	Singles: $150, doubles: $170, suites: $190 and up
GUEST ROOMS	800 rooms on 22 floors, primarily nonsmoking
ROOM AMENITIES	AC, cable TV, phone with voice mail
RESTAURANTS	Café Edison, Sofia's Italian restaurant, The Supper Club
BARS	The Rum House
CLIENTELE	Business and leisure travelers
GUEST SERVICES	Concierge, $10 pass to health club, internet kiosk, gift shop, beauty salon
PARKING	None
CANCELLATION POLICY	24 hours before check-in
WHEELCHAIR ACCESS	Yes

The Edison Hotel was launched in 1931, when Thomas Edison turned on the lights by remote control from his home in Menlo Park. Its lights promise to stay bright for many years to come. Designed in the same Art Deco style as the famed Radio City Music Hall, the hotel features one of the largest and most attractive sitting areas in New York. Its sky-high ceilings and creative use of space make it a popular spot for a midtown rendezvous.

Guest accommodations don't have the same "wow" appeal as the lobby, but they fulfill most people's basic requirements. Considering you're so close to Times Square, the calming décor is perfect. Rooms are certainly not spacious, but at least you don't trip over the furniture on your way to the door. The desks are adequate for business travelers, and closets have plenty of hangers. We were disappointed in the tiny bathrooms and nonexistent bath products, but appreciated the heavy, soundproofed doors and electronic keycards.

Of the hotel's three restaurants, only the Café Edison allows guests to charge meals to their room. The Supper Club features dining and dancing, and the Rum House provides a warm, tavern ambience for those tired of the city's "we're too cool to be comfortable" bars. Unfortunately, none of these establishments offers room service, but they do offer food to go. To make up for its lack of a business center, the front desk supplies some basic business services. Guests also get a $10 pass to the nearby New York Sports Club.

It's always refreshing when one of Manhattan's landmark midtown hotels turns out to be affordable.

The Edison's Art Deco lobby is a popular midtown meeting place. Credit: Lisa Mullenneaux

414 INN

414 W. 46th St.
New York, NY 10036

(BETWEEN NINTH AND 10TH AVENUES)

VALUE ★ ★ ★ ★

CLEANLINESS ★ ★ ★ ★ ★

GUEST SERVICES ★ ★ ★

SECURITY ★ ★ ★ ★

(★POOR - ★★★★★EXCELLENT)

CATEGORY	Euro-style
PHONE	(212) 399-0006
FAX	(212) 957-8716
EMAIL	p414inn@hotmail.com
WEBSITE	www.414inn.com Offers seasonal promotions
RATES	$110-$210
GUEST ROOMS	22 rooms in 2 four-story buildings, 8 smoking rooms, no elevator
ROOM AMENITIES	AC, cable TV, VCR, phone with voice mail and dataport, safe
RESTAURANTS	None
BARS	None
CLIENTELE	A mix of leisure and business travelers
GUEST SERVICES	Continental breakfast; video rentals; fruit, coffee, and tea all day
PARKING	None
CANCELLATION POLICY	24 hours before check-in
WHEELCHAIR ACCESS	None

What a delight to discover this charming inn in a relatively charmless stretch of midtown. Only about two years old, the inn is made up of two four-story buildings separated by a courtyard.

Decorated in soft grays, blues, and greens, rooms feature queen-sized beds, except for two with king-sized beds and two with twin beds. Closets are only average-sized, but the armoire houses drawers as well as the television. Most of the rooms have a full desk. All private, the bathrooms are larger than expected in a small inn. No hair dryer, but the vanity shelf is large enough for a starlet's bag of cosmetics. The rear townhouse caters to smokers.

The inn provides a continental breakfast of fresh juice and fruits, breads, and hot and cold cereals. The seating area in the small lobby where breakfast is served is also a hot spot in the evening because of the large-screen television and working fireplace. If you need some time alone, rent a video from the hotel's well-stocked library for $4.

This neighborhood has improved much over the past several years, but security is still important. Guests must be buzzed in, and the hotel uses electronic keycards, unusual for a small property. Less than one block away you'll find Restaurant Row, and it's an easy walk to the Theater District, Port Authority Building, and Times Square.

Hotels appear and disappear quickly in Manhattan. We hope this one survives.

HAMPSHIRE HOTEL AND SUITES

157 W. 47th St.
New York, NY 10036
(BETWEEN SIXTH AND SEVENTH AVENUES)

VALUE ★★★★★

CLEANLINESS ★★★★★

GUEST SERVICES ★★★

SECURITY ★★★★★

(★POOR - ★★★★★EXCELLENT)

CATEGORY	Boutique
PHONE	(212) 768-3700
	(800) 334-4667 Reservations
FAX	(212) 768-7573 Reservations
	(212) 921-2819
EMAIL	None
WEBSITE	www.bestnyhotels.com\hhs
RATES	$109–$379
	10 percent discount to AAA and AARP members
GUEST ROOMS	160 rooms on 10 floors, 2 smoking floors

ROOM AMENITIES	AC, cable TV with pay movies, phone with voice mail and dataport; hair dryer, iron and ironing board, and mini-fridge available on request
RESTAURANTS	None
BARS	None
CLIENTELE	Primarily European business travelers; 45 percent Americans
GUEST SERVICES	Continental breakfast, valet laundry, concierge, meeting room for up to 30 people
PARKING	None
CANCELLATION POLICY	24 hours before check-in
WHEELCHAIR ACCESS	10 rooms

This boutique hotel offers a reassuringly quiet and comfortable lobby with a savvy concierge and front desk staff. Guest rooms on seven of 10 floors have been refurbished since 1997, when the property was purchased from Quality Hotels. Hallways are sparkling with elegant red and gold carpets and marbled walls. All rooms have bathrooms with a marble commode and a cramped tub/shower, walk-in closets, phones with voice mail, and sophisticated, even regal, furnishings.

You can request a mini-fridge for your room at no charge. Ninety percent of the suites have Jacuzzi tubs and all feature sitting rooms, some with sofa beds. Standard rooms are more compact but offer similar amenities and handsome décor, like antique prints in gilt-edged frames. As with any Times Square hotel, request an inside room unless you're a junkie for street action.

Corporate clients can choose the luxurious CEO suites with large desks and living rooms. Or they can move up to the Presidential Suite and use the Penthouse Conference Room with its state-of-the-art equipment.

Sales Director Jeanette Alicea boasts a return rate of 85 percent because "our suites match a standard room at four-star properties—like the Sheratons, Hyatts, and Marriotts." A good value just steps from Rockefeller Center and the Theater District.

MIDTOWN WEST

HERALD SQUARE HOTEL
19 W. 31st St.
New York, NY 10001
(BETWEEN FIFTH AVE. AND BROADWAY)

VALUE ★ ★ ★
CLEANLINESS ★ ★ ★
GUEST SERVICES ★
SECURITY ★ ★ ★ ★
(★POOR - ★★★★★EXCELLENT)

CATEGORY	Bare Essentials
PHONE	(212) 279-4017
	(800) 727-1888 Reservations
FAX	(212) 643-9208
EMAIL	info@heraldsquarehotel.com
WEBSITE	www.heraldsquarehotel.com
RATES	$65-$160
	Discounts to ISI card holders
GUEST ROOMS	125 rooms on 9 floors, some singles share baths, all smoking
ROOM AMENITIES	AC, cable TV, phone with voice mail, safe; hair dryers and irons available on request
RESTAURANTS	None
BARS	None
CLIENTELE	Mostly international tourists
GUEST SERVICES	Lockers, internet access
PARKING	None
CANCELLATION POLICY	24 hours before check-in
WHEELCHAIR ACCESS	None

A golden cherub, known as Winged Life, heralds your entrance into what were once the offices of *Life* magazine. Magazine covers displayed in the lobby and upstairs hallways toast those glory days of publishing. Unfortunately, there's nothing glorious about the present occupant. It offers no-frills lodging and you get what you pay for.

Your first challenge may be locating your room because hallways have no directional signs. Those hallway floors are tiled, not carpeted, and the scenery's pretty grim. The least expensive room is a single with a twin bed and shared bath. It's no bigger than a bread box, but it's clean. The rest—single, standard double, double/double, triple, and quad—have private bathrooms. They are clean and comfortable, but short on amenities. In size and décor, they match rooms at the Portland Square. The double/double room is the most attractive, but at $140 is undercut by other budget hotels in this neighborhood. Lack of control over room temperature can make you feel like you're being slow-roasted during winter months.

The Herald Square is identical in price and appearance to its uptown sister hotel, the Portland Square. They are popular with singles, who can ignore the primitive shared baths and cramped quarters. Maybe someday the owners will realize they have a diamond in the rough and give this place the polish to match its angelic Beaux Arts exterior.

White-and-gold façade of the birthplace of *Life* Magazine serves as the no-frills Herald Square Hotel.
Credit: Desmond Shaw

MIDTOWN WEST

HOTEL METRO

45 W. 35th St.
New York, NY 10001
(BETWEEN FIFTH AND SIXTH AVENUES)

VALUE ★ ★ ★ ★
CLEANLINESS ★ ★ ★ ★ ★
GUEST SERVICES ★ ★ ★ ★
SECURITY ★ ★ ★
(★POOR - ★★★★★EXCELLENT)

CATEGORY	Boutique
PHONE	(212) 947-2500
	(800) 356-3870 Reservations
FAX	(212) 279-1310
EMAIL	None
WEBSITE	www.hotelmetronyc.com
	Excellent information and design
RATES	$150-$275
GUEST ROOMS	180 rooms on 14 floors, 19 suites, 2 nonsmoking floors
ROOM AMENITIES	AC, cable TV with HBO, 2-line phone with voice mail and dataport, mini-fridge, iron and ironing board, hair dryer
RESTAURANTS	Metro Grill
BARS	Terrace Bar in summer
CLIENTELE	A mix of business and leisure travelers
GUEST SERVICES	Continental breakfast, valet laundry, exercise room, meeting room, room service, *New York Times* available at the front desk
PARKING	None
CANCELLATION POLICY	24 hours before check-in
WHEELCHAIR ACCESS	Yes

For once the brochure doesn't lie: the Hotel Metro does set the standard for moderately priced accommodations in New York City. Its Art Deco lobby is a handsome space with mirrored walls and pillars in a black-and-gold motif surrounded by stylish photos of the Great Garbo.

Garbo stares back at you from the walls of the Metro's handsome lobby. Credit: Desmond Shaw

Extending back from the lobby, a lounge and library provide quiet space for chatting or reading with a cup of complimentary tea or coffee. (Pull a book from their shelves if you forgot to bring one of your own.)

Each of the 180 guest rooms has the same Art Deco design, and they are spotless. Marble bathrooms offer a tub/shower, some only tubs, and some only showers. State your preference. Two guest elevators whisk you to the 14th floor, where a small fitness room is equipped with weight machines, bikes, treadmills, and a large-screen TV. Business travelers have a range of support services, including a boardroom for groups up to 25.

In warm weather, the Terrace Bar serves drinks and finger food on a deck that faces the Empire State Building. As if that weren't enough, they feed you breakfast in the downstairs lounge. If you prefer a full breakfast, try the Metro Grill next door. It also serves lunch and dinner at prices that won't stretch the seams in your wallet.

MIDTOWN WEST

HOTEL PENNSYLVANIA

401 Seventh Ave.
New York, NY 10001
(BETWEEN W. 32ND AND W. 33RD STREETS)

VALUE ★ ★ ★ ★

CLEANLINESS ★ ★ ★

GUEST SERVICES ★ ★ ★ ★ ★

SECURITY ★ ★ ★ ★

(★POOR - ★★★★★EXCELLENT)

CATEGORY	Limited Services
PHONE	(212) 736-5000
	(800) 223-8585 Reservations
FAX	(212) 502-8799
	(212) 502-8712 Reservations
EMAIL	sales@hotelpenn.com
WEBSITE	www.hotelpenn.com
	Offers special packages
RATES	$119-$250
	Discounts for AAA and AARP members
GUEST ROOMS	1,700 rooms includes 20 suites on 16 floors, some nonsmoking
ROOM AMENITIES	AC, cable TV, phone with voice mail; 2-line phones with dataport and mini-fridges available on request
RESTAURANTS	3
BARS	2
CLIENTELE	Mostly international tourists
GUEST SERVICES	Concierge, valet laundry, meeting and function rooms, business center, tour and travel desk, vending and ice machines on each floor, use of Bally's Health Club for $12 a day
PARKING	None
CANCELLATION POLICY	24 hours before check-in
WHEELCHAIR ACCESS	Yes

On weekends, the crowded lobby here could be an extension of Penn Station across the street. In fact, it was built in 1919 by the Pennsylvania Railroad to accommodate its passengers. Later, the hotel's Café Rouge Ballroom hosted

Big Band Era greats like Count Basie and the Glenn Miller Orchestra, which immortalized the hotel's phone number in its 1938 hit "Pennsylvania 6-500." But this landmark's glory is solidly in the past. Management needs to make a much greater financial commitment if it wants to own a crowd-pleaser and not a crowd-teaser.

Seven front desk clerks are available to check guests in, but no chairs or sofas for those guests to rest their weary limbs. The resulting gridlock can be overwhelming when you first arrive. Space is not a problem: you could drive a tractor trailer through the hallways. But you'd have to ignore stained carpet, cracked paint, and other symptoms of neglect.

The trick here is to ask for a renovated room, and as of press time 900 had been completed. The refurbished ones feature either a king bed or double/doubles and cost a bit more than the older rooms. The older "Tour and Travel" accommodations feature queen beds, twins, a single double, and a double/double. If an older room is your only option, bring some deodorizer. They smell. Bathrooms have either a tub or stall shower, minimal toiletries, and no hair dryer. There's cable TV, a phone with voice mail, a mini-fridge and double-paned windows. An encouraging sign are the new computerized, high-speed elevators.

This landmark hotel faces Penn Station and Madison Square Garden.
Credit: Hotel Pennsylvania

MIDTOWN WEST

HOTEL STANFORD

43 W. 32nd St.
New York, NY 10001
(BETWEEN BROADWAY AND FIFTH AVE.)

VALUE ★ ★ ★ ★
CLEANLINESS ★ ★ ★ ★
GUEST SERVICES ★ ★ ★
SECURITY ★ ★ ★ ★
(★POOR - ★★★★★EXCELLENT)

CATEGORY	Limited Services
PHONE	(212) 563-1500
	(800) 365-1114 Reservations
FAX	(212) 643-0157
	(212) 629-0043 Reservations
EMAIL	stanfordny@aol.com
WEBSITE	www.hotelstanford.citysearch.com
RATES	$120-$250
GUEST ROOMS	121 smoking rooms on 12 floors, 20 suites
ROOM AMENITIES	AC, cable TV, phone with voice mail, mini-fridge, hair dryer, safe
RESTAURANTS	Pastry café and Korean restaurant
BARS	Maxim on second floor
CLIENTELE	60 percent business clients, 40 percent American and European tourists
GUEST SERVICES	Continental breakfast, valet laundry, luggage room
PARKING	None
CANCELLATION POLICY	24 hours before check-in
WHEELCHAIR ACCESS	None

This is a clean and affordable lodging in the heart of Little Korea. At least 60 percent of its guests are business travelers; the rest are American and European bargain hunters. (For guests' convenience, lobby clocks are set for London, New York, and Seoul/Tokyo time.) Friendly front desk staff set the tone for this little gem. They can help you arrange tours and transportation and delight in sharing insiders' tips about what's hot and what's not in the Big Apple.

Singles with a double bed are equipped with a desk; dresser; cable TV; phone with voice mail; mini-fridge; walk-in closet; and medium-sized bathroom with a tub/shower, hair dryer, and toiletries. Doubles with a queen bed are roomier with similar furnishings and amenities plus a safe. Suites are cavernous. Ask for a refurbished room; the 30 percent that have not been spruced up are clean but dingy. As always, if you crave quiet, ask for an off-street room on a top floor.

A pastry café and pleasant Korean restaurant are convenient, especially in winter months, and the free breakfast adds value. In sum, this oldie but goodie delivers the goods at moderate prices.

HOTEL WOLCOTT

4 W. 31st St.
New York, NY 10001
(BETWEEN FIFTH AVE. AND BROADWAY)

VALUE ★ ★ ★ ★ ★

CLEANLINESS ★ ★ ★ ★

GUEST SERVICES ★ ★ ★ ★

SECURITY ★ ★ ★ ★

(★POOR - ★★★★★EXCELLENT)

CATEGORY	Limited Services
PHONE	(212) 268-2900
FAX	(212) 563-0096
EMAIL	sales@wolcott.com
WEBSITE	www.wolcott.com Extensive and informative
RATES	$99-$180
GUEST ROOMS	165 rooms on 14 floors include 23 suites, all smoking
ROOM AMENITIES	AC; cable TV with pay movies, games, and internet access; phone with voice mail and dataport; mini-fridge; safe; hair dryer
RESTAURANTS	None
BARS	None

CLIENTELE	Mix of leisure and business travelers
GUEST SERVICES	Self-service laundry, concierge, gift shop, fitness room, small meeting room, lockers, free use of printers and computers
PARKING	$17 discounted rate
CANCELLATION POLICY	24 hours before check-in
WHEELCHAIR ACCESS	One room

The Wolcott is famous for its Louis XVI-style, marble-pillared lobby. Dazzled by gilt and mirrors, you might think you've stumbled into Versailles. But the lobby isn't a tease; guest rooms feature the same ornate ceilings and oversized space. They have recently been "improved" with

Versailles west. Wolcott's famous lobby is all gilt and mirrors.
Credit: Desmond Shaw

new mahogany furniture, striped wallpaper, green carpet, and matching green and rose spreads. All rooms offer a three-drawer dresser, writing desk, clock radio, good-sized bathrooms, and those without a closet have a clothes rack. Some have mini-fridges.

Complementing the in-room amenities are abundant guest services like exercise equipment, computers, and a self-service laundry. The hotel is within strolling distance of Macy's, the Jacob Javits Convention Center, Times Square amusements, and the Empire State Building. A concierge can get you discounted theater tickets, but TKTS at Broadway and 47th Street in Times Square offers as much as 50 percent off top shows.

The Wolcott's Old World charm and reasonable rates have charmed many a traveler, who will be well pleased with its comforts and services. The building may be out-of-fashion, but its new room décor and amenities are right up to date.

HOWARD JOHNSON PLAZA HOTEL

851 Eighth Ave.
New York, NY 10019
(AT W. 51ST ST.)

VALUE ★ ★ ★ ★

CLEANLINESS ★ ★ ★ ★

GUEST SERVICES ★ ★ ★ ★

SECURITY ★ ★ ★ ★

(★POOR - ★★★★★EXCELLENT)

CATEGORY	Limited Services
PHONE	(212) 581-4100
	(800) 426-HOJO Reservations
FAX	(212) 974-7502
EMAIL	None
WEBSITE	www.hojo.com
RATES	$99-$499
	Discount to AAA and AARP members
GUEST ROOMS	300 rooms on 11 floors, smoking rooms on floors 2, 3, and 4

ROOM AMENITIES	AC, cable TV with pay movies, phone with voice mail, iron, ironing board and hair dryer; mini-fridge available on request
RESTAURANTS	Beefsteak Charlie's
BARS	In the restaurant
CLIENTELE	A mix of business and leisure travelers
GUEST SERVICES	Valet laundry, concierge, gift shop, room service, ATM and fax machine in lobby, vending and ice machines on each floor
PARKING	None
CANCELLATION POLICY	24 hours before check-in
WHEELCHAIR ACCESS	2 rooms

This Hojo is owned by Hampshire Hotels and Resorts, which also owns the Days Hotel. Guest rooms, rates, and amenities are virtually identical in the two hotels, down to the beige walls, rose carpets, and mahogany furniture.

Each offers double/doubles, queen-, or king-sized beds in comfortable quarters with a sitting area, large-screen TV with cable channels and pay movies, climate control, double-paned windows, and phones with voice mail. Bathrooms are good-sized with sparse toiletries and hair dryers. Mini-fridges are available on request. Like its twin, the Hojo has executive rooms on the 11th floor, which provide extra space, a microwave, mini-fridge, coffee-maker, and two walk-in closets with an iron and hair dryer. A nice perk here is room service from Beefsteak Charlie's.

This Hojo offers good value for business guests attending events at the nearby Jacob Javits Convention Center and vacationers who crave lots of theater action. A tip of the chapeau to management for hiring smart, gracious front desk staff. They really know how to welcome new arrivals.

SLEEP CHEAP IN NEW YORK

MAYFAIR NEW YORK

242 W. 49th St.
New York, NY 10019
(BETWEEN BROADWAY AND EIGHTH AVE.)

VALUE ★ ★ ★ ★ ★

CLEANLINESS ★ ★ ★ ★ ★

GUEST SERVICES ★ ★ ★

SECURITY ★ ★ ★ ★ ★

(★POOR - ★★★★★EXCELLENT)

CATEGORY	Boutique
PHONE	(212) 586-0300 (800) 556-2932 Reservations
FAX	(212) 307-5226
EMAIL	mayfairny@aol.com
WEBSITE	www.mayfairnewyork.com
RATES	$90–$290
GUEST ROOMS	78 rooms on 7 floors, all nonsmoking
ROOM AMENITIES	AC, cable TV, 2-line phone with voice mail and dataport, safe, hair dryer
RESTAURANTS	The Garrick, named for a 17th-century Shakespearean actor, serves lunch and dinner
BARS	Yes
CLIENTELE	70 percent American business and leisure travelers, 30 percent foreigners
GUEST SERVICES	Valet laundry, discount at Mid City Gym
PARKING	$18 discounted rate
CANCELLATION POLICY	24 hours before check-in
WHEELCHAIR ACCESS	Yes

When Robert Ernstoff rehabilitated a drug-infested neighborhood eyesore, he made a lot of smart choices, beginning with the design of this hotel's chic lounge/lobby. He covered the walls with the warm red-gold tones of cherry wood, laid terrazzo floors, and installed leather banquettes where guests can relax over a cup of cappuccino from the restaurant next door. Vintage photos from the Museum of the City of New York capture the Theater District's legendary performers.

Problems begin when you board the tiny, erratic elevator. For guests on lower floors, the stairs are a better option. Like most boutique hotels, the Mayfair sacrifices space for style. Rooms are either standard (cramped) or deluxe (small), but the décor is perky, especially the red-and-white matching spreads and curtains, striped wallpaper, and Biedermeier-style furniture.

Guests can expect firm mattresses, Irish linen and towels, phones with voice mail and dataports, cable TVs, wall safes, and small closets. The smallest room has a stall shower; others have a tub and shower, and they are fully equipped. All rooms offer lots of mirrors, which add the illusion of space—a smart idea. Hall and stairway carpets need to be replaced, but otherwise this property looks impressive. There's a lot of room for choice so sample some rooms before you decide.

Adjacent to the Eugene O'Neill Theater in one of the city's most exciting venues, the Mayfair New York combines classic Old World elegance with modern conveniences that ensure a memorable stay.

MILFORD PLAZA

270 W. 45th St.
New York, NY 10036
(AT EIGHTH AVE.)

VALUE ★ ★ ★ ★

CLEANLINESS ★ ★ ★ ★

GUEST SERVICES ★ ★ ★ ★ ★

SECURITY ★ ★ ★ ★ ★

(★POOR - ★★★★★EXCELLENT)

CATEGORY	Full Services
PHONE	(212) 869-3600
	(800) 221-2690 Reservations
FAX	(212) 944-8357
EMAIL	None
WEBSITE	www.milfordplaza.com
RATES	Singles: $129-$179
	Doubles: $144-$194
	10 percent discount to AAA members and 15 percent to AARP members

GUEST ROOMS	1,300 rooms on 24 floors, 15 floors nonsmoking, 550 rooms reserved for airline personnel
ROOM AMENITIES	AC, cable TV with pay movies, 2-line phone with voice mail and dataport; iron and ironing board, hair dryer and mini-fridge available on request
RESTAURANTS	Celebrity Deli
BARS	Harvey's Pub
CLIENTELE	Mix of business guests and tourists
GUEST SERVICES	Valet laundry, room service, concierge, game room, ATMs, fitness room
PARKING	None
CANCELLATION POLICY	Same day by 4 p.m.
WHEELCHAIR ACCESS	None

This Times Square stalwart ended its relationship with Ramada Inns in August 2000 and, as of press time, was in the process of remodeling all 1,300 guest rooms. The new rooms are handsome, if you like a green and goldenrod palette. We prefer the older décor of rose and aqua.

Older rooms show wear and tear, but they are clean and even the singles offer desks, huge wall mirrors, walk-in closets, 2-line phones with voice mail and dataport, and cable TV with pay movies. Mattresses are firm and lighting is adequate. Windows in both new and older rooms are single-paned, and there's central heating, rather than individual thermostats. The corner rooms on each floor are oversized; ask for one on a top floor for better views and less noise.

Then there are those extra services, so convenient for guests with limited time. Eight good-sized elevators help move traffic swiftly among 28 floors. There are vending and ice machines on each floor. Once in the lobby, you can book your airport shuttle, tours, and theater tickets at the tour desk, get your hair done, buy souvenirs and sundries, and use their fax and photocopy machines. An exercise room opens at 6 a.m., and a game room will attract the young folks in your group and keep them from wandering the halls. Finally, the Celebrity Deli is famous for its mile-high sandwiches and New York cheesecake, as is Harvey's Pub for liquid refreshment.

Not a bad choice for the price, but be aware that almost half the hotel is reserved for airline crews. We saw so many uniformed personnel wheeling their soft-sided luggage we thought we'd taken a wrong turn and landed at JFK Airport.

MODERNE

243 W. 55th St.
New York, NY 10019
(BETWEEN BROADWAY AND EIGHTH AVE.)

VALUE ★★★★

CLEANLINESS ★★★★

GUEST SERVICES ★★★

SECURITY ★★★★

(★POOR - ★★★★★EXCELLENT)

CATEGORY	Boutique
PHONE	(212) 397-6767
	(888) 66-HOTEL Reservations
FAX	(212) 397-8787
EMAIL	None
WEBSITE	www.nycityhotels.net
	Offers special packages
RATES	$110-$350
GUEST ROOMS	34 rooms on 8 floors include 4 suites, some nonsmoking rooms
ROOM AMENITIES	AC, TV with VCR, CD player, 2-line phone with voice mail and dataport, iron and ironing board, hair dryer, Belgian linens
RESTAURANTS	None
BARS	None
CLIENTELE	A mix of business and leisure travelers
GUEST SERVICES	Continental breakfast, copies of *USA Today*, valet laundry
PARKING	None
CANCELLATION POLICY	24 hours before check-in
WHEELCHAIR ACCESS	None

The aptly named "Moderne" showcases avant-garde art and furniture to create a playful, original décor. A closer look at this renovated older building, however, reveals slap-dash carpentry and painting. Nothing artistic about that. As with all of the properties owned by the Amsterdam Hospitality Group, space is minimal, but the ambience is cheerful and hotel staff are anxious to please.

Hallways are very narrow but brightly lit. Guest rooms are painted in primary colors and equipped with blond maple furniture and upholstered headboards with built-in night tables. Many of them feature Andy Warhol's silk-screened image of Marilyn Monroe. Bathrooms are either green or white marble with a sprinkling of amenities. Closets are tiny, but they do store an iron and safe. Because room size varies while the rate stays the same, ask for the largest room available.

At press time, nights were quiet, but construction on 55th Street was an annoyance during the day. And that's a pity because the glassed-in breakfast room overlooking

Even Marilyn approves of the Moderne's playful décor.
Credit: Amsterdam Hospitality Group

55th Street with its library of books can also serve as a cozy lounge for reading, chatting, or entertaining guests.

This is a unique lodging in a desirable midtown locale. Too bad that shoddy workmanship and poor maintenance diminish its appeal.

NEW YORK INN

765 Eighth Ave.
New York, NY 10036
(BETWEEN W. 46TH AND W. 47TH STREETS)

VALUE ★★
CLEANLINESS ★
GUEST SERVICES ★★
SECURITY ★★★
(★POOR - ★★★★★EXCELLENT)

CATEGORY	Bare Essentials
PHONE	(212) 247-5400
	(888) 450-5555 Reservations
FAX	(212) 586-6201
EMAIL	nyinn@aol.com
WEBSITE	www.newyorkinn.com
RATES	$89–$130
GUEST ROOMS	40 rooms on 4 floors, all smoking
ROOM AMENITIES	AC, cable TV, phone, hair dryer
RESTAURANTS	Subway sandwich shop
BARS	None
CLIENTELE	International tourists
GUEST SERVICES	Continental breakfast
PARKING	None
CANCELLATION POLICY	48 hours before check-in
WHEELCHAIR ACCESS	None

The tiny lobby up one flight from Eighth Avenue is pungent with the aroma of hot meatball sandwiches. At any other hotel that might be a liability. Here it's about the best odor you'll sniff. Most rooms reek of either smoke (all rooms are open to smokers) or disinfectant. To compound the misery, there's no elevator. The hotel manager insisted there was a bellman when we visited, but no one was in sight. Maybe he stepped out for a hot meatball sandwich.

Hallways are shabby with antediluvian carpets. Singles and doubles have thin, lumpy mattresses and grimy windows. At least one air conditioner we saw was open to frigid winter air. Bathrooms are cramped, but they do offer hair dryers. Shower curtains look like the murder scene from *Psycho*. Rooms are identical down to the grit and noise from Eighth Avenue. Management talks about refurbishing. Give them plenty of time. Better bang for the buck elsewhere makes this midtown hotel a nonstarter.

NEW YORKER-RAMADA PLAZA

481 Eighth Ave.
New York, NY 10001
(AT W. 34TH ST.)

VALUE ★ ★ ★ ★ ★
CLEANLINESS ★ ★ ★ ★ ★
GUEST SERVICES ★ ★ ★ ★ ★
SECURITY ★ ★ ★ ★ ★
(★POOR - ★★★★★EXCELLENT)

CATEGORY	Full Services
PHONE	(212) 971-0101
	(800) 764-4680 Reservations
FAX	(212) 563-6136
EMAIL	info@nyhotel.com
WEBSITE	www.nyhotel.com
	Complete and informative with lots of historical detail
RATES	$129-$199
	Discounts for AAA and AARP members
GUEST ROOMS	1,012 rooms on 22 floors, some nonsmoking
ROOM AMENITIES	AC, cable TV with pay movies, 2-line phone with voice mail and dataport, some with mini-fridge
RESTAURANTS	Tick Tock Diner (open 24 hours, will deliver), La Vigna Ristorante/Bar and Grill, the Lobby Café
BARS	Yes

The New Yorker has been a beacon of hospitality for seventy years.
Credit: New Yorker-Ramada Plaza

CLIENTELE	Half tourist, half business
GUEST SERVICES	Fitness equipment, valet laundry, room service, business center, theatre desk
PARKING	None
CANCELLATION POLICY	Day of arrival by 4 p.m.
WHEELCHAIR ACCESS	Yes

The New Yorker proves that with enough financial commitment you can resurrect a fallen idol and make it shine. (Listen up, Hotel Pennsylvania.) It was a marvel when it opened in 1930 with 2,500 guest rooms, five restaurants, a barber shop with 42 chairs, 92 telephone operators, and 150 laundry staff. They were all supported by America's biggest private power plant. Like the Hotel Pennsylvania, its ballrooms hosted the Big Bands of the day and most of society's elite.

The New Yorker is now affiliated with Ramada, and refurbishment of guest rooms and public areas is ongoing. Management spent $4 million on new elevators alone. They move traffic speedily among 40 floors, 22 of which are open to hotel guests. Security is exemplary. All guests must show room keys to board the elevators, and keys are required to use the self-service laundry, fitness center, and business center.

Even the smallest room is comfortable and comes equipped with a phone with dataport, TV with pay movies and HBO, double-paned windows, and a thermostat to control the air and heat. Bathrooms have tub/showers, but no hair dryers. Tower rooms give more bang for slightly bigger bucks, but at $195 a night they are a steal. Among their amenities are fully-equipped marble bathrooms, fax machines, continental breakfast, wet bar, and mini-fridge.

Whichever room you choose, ask for one on an upper floor and enjoy views of the Hudson River, Chrysler Building, and the Empire State Building. All of the rooms we visited smelled fresh and looked brand new. The New Yorker is a model for other vintage hotels, and what they don't do right doesn't matter.

MIDTOWN WEST

PARK SAVOY

158 W. 58th St.
New York, NY 10019
(BETWEEN SIXTH AND SEVENTH AVENUES)

VALUE ★★★

CLEANLINESS ★★★★

GUEST SERVICES NONE

SECURITY ★★★★

(★POOR - ★★★★★EXCELLENT)

CATEGORY	Euro-style
PHONE	(212) 245-5755
FAX	(212) 765-0668
EMAIL	parksavoy@aol.com
WEBSITE	None
RATES	$85-$185 Breakfast is free for guests who stay more than 5 nights Rates include taxes
GUEST ROOMS	80 rooms on 9 floors, all allow smoking
ROOM AMENITIES	AC, TV, phone with voice mail
RESTAURANTS	None
BARS	None
CLIENTELE	Mostly travelers from abroad
GUEST SERVICES	None
PARKING	None
CANCELLATION POLICY	24 hours prior to arrival
WHEELCHAIR ACCESS	None

In the grand opera of midtown Manhattan, the Park Savoy is a stagehand surrounded by divas like the Essex and Plaza. But divas are expensive, and this low-maintenance lodging may be just the place if you want a clean, comfortable room you'll probably only face at night.

There's no lobby, just a long, narrow hallway that leads to a front desk. Staff are chatty and very helpful. Ask them about restaurants, tours, and tickets, but also about the best room available. At certain times of the year, you can get a spacious double with a queen bed for as little as $85, including taxes. Bunk here and you'll be able to afford a cocktail at the Plaza's Oyster Bar.

The smallest room is tiny with a full-sized bed, armoire, desk, TV with limited channels, phone that you'll need a calling card to use (buy one at the front desk), new AC, stall shower, and Calla Royal Orchards toiletries. Doubles are three times larger than singles with either a queen or two full-sized beds. They come equipped with similar furnishings, plus a mini-fridge, walk-in closet, and tub/shower. Carpets and textiles in all the rooms are new and perky, but the building itself could be better maintained. Double-paned windows help filter out some traffic noise, but don't expect a Zen-like silence.

PORTLAND SQUARE

132 W. 47th St.
New York, NY 10036
(BETWEEN BROADWAY AND SIXTH AVE.)

VALUE ★★
CLEANLINESS ★★★
GUEST SERVICES ★★★
SECURITY ★★★★
(★POOR - ★★★★★EXCELLENT)

CATEGORY	Bare Essentials
PHONE	(212) 382-0600
	(800) 388-8988 Reservations
FAX	(212) 382-0684
EMAIL	portlandsq@aol.com
WEBSITE	www.portlandsquarehotel.com
RATES	$65–$160
GUEST ROOMS	145 rooms, some shared baths, all smoking
ROOM AMENITIES	AC, cable TV, safe, phone with voice mail
RESTAURANTS	None
BARS	None
CLIENTELE	International tourists, primarily
GUEST SERVICES	Self-service laundry, small gym, lockers, internet kiosk, phone cards for sale, vending machines
PARKING	None

CANCELLATION POLICY   Day of arrival by 6 p.m.
WHEELCHAIR ACCESS   None

Style and comfort are not the Portland Square's strong suit. Like the Herald Square Hotel, which it matches in both price and appearance, guests are buzzed into a bare-bones lobby, and check in with staff shielded by protective glass. They will take your $25 deposit to open an outside phone line and more if you need a hair dryer or iron. Rooms that face 47th Street are brighter than inside rooms and offer better views. The only breach of this property's institutional armor are pink-painted walls in the lobby and upstairs halls. Otherwise, it's as cheerless as a prison.

A single with private bath is pint-sized. If claustrophobia is a problem, seek lodging elsewhere. Those beige walls, green carpets, and floral bedspreads are going to seem like a second skin. There's cable TV, a safe, toiletries, a window AC unit, phone with voice mail, and a Gideon's Bible, which is standard issue for hotels but might be your salvation if you stay here long term. A single with a shared bath is a cubby hole with the same features plus a sink. Hallway bathrooms are tiny with stall showers and a toilet. They are best avoided.

A double with private bath for $125 is smaller than average with a small dresser, desk, and closet, but, inexplicably, no safe. The medium-sized bathroom has a tub/shower combo and toiletries.

The Portland Square bills itself as the longest-running show on Broadway, but we feel its appeal is strictly limited to those free-spirited singles who are short on cash and long on tolerance. They can get a clean room with a shared bath for $65. But couples and families who want a private bath and some stretching room can find better bang for the buck nearby.

QUALITY HOTEL AND SUITES MIDTOWN

59 W. 46th St.
New York, NY 10036
(BETWEEN FIFTH AND SIXTH AVENUES)

VALUE ★ ★ ★
CLEANLINESS ★ ★ ★
GUEST SERVICES ★ ★ ★ ★
SECURITY ★ ★ ★
(★POOR - ★★★★EXCELLENT)

CATEGORY	Limited Services
PHONE	(212) 719-2300 (800) 567-7720 Reservations
FAX	(212) 768-3477 (212) 790-2760 Reservations
EMAIL	None
WEBSITE	www.applecorehotels.com
RATES	$89-$329 10 percent discount for AAA and AARP members for rates above $109 Children 13 and under stay free
GUEST ROOMS	206 rooms in 2 buildings, some nonsmoking
ROOM AMENITIES	AC; cable TV with pay movies, games, and internet access; phone with voice mail (free local calls); iron and ironing board; safe; hair dryer; coffeemaker
RESTAURANTS	None
BARS	Sky Bar on second floor
CLIENTELE	Mix of business and leisure travelers
GUEST SERVICES	Concierge, valet laundry, business center, continental breakfast, fitness center
PARKING	None
CANCELLATION POLICY	48 hours before check-in
WHEELCHAIR ACCESS	Yes

At press time, this hotel was completing a renovation. The new lobby offers adequate lounging space in a handsome setting of mahogany-paneled pillars and wainscotting, white marble floors, alabaster-petal ceiling lamps, lemon wallpaper, and a colorful mural of New York City.

Older guest rooms pass muster, but they don't sparkle. In fact, they smell fresher than they look. Singles don't give you much elbow room nor would the tiny closets relieve your suitcases of their contents. They do house an iron, ironing board, and safe. Doubles vary in size, so ask for the largest available. A double with two queens is roomy with an average-sized bathroom equipped with a tub/shower, hair dryer, and toiletries. Central heat and air; no thermostats. Mattresses vary in quality but are generally firm. To get the most for your money, try to book a newer room; they are brightly decorated and nicely appointed.

A granite staircase leads down from the lobby to a breakfast room and fitness center, regrettably not locked to outsiders. A small business center, operated with your credit card, adds convenience to a very attractive hotel package.

A colorful New York mural is the centerpiece of the Quality Hotel's lobby. Credit: Lisa Mullenneaux

SLEEP CHEAP IN NEW YORK

RADIO CITY APARTMENTS

142 W. 49th St.
New York, NY 10019
(BETWEEN SIXTH AND SEVENTH AVENUES)

VALUE ★ ★ ★ ★

CLEANLINESS ★ ★ ★ ★

GUEST SERVICES ★

SECURITY ★ ★ ★ ★ ★

(★POOR - ★★★★★EXCELLENT)

CATEGORY	Limited Services
PHONE	(212) 730-0728
	(877) 921-9321 Reservations
FAX	(212) 921-0572
EMAIL	radiocityapt@earthlink.net
WEBSITE	www.radiocityapartments.com
RATES	Studios: $132
	One bedrooms: $175
	Two bedrooms: $205
GUEST ROOMS	96 rooms on 12 floors, all smoking
ROOM AMENITIES	AC, cable TV, kitchenette, phone with voice mail
RESTAURANTS	None
BARS	None
CLIENTELE	International and domestic tourists
GUEST SERVICES	Self-service laundry
PARKING	None
CANCELLATION POLICY	48 hours before check-in
WHEELCHAIR ACCESS	None

A pleasant lobby embellished with ornately painted ceilings, marble floors, and crystal chandeliers reminds us of this building's former elegance. But Radio City's greatest asset these days isn't aesthetics; it's the economizing potential of its studio, one-, and two-bedroom apartments. All are showing some age, but are clean. Those rooms that have been refurbished offer marble baths and new appliances.

If you rent a studio, you can choose either two twins or a double bed. All rooms come with a fully equipped kitch-

MIDTOWN WEST

enette with a range, microwave, and mini-fridge; a satellite TV; coffeemaker; bath with hair dryer and toiletries; a firm mattress; an intercom for receiving guests; and a phone with voice mail. One- and two-bedroom apartments are good-sized, but some inexplicably have just a mini-fridge and microwave instead of a kitchenette. As the rate is the same, ask for an apartment with a kitchenette. Hotel security is reassuringly tight, but front desk staff could benefit from a course in congeniality.

Radio City Apartments is a reasonable resource for visitors staying more than a few days. One New York breakfast alone can cost $10, so it helps to be able to eat in. You can even wash the grit from your clothes in the coin-operated laundry.

RED ROOF INN

6 W. 32nd St.
New York, NY 10001
(BETWEEN BROADWAY AND FIFTH AVE.)

VALUE ★ ★ ★ ★ ★

CLEANLINESS ★ ★ ★ ★ ★

GUEST SERVICES ★ ★ ★ ★ ★

SECURITY ★ ★ ★ ★ ★

(★POOR - ★★★★★EXCELLENT)

CATEGORY	Limited Services
PHONE	(212) 643-7100
	(800) 567-7720 Reservations
FAX	(212) 643-7101
	(212) 790-2760 Reservations
EMAIL	None
WEBSITE	www.redroof.com
RATES	$89.99-$339
	5 percent discount to AAA and AARP members for rates above $109
GUEST ROOMS	171 rooms, floors 8-17 are nonsmoking
ROOM AMENITIES	AC; cable TV with pay movies, games, and internet access; 2-line phone with voice mail and dataport; coffeemaker; hair dryer; iron and ironing board; some with mini-fridge and microwave

RESTAURANTS	None
BARS	Yes
CLIENTELE	70 percent are business clients, a mix of American, European, Indian, and Korean
GUEST SERVICES	Continental breakfast, valet laundry, fitness center, meeting room for up to 15 people, concierge
PARKING	None
CANCELLATION POLICY	24 hours before check-in
WHEELCHAIR ACCESS	10 rooms

A lofty, polished lobby with no "Red Roof" in sight.
Credit: Apple Core Hotels

Note: this is not the Red Roof Inn you saw off Interstate 80 on your last trip through Ohio. Apple Core Hotels invested $23 million to buy and convert a 17-story office building into a stylish, yet functional, budget hotel. Its $89.99 rate, usually available in January and February, is the hottest ticket in town. One sure draw is the hotel's proximity to Times Square, Fortune 500 headquarters, the Empire State Building, and Madison Square Garden.

Just off Fifth Avenue, it presents a modern, high-ceilinged lobby with a mezzanine bar, where you can read or wait for visiting friends. At 4 p.m. the bar opens for business, and shuts down at 11 p.m.

Standard double rooms feature a king-sized bed or two doubles, large-screen cable TV with all the extras, walk-in closets, a good-sized tub/shower, and toiletries. New furniture, pine green carpets, and matching green-and-rose curtains and spreads add a touch of panache. If you need a room with a desk, mini-fridge, or microwave, ask for them when you make your reservation.

Front rooms on the top floors enjoy a view of the Empire State Building and also some street noise. An exercise room, open 24 hours a day, offers two bikes, three treadmills, and a step machine. A business center completes the array of guest services.

SKYLINE HOTEL

725 10th Ave.
New York, NY 10019
(AT W. 49TH ST.)

VALUE ★ ★ ★ ★ ★

CLEANLINESS ★ ★ ★ ★ ★

GUEST SERVICES ★ ★ ★ ★ ★

SECURITY ★ ★ ★ ★ ★

(★POOR - ★★★★★EXCELLENT)

CATEGORY	Full Services
PHONE	(212) 586-3400
	(800) 433-1982 Reservations
FAX	(212) 541-7355
	(212) 582-4604 Reservations
EMAIL	skylinehot@aol.com

WEBSITE	www.skylinehotelny.com
RATES	$129-$189
GUEST ROOMS	230 rooms in 2 buildings, 3 floors are nonsmoking
ROOM AMENITIES	AC; cable TV with pay movies, games, and internet access; phone with voice mail; iron and ironing board; hair dryer; safe
RESTAURANTS	1050 restaurant serves American/Italian meals at moderate prices
BARS	In the restaurant
CLIENTELE	International tourists mostly
GUEST SERVICES	Continental breakfast, internet kiosk, concierge, two meeting rooms hold up to 100 and 200 people, indoor swimming pool on the 8th floor open to guests 5 p.m.-10 p.m. weeknights and during the day on weekends
PARKING	Yes, but you must leave it parked or pay a fee
CANCELLATION POLICY	Day of arrival by 4 p.m.
WHEELCHAIR ACCESS	9 rooms

Space is one of the Skyline's competitive advantages. It's apparent as soon as you breeze into the large lobby off busy 10th Avenue. You'll have lots of lounging area and competent front desk staff to greet you. Luis, the bellman, will not only schlep your bags; he'll give you a chatty tour.

Most guest rooms are double/doubles. There are a few king-sized beds, and 16 rooms with one double bed. Junior suites have a combined living/sleeping area, and two-bedroom suites have a living room with a pull-out sofa bed and double/doubles in the bedroom. They are all attractively decorated in peach walls with matching bedspreads and pine green carpets.

You can rest comfortably on a firm mattress and watch a large-screen TV that offers 19 cable channels, pay movies and games, and internet access. Bathrooms are white-tiled with marble sinks. Twelve rooms still have stall showers, the rest a tub/shower combination with a hair dryer and toiletries. A thermostat allows you to control the air and heat. Walk-in closets with a safe, iron, and ironing board add plenty of storage space. Windows of a European design are fairly effective in blocking traffic noise. Best of all, the rooms we visited were spotless.

The indoor pool is glass-enclosed and overlooks the Hudson River. Pool hours are limited. Because of this hotel's commercial location on the far West Side, the 1050 restaurant and lounge is handy, especially in the a.m. when breakfast is served. Ask the front desk for other dining suggestions in this area. Security is acceptable: surveillance cameras are installed in public areas and the front door is locked to visitors after 11 p.m. A short hike to midtown attractions is a fair trade for the Skyline's stellar accommodations and services.

Spacious surroundings and plentiful services are hallmarks of The Skyline. Credit: Skyline Hotel

SLEEPING DEAL

337 W. 55th St.
New York, NY 10019
(BETWEEN EIGHTH AND NINTH AVENUES)

VALUE ★ ★ ★

CLEANLINESS ★ ★ ★ ★

GUEST SERVICES NONE

SECURITY ★ ★

(★POOR - ★★★★★EXCELLENT)

CATEGORY	Euro-style
PHONE	(212) 397-9686
FAX	(212) 397-1494
EMAIL	1291@1291.com or info@1291.com
WEBSITE	www.1291.com
RATES	$90 and up Ask about weekly/monthly rates and seasonal discounts
GUEST ROOMS	11 rooms, 1 with private bath
ROOM AMENITIES	AC, cable TV, VCR, stereo, CD player, clock radio, mini-fridge, toiletries, phone with free local calls
RESTAURANTS	None
BARS	None
CLIENTELE	Independent travelers, who prefer apartment-like living to hotels
GUEST SERVICES	None
PARKING	None
CANCELLATION POLICY	72 hours before check-in
WHEELCHAIR ACCESS	None

1291 Accommodations, which also owns Manhattan Youth Castle, offers 11 rooms in an unrenovated apartment building on a quiet street close to Theater District action and Columbus Circle subway transit. Each room has a sink, cable TV with a VCR, CD and stereo player, king-sized bed, walk-in closet, phone and mini-fridge. Ten rooms share tub/shower facilities, and unlike most hotels, pets are permitted. Rooms are named for their color schemes, vary slightly in size, and are very pretty, though small. Keith Haring prints add a contemporary flair.

An extra mattress is available for guests.

It's questionable what the "sleeping deal" is here. Location and quiet are certainly assets, and many guests lodge here while they are shopping for an apartment. The best deal may be negotiating your room rate with reservations, depending on season and availability. Don't be shy.

TRAVEL INN

515 W. 42nd St.
New York, NY 10036
(BETWEEN 10TH AND 11TH AVENUES)

VALUE ★ ★ ★ ★
CLEANLINESS ★ ★ ★ ★
GUEST SERVICES ★ ★ ★ ★
SECURITY ★ ★ ★ ★ ★
(★POOR - ★★★★★EXCELLENT)

CATEGORY	Full Services
PHONE	(212) 695-7171
	(800) 869-4630 Reservations
FAX	(212) 268-3542
	(212) 967-5025 Reservations
EMAIL	travelinn@newyorkhotel.com
WEBSITE	www.newyorkhotel.com
	Offers special packages
RATES	$115-$300
	Discount for AAA and AARP members
GUEST ROOMS	160 rooms in 2 buildings, one-half nonsmoking
ROOM AMENITIES	AC; cable TV with pay movies, games, and internet access; phone with voice mail; iron and ironing board; mini-fridge on request
RESTAURANTS	None
BARS	None
CLIENTELE	Families and those attending the Jacob Javits Convention Center
GUEST SERVICES	24-hour room service, internet kiosk in lobby, outdoor swimming pool, fitness equipment, conference room, gift shop/tour desk
PARKING	Yes

CANCELLATION POLICY 24 hours before check-in

WHEELCHAIR ACCESS None

Built like a square doughnut that occupies most of 10th Avenue between 42nd and 43rd streets, this hotel is popular with business types attending trade shows at the nearby Javits Center. For tourists, however, its location near the Hudson River is neither scenic nor very convenient, unless you need to park your car. Parking is free and indoors, with none of the usual in-and-out charges.

It will remind you of a Florida motel with an outdoor pool and rooms with balconies. But what may be a summer bonus becomes a winter liability. You must enter the balcony rooms from the outside, a bit nippy in 20-degree weather. (Of course, you can always use the balcony to chill beverages; the ice machine is inconveniently located on the third floor.)

On the plus side, rooms were renovated in 1999, are nicely furnished, and offer plenty of entertainment—movies, games, cable channels, and internet access. Thermostats allow you to control the air and heat. Large closets allow you to hang up your wardrobe. Mattresses are nice and firm. Double-paned windows help shield out traffic noise, but ask for an inside room anyway. (Tenth Avenue can be deafening.) Small bathrooms provide a hair dryer and Gilchrist & Soames toiletries.

There's plenty of space to spread out around the pool or, if you feel energetic, to work out in the small fitness center next to it. If you really want to feel pampered, order room service from the River West Café/Deli.

MIDTOWN WEST

WASHINGTON-JEFFERSON HOTEL

318 W. 51st St.
New York, NY 10019
(BETWEEN EIGHTH AND NINTH AVENUES)

VALUE ★ ★ ★
CLEANLINESS ★ ★ ★ ★
GUEST SERVICES NONE
SECURITY ★ ★ ★
(★POOR - ★★★★★EXCELLENT)

CATEGORY	Limited Services
PHONE	(212) 246-7550
	(888) 567-7550 Reservations
FAX	(212) 246-7622
EMAIL	reservations@wjhotel.com
WEBSITE	www.wjhotel.com
	Offers special packages
RATES	$139 -$259
GUEST ROOMS	165 rooms on 6 floors in 2 buildings, most nonsmoking. Full-time tenants share the property with guests
ROOM AMENITIES	AC, cable TV, phone with voice mail and dataport, hair dryer
RESTAURANTS	Coming in 2002
BARS	Coming in 2002
CLIENTELE	European tourists mostly
GUEST SERVICES	None
PARKING	None
CANCELLATION POLICY	72 hours before check-in
WHEELCHAIR ACCESS	None

Once seedy, the neighborhood called Hell's Kitchen now pulses with outdoor cafés and chic bars. Fortunately, after years of decrepitude, the W-J is catching up. The hotel is like a Dickens novel: "It was the best of times, it was the worst of times." Brace yourself when you enter the lobby because you're seeing the worst. As you walk across the threadbare carpet, floor boards creak and sag.

A single with a twin bed is the least expensive of the remodeled rooms. It's very small, even by Manhattan standards, but nicely appointed, in a contemporary décor with an armoire, tiny sink, and stall shower. Rooms with a double or two twin beds are double in size with a tub/shower and vanity, two phones, a writing desk, and walk-in closet. A spacious superior king room is the top of the line at $199; it offers a Jacuzzi tub.

All the older rooms with shared baths are being converted to rooms with private baths. If you stand where the two buildings that comprise this hotel join, you see reconstruction "before and after." The new hallways gleam with ivory wallpaper and cherry red carpet; the old hallways' grimy tiled floors and walls look like something out of *Bleak House*. While construction is underway, guests should expect some daytime noise.

It's clear the W-J's owners have spent wisely, and their plans for the hotel include a new entrance, expanded lobby, gym, and restaurant. 'Round about spring 2002 when the dust has settled and the makeover is completed, the seedy W-J will be history and the new W-J a welcomed addition to this exciting neighborhood.

WESTPARK HOTEL

308 W. 58th St.
New York, NY 10019
(BETWEEN EIGHTH AND NINTH AVENUES)

VALUE ★ ★ ★ ★

CLEANLINESS ★ ★ ★ ★

GUEST SERVICES ★ ★

SECURITY ★ ★ ★ ★

(★ POOR - ★ ★ ★ ★ ★ EXCELLENT)

CATEGORY	Limited Services
PHONE	(212) 445-0200
FAX	(212) 246-3131
EMAIL	westparkny@aol.com
WEBSITE	www.westparkhotel.com Offers internet-only rates
RATES	Singles: $109 Doubles: $159 Queens: $169-$179 Double/doubles: $179 Suites: $199-$249

GUEST ROOMS	90 rooms on 9 floors includes 8 suites, 2 nonsmoking floors
ROOM AMENITIES	AC, cable TV, phone with voice mail and dataport, hair dryer, iron, and safe
RESTAURANTS	None
BARS	None
CLIENTELE	A mix
GUEST SERVICES	Continental breakfast, coffee and tea available daily, valet laundry
PARKING	None
CANCELLATION POLICY	24 hours before check-in
WHEELCHAIR ACCESS	None

Front rooms at the Westpark overlook Columbus Circle and scenic south Central Park. Unfortunately, for the short term, they also overlook a very unscenic and clamourous AOL/Time-Warner construction site. Hotel renovations are ongoing and probably overdue. Hallways and untouched rooms show chipped and marred furniture and drab décor. The downstairs breakfast room especially needs attention. It's a depressing way to begin your day.

Singles come with a twin bed; doubles with either one bed, two double beds, or a queen. There are walk-in closets with a safe, iron and ironing board, cable TV, two-line phone with voice mail and a place to plug in your laptop, central heat, and an average-sized bathroom with a tub/shower, hair dryer, and toiletries. Suites are the standard bedroom plus a sitting room with a sofa bed, two TVs, and a mini-fridge. Plush carpeting and mattresses are new.

Rooms at the back of the hotel are both quieter and cheaper than those at the front, and service staff can be especially attentive to your needs. Those assets and an ideal location near Central Park keep guests coming back.

THE WYNDHAM

42 W. 58th St.
New York, NY 10019
(BETWEEN FIFTH AND SIXTH AVENUES)

VALUE ★ ★ ★ ★ ★

CLEANLINESS ★ ★ ★ ★

GUEST SERVICES ★

SECURITY ★ ★ ★ ★

(★ POOR - ★ ★ ★ ★ ★ EXCELLENT)

CATEGORY	Limited Services
PHONE	(212) 753-3500
	(800) 257-1111 Reservations
FAX	(212) 754-5638
EMAIL	None
WEBSITE	None
RATES	Singles: $135-$150
	Doubles: $150-$165
	Suites: $195-$240
GUEST ROOMS	135 rooms on 16 floors, all smoking
ROOM AMENITIES	AC, cable TV, phone with voice mail and dataport, *New York Times* on request
RESTAURANTS	Minotaur
BARS	In the restaurant
CLIENTELE	Mixed business and leisure crowd
GUEST SERVICES	Valet laundry
PARKING	None
CANCELLATION POLICY	48 hours before check-in
WHEELCHAIR ACCESS	None

This hotel has been a favorite with the theater and film crowd since the 1920s. It's not part of the Wyndham chain, and its idiosyncrasies probably wouldn't appeal to those who favor the standardization of chain hotels.

Considering how large even their smallest rooms are, we were surprised how affordable the hotel is throughout the year. Most hotel rooms on the East Side and midtown are one-third smaller, but one-third more expensive. The Wyndham's already attractive rates drop at least 25 percent in January, February, July, and August, making it an incredibly good deal in low season.

Guest accommodations are beautifully appointed in floral motifs and pastel colors. Perhaps the best compliment one can make is that they don't look like hotel rooms. The cheapest rooms may remind you of European hotels, in which two twin beds are pushed together to make one. Most rooms, however, offer either queen- or king-sized beds. Closets are larger than average, bathrooms smaller. The hotel's new restaurant, Minotaur, serves three meals a day in a spacious dining area and bar. At press time, room service was not available.

Guest rooms use keys instead of electronic locks, but security is not an issue. The front desk is staffed 24 hours and unless they recognize you as a guest, you'll be stopped. A bellman is stationed at the doors, and hotel staff operate the elevators. The hotel offers easy access to the most popular sections of Fifth Avenue, Madison Avenue, and Central Park.

With its oversized rooms and undersized prices, the Wyndham is the kind of place you could stay for an extended period and still feel at home. Many people do.

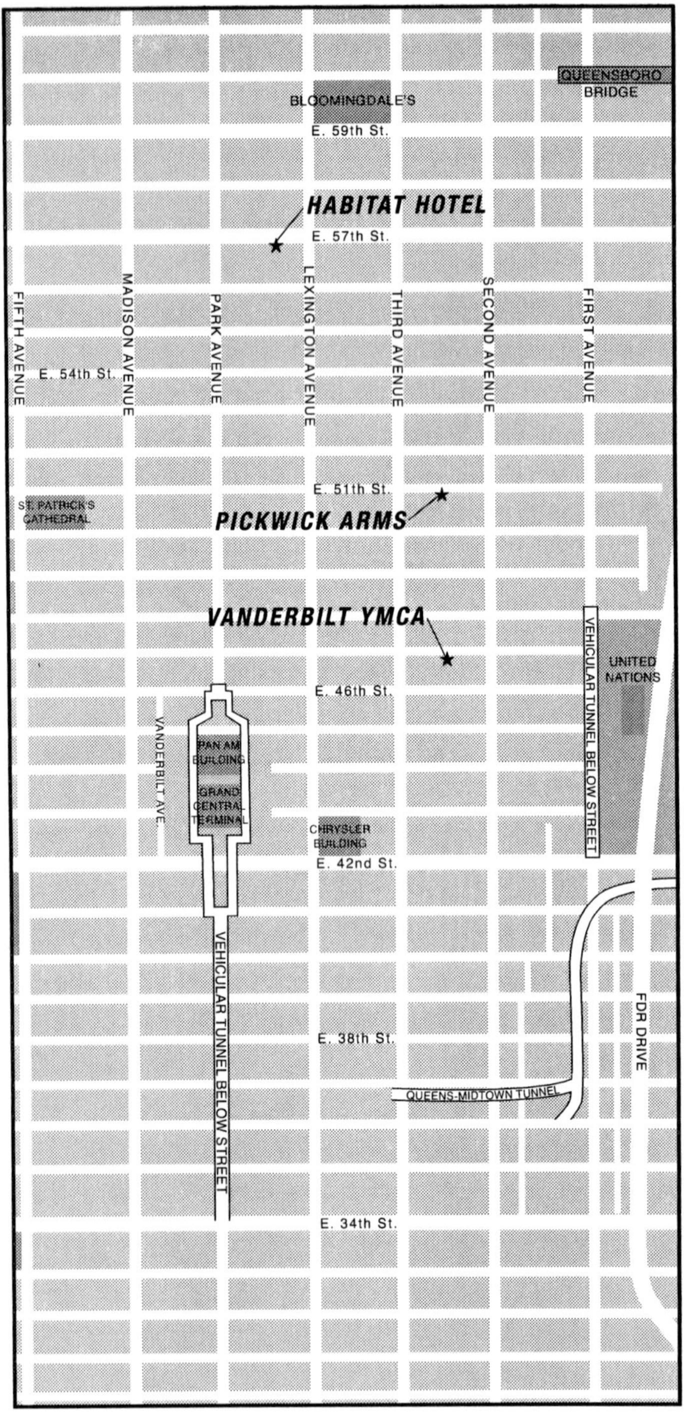
QUEENSBORO
BRIDGE
BLOOMINGDALE'S
E. 59th St.
HABITAT HOTEL
E. 57th St.
FIFTH AVENUE
MADISON AVENUE
PARK AVENUE
LEXINGTON AVENUE
THIRD AVENUE
SECOND AVENUE
FIRST AVENUE
E. 54th St.
E. 51th St.
ST. PATRICK'S
CATHEDRAL
PICKWICK ARMS
VANDERBILT YMCA
VEHICULAR TUNNEL BELOW STREET
UNITED
NATIONS
E. 46th St.
VANDERBILT AVE
PAN AM
BUILDING
GRAND
CENTRAL
TERMINAL
CHRYSLER
BUILDING
E. 42nd St.
VEHICULAR TUNNEL BELOW STREET
FDR DRIVE
E. 38th St.
QUEENS-MIDTOWN TUNNEL
E. 34th St.

MIDTOWN EAST

> *"He left Fifth Avenue and walked west towards the movie houses. Here on 42nd Street it was less elegant but no less strange. He loved this street, not for the people or the shops, but for the stone lions that guarded the great main building of the Public Library...."*
> —James Baldwin

Fifth Avenue divides Midtown East from West, and it attracts business travelers, shoppers, and sightseers in great numbers. The flagship stores of Tiffany's, FAO Schwarz, Lord & Taylor, Saks Fifth Avenue, and Bergdorf Goodman are here with more recent competition from retailers like the Gap and Gianni Versace. Saint Patrick's Cathedral is one of several famous churches on or east of Fifth Avenue. Over on the East River stands the United Nations and in between are some of the city's ritzier hotels, the Waldorf-Astoria, Four Seasons, Pierre, Sherry-Netherland, and St. Regis (great for a drink when you're bedding elsewhere). But perhaps the steel-and-glass spires owned by MetLife, CitiCorp, IBM, Seagram, and (originally) by Chrysler define this neighborhood best as the nerve center of Corporate America.

SLEEP CHEAP IN NEW YORK

HABITAT HOTEL

130 E. 57th St.
New York, NY 10022
(AT LEXINGTON AVE.)

VALUE ★ ★ ★
CLEANLINESS ★ ★ ★ ★
GUEST SERVICES ★ ★
SECURITY ★ ★ ★ ★

(★POOR - ★★★★★EXCELLENT)

CATEGORY	Euro-style
PHONE	(212) 753-8841 (800) 497-6028 Reservations
FAX	(212) 838-4767 (917) 441-0295 Reservations
EMAIL	info@stayinny.com
WEBSITE	www.habitatny.com
RATES	Single shared bath: $85-$105 Double shared bath: $95-$115 Single private bath: $135-$175 Double private bath: $145-$185 Suites: $220-$280
GUEST ROOMS	330 rooms on 17 floors, some share baths, 1 smoking floor
ROOM AMENITIES	AC, cable TV, phone with voice mail and dataport, iron and ironing board, clock radio; hair dryers on request
RESTAURANTS	Opia serves lunch and dinner
BARS	Yes
CLIENTELE	60 percent internationals to 40 percent Americans
GUEST SERVICES	Internet kiosk, concierge, luggage room
PARKING	None
CANCELLATION POLICY	24 hours before check-in
WHEELCHAIR ACCESS	None

New in 1999, Habitat Hotel is at the low-priced end of a trio owned by Citylife Hotel Group; ThirtyThirty is considered mid-range and On the Ave upscale. The cheapest rooms share a bath, and they fulfill all the basic requirements as long as your requirements are very minimal. They're clean and stylish with bedding and plush towels, a pedestal sink, cable TV, a clock radio, voice mail, a few toiletries, and a small armoire that contains a tiny iron and ironing board. Rooms with private bath are slightly larger, but it's a tight squeeze when you pull out the trundle (second mattress) to form a double bed. Only a few queen beds are available.

Unfortunately, noisy plumbing, chipped paint, and frayed hallway carpet are all evidence of the cheap renovation and poor maintenance of this older building. In one room we visited, the radiator coil was fully exposed. A brush with bare skin would leave a lasting impression. Windows are double-paned, but, as always, ask for a top, inside room to ensure sweet dreams. The restaurant and bar on the mezzanine level were unveiled last year.

If you want a room with a private bath, there are better choices elsewhere. There's less here than meets the eye.

PICKWICK ARMS HOTEL

230 E. 51st St.
New York, NY 10022
(BETWEEN SECOND AND THIRD AVENUES)

VALUE ★ ★ ★ ★ ★

CLEANLINESS ★ ★ ★ ★

GUEST SERVICES ★ ★

SECURITY ★ ★ ★ ★

(★POOR - ★★★★★EXCELLENT)

CATEGORY	Euro-style
PHONE	(212) 355-0300
	(800) 742-5945 Reservations
FAX	(212) 755-5029
EMAIL	info@pickwickarms.com
WEBSITE	www.pickwickarms.com

RATES	Single shared bath: $75-$90 Single private bath: $120 Double private bath: $145-$155 Triple private bath: $170 Studios: $225
GUEST ROOMS	370 rooms on 14 floors include 7 studios, singles share a bath, all smoking
ROOM AMENITIES	AC, cable TV, phone with voice mail
RESTAURANTS	Le Bateau Ivre, Montparnasse
BARS	Yes
CLIENTELE	70 percent international tourists and those doing business at the U.N.
GUEST SERVICES	Internet kiosk, roof garden, luggage room, airport shuttles
PARKING	None
CANCELLATION POLICY	24 hours before check-in
WHEELCHAIR ACCESS	None

The expensive Upper East Side claims one of the city's best budget hotels. Built in 1930, the Pickwick Arms was a favorite with Hollywood celebrities. According to owner Harry Wittlin, it is still popular with the film crowd, both as a lodging and shooting location. That location—on a tree-lined residential street—is handy for Bloomingdale shoppers as well as those doing business at the United Nations. On a typical day, the comfortable lobby actually resembles the United Nations; we spoke to travelers from Mauritius, Finland, and New Zealand the afternoon we visited.

Some of the cheaper single rooms share a bath in the hallway with a tub/shower combination. Doubles and triples have private baths with stall showers and tiny toilets. They are clean, tiny, and uniform with the same décor in dull beige tones. Hallways would benefit from some air freshener. Each room has a sink, phone with voice mail, TV with cable, and a desk.

Studios boast custom-made furniture and fixtures, marble baths, recessed lighting (for romantic effect), large walk-in closets, fridges, large-screen TVs, desks, and firm queen-sized mattresses. Access to them is off the lobby in an adjacent townhouse, and at $225, they are a deal.

Pickwick Arms guests come for the ambience and a superfriendly, multilingual staff. What they save on room rates, they can spend on a Gallic meal at Montparnasse or Le Bateau Ivre.

For decades, one of the East Side's best lodging buys.
Credit: Pickwick Arms Hotel

SLEEP CHEAP IN NEW YORK

VANDERBILT YMCA
224 E. 47th St.
New York, NY 10017
(BETWEEN SECOND AND THIRD AVENUES)

VALUE ★ ★ ★ ★

CLEANLINESS ★ ★ ★ ★

GUEST SERVICES ★ ★ ★ ★

SECURITY ★ ★ ★

(★POOR - ★★★★★EXCELLENT)

CATEGORY	YMCA
PHONE	(212) 756-9600
FAX	(212) 752-0210
EMAIL	vanderbiltguestrooms@ymcanyc.org
WEBSITE	www.ymcanyc.org
RATES	$85-$150
GUEST ROOMS	430 rooms on 10 floors, all but 4 share a bathroom, all allow smoking
ROOM AMENITIES	AC, cable TV, no phone, mini-fridge on request
RESTAURANTS	Cafeteria
BARS	None
CLIENTELE	Half American, half international tourists
GUEST SERVICES	Coin-operated laundry, concierge, lockers, gift shop, health club, meeting rooms
PARKING	None
CANCELLATION POLICY	24 hours before check-in
WHEELCHAIR ACCESS	Yes

The Y is an acceptable lodging for those who don't want to spend a lot of time in a guest room. Accommodations are cell-like with linoleum floors, no phones, shared baths (four with a queen bed have a private bath and they are the most expensive), fluorescent overhead lighting, small TVs with cable, AC, a rack to hang your clothes on, a three-drawer dresser, a towel, and soap. Thin mattresses don't encourage lengthy stays. Doubles have bunk beds. But if you're not opposed to dormitory living, the large toilets, showers, and hallways are immaculate.

The Y offers plenty of extras, like free use of a health club next door, washers and dryers, a cafeteria-style restaurant, and a concierge who will entertain you with his comic patter while he arranges such entertainment as a gospel tour of Harlem or tickets to *Kiss Me Kate*. He really knows how to make out-of-towners feel at home.

Security is highly touted, and a house phone on each floor is handy in case of emergencies. However, when we visited, guards were too distracted to stop people and insist they show their room keys, and those keys are numbered. We were able to take the elevators and walk around unchecked. This suggests that security breaches would be a snap.

The Y is an improvement over most hostels and a real draw for fitness buffs, who can swim, work out with weights, run laps, sign up for over 135 exercise classes, and sweat in the steam room or sauna. Not a bad perk for budget travelers.

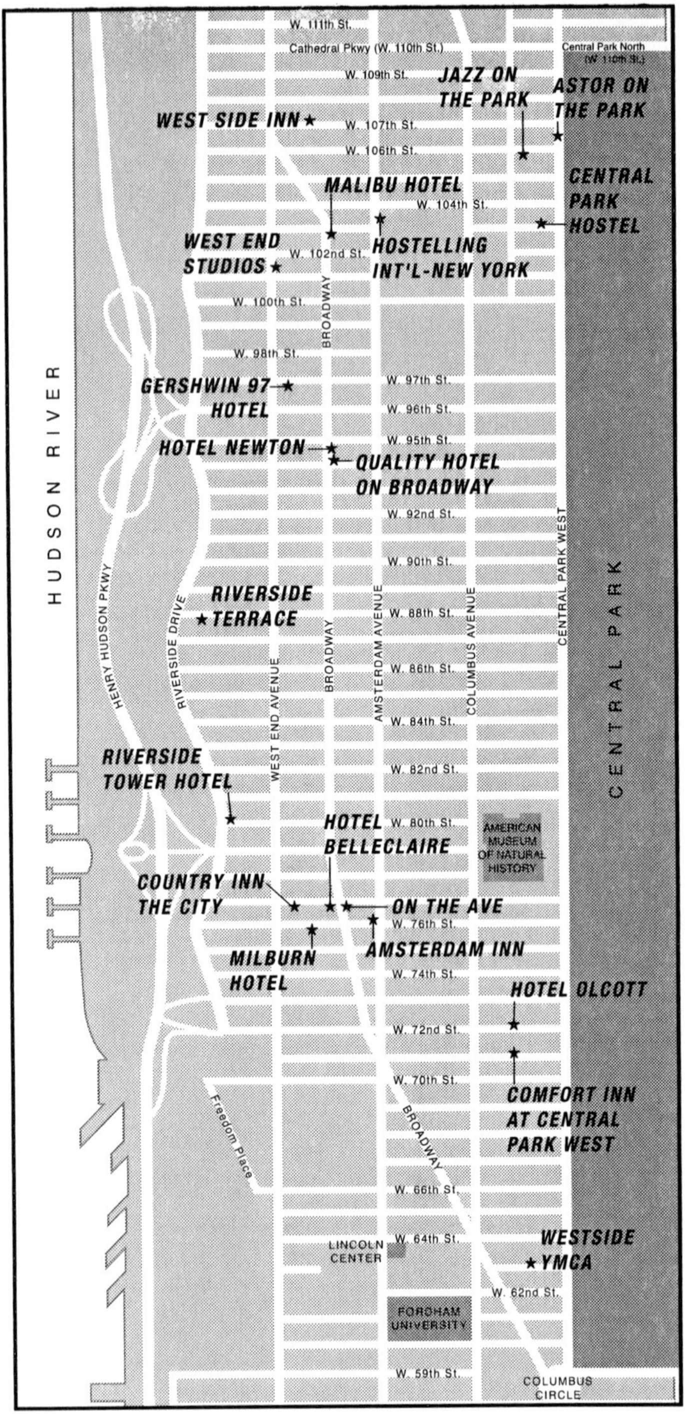

W. 111th St.
Cathedral Pkwy (W. 110th St.)
Central Park North (W. 110th St.)
W. 109th St.
JAZZ ON THE PARK
ASTOR ON THE PARK
WEST SIDE INN
W. 107th St.
W. 106th St.
MALIBU HOTEL
CENTRAL PARK HOSTEL
W. 104th St.
WEST END STUDIOS
W. 102nd St.
HOSTELLING INT'L-NEW YORK
W. 100th St.
BROADWAY
W. 98th St.
GERSHWIN 97 HOTEL
W. 97th St.
W. 96th St.
W. 95th St.
HOTEL NEWTON
QUALITY HOTEL ON BROADWAY
HUDSON RIVER
W. 92nd St.
W. 90th St.
CENTRAL PARK WEST
RIVERSIDE TERRACE
W. 88th St.
HENRY HUDSON PKWY
RIVERSIDE DRIVE
AMSTERDAM AVENUE
COLUMBUS AVENUE
CENTRAL PARK
W. 86th St.
W. 84th St.
WEST END AVENUE
RIVERSIDE TOWER HOTEL
W. 82nd St.
HOTEL BELLECLAIRE
W. 80th St.
AMERICAN MUSEUM OF NATURAL HISTORY
COUNTRY INN THE CITY
ON THE AVE
W. 76th St.
AMSTERDAM INN
MILBURN HOTEL
W. 74th St.
HOTEL OLCOTT
W. 72nd St.
W. 70th St.
COMFORT INN AT CENTRAL PARK WEST
Freedom Place
W. 66th St.
WESTSIDE YMCA
W. 64th St.
LINCOLN CENTER
W. 62nd St.
FORDHAM UNIVERSITY
W. 59th St.
COLUMBUS CIRCLE

UPPER WEST SIDE

> *"If you should happen after dark*
> *To find yourself in Central Park,*
> *Ignore the paths that beckon you*
> *And hurry, hurry to the zoo,*
> *And creep into the tiger's lair.*
> *Frankly, you'll be safer there."*
> —Ogden Nash

This neighborhood is one of the city's most desirable addresses and tends to attract New York's cultural elite. Its main artery is Broadway, which travels north from Columbus Circle at 59th Street, past Lincoln Center and the Juilliard School between W. 63rd and W. 66th streets. Then, Broadway curves west and Ninth Avenue becomes Columbus Avenue, a popular pedestrian thoroughfare, especially on summer weekends when its outdoor cafés and coffee shops are jammed.

Imposing Art Deco apartment houses like the Majestic, Dakota, San Remo, and Kenilworth give a Central Park West address its cachet. Farther north on CPW is the New York Historical Society and American Museum of Natural History. Skaters, joggers, and strollers enter Central Park from CPW at 72nd or 96th Street. On the river side, West End Avenue is purely residential, lined with elegant prewar townhouses and a few modern highrises. Riverside Drive has its park, its palatial townhouses, and scenic views of the Hudson River. After 110th Street, this neighborhood becomes Morningside Heights.

AMSTERDAM INN

340 W. 76th St.
New York, NY 10023
(AT AMSTERDAM AVE.)

VALUE ★ ★ ★

CLEANLINESS ★ ★ ★

GUEST SERVICES NONE

SECURITY ★ ★ ★ ★

(★POOR - ★★★★★EXCELLENT)

CATEGORY	Bare Essentials
PHONE	(212) 579-7500
FAX	(212) 579-6127
EMAIL	info@amsterdaminn.com
WEBSITE	www.amsterdaminn.com Occasionally offers specials
RATES	Shared bath: $75-$105 Private bath: $125 Cash and traveler's checks only
GUEST ROOMS	25 rooms on 4 floors are mostly nonsmoking with about one-half shared baths, no elevator
ROOM AMENITIES	AC, cable TV, phone ($5 deposit to activate line), sink in shared-bath accommodations
RESTAURANTS	None
BARS	None
CLIENTELE	Leisure travelers
GUEST SERVICES	None
PARKING	None
CANCELLATION POLICY	Must call 48 hours before check-in to confirm reservation
WHEELCHAIR ACCESS	None

The Amsterdam Inn's advantages are its low prices and location, but that's really all the hotel has going for it. In the heart of the Upper West Side, the inn is surrounded by restaurants and shops, and near two subway stations. Central Park, Lincoln Square, and the neighborhood's other attractions are within an easy walk.

The hotel itself is fairly forgettable. After walking up

two flights of steep stairs, you find yourself in a check-in area that resembles a doctor's office minus the chairs and old magazines. About one-half of the 25 rooms have a private bathroom. All have a television, chest of drawers, and nightstand. Bars instead of hooks serve as the closet. Some of the rooms have bunk beds. Several of the phones feature dataport jacks. Bathrooms, both private and shared, are clean. A hair dryer as well as iron and ironing board are available on request.

The hotel's reservation policy is a bit cumbersome. Guests must confirm reservations by telephone within 48 hours prior to arrival, or pay one night's deposit two weeks in advance either by check or money order. Security could be improved. Although guests must be buzzed in, they still use numbered room keys. As of press time, a large construction project was going up across the street. They only work during the day, but it would be prudent to get a room in the back of the hotel.

ASTOR ON THE PARK

465 Central Park West
New York, NY 10025
(BETWEEN W. 106TH AND W. 107TH STREETS)

VALUE ★ ★ ★ ★

CLEANLINESS ★ ★ ★ ★

GUEST SERVICES ★ ★

SECURITY ★ ★ ★

(★POOR - ★★★★★EXCELLENT)

CATEGORY	Boutique
PHONE	(212) 866-1880
FAX	(212) 316-9555
EMAIL	None
WEBSITE	www.nychotels.com Offers promotional rates in January, February, and certain summer months
RATES	$99-$180
GUEST ROOMS	80 rooms on 7 floors, one-half smoking
ROOM AMENITIES	AC, TV without cable, phone with dataport, iron and ironing board, hair dryer

RESTAURANTS	None
BARS	None
CLIENTELE	Business and leisure travelers
GUEST SERVICES	Continental breakfast, valet laundry
PARKING	None
CANCELLATION POLICY	24 hours before check-in
WHEELCHAIR ACCESS	None

Astor on the Park is a great find, especially when it's offering a promotional rate. You can expect a sleek, minimalist approach in the public areas and guest rooms. Hotel staff is courteous and professional. The subway is only three blocks away, and Central Park is right across the street. This is not the safest area of the park, however.

Accommodations feature walnut and ash furniture and a soothing décor of mint green. The beds are soft; in fact, some of them are too soft. Instead of a separate closet,

Lobby and guest rooms at Astor On The Park feature hip décor. Credit: Amsterdam Hospitality Group

the armoire doubles as an entertainment center and closet; so pack light or expect to use your suitcase as a closet. Fortunately, all the guest accommodations have an iron and ironing board to smooth out wrinkled trousers. Some of the televisions look tired and they don't offer cable channels. We like the full-length mirrors, although we'd trade them for voice mail in a jiffy. Bathrooms aren't spacious, but they do the job and offer a vanity shelf and ceiling fan as well as bath products.

A continental breakfast—the usual breads and coffee plus a bit extra—is served in a room below the lobby. That's also where guests can watch TV with the cable channels that aren't available on the TVs in their rooms. The hotel uses keys rather than an electronic lock system, which is always a security risk.

Overall, Astor on the Park has a lot to offer. We'd just like it a lot more with cable TV, voice mail, and bigger towels.

CENTRAL PARK HOSTEL

19 W. 103rd St.
New York, NY 10025
(BETWEEN CENTRAL PARK WEST AND MANHATTAN AVE.)

VALUE ★ ★ ★ ★

CLEANLINESS ★ ★ ★ ★

GUEST SERVICES ★ ★ ★

SECURITY ★ ★ ★ ★ ★

(★POOR - ★★★★★EXCELLENT)

CATEGORY	Hostel
PHONE	(212) 678-0491
FAX	(212) 678-0453
EMAIL	cph103rd@aol.com
WEBSITE	www.centralparkhostel.com
RATES	Dorm beds: $26-$36 Double private rooms: $75 Only cash or traveler's checks Prices include taxes and tariffs
GUEST ROOMS	231 rooms on 5 floors, all shared baths, no elevator
ROOM AMENITIES	AC, locker, bedding and towels

RESTAURANTS	Coming in 2002
BARS	None
CLIENTELE	Budget travelers at least 18 years old, unless accompanied by an adult
GUEST SERVICES	Small kitchen, vending machines, ATM, TV lounge, internet kiosk, public phones
PARKING	None
CANCELLATION POLICY	48 hours before check-in
WHEELCHAIR ACCESS	None

Unveiled in Fall 2000, this hostel is a valid alternative to its much larger neighbor around the corner, Hostelling International-New York.

Each room sleeps from two to eight people, primarily in bunk beds. Double private rooms offer a small desk, chair, mirror, and lockers, but no sink. Carpet covers the floors instead of tile. Each floor has three full bathrooms with shower stalls and soap dispensers. The hostel provides all bed sheets and towels. You can buy phone cards and a padlock for the lockers at the front desk. A small kitchen on the second floor features a stove and full-sized refrigerator. Smoking is permitted in the common areas. A TV lounge, ping pong table, internet kiosk, and ATM machine are also available to guests.

A valid passport and payment in full is required upon check-in. Call two days prior to arrival to confirm reservations. During off-peak months, such as January and February, discounts of $5 to $10 are common. The security system is reassuring. A big metal door is the only way into the sleeping quarters. Everyone must be buzzed in by the front desk, which is staffed 24 hours.

The hostel is located on a quiet street sandwiched between Central Park and several large housing projects. At night, don't take the shortcut through this development. Also, be aware that the portion of the park above 97th Street isn't considered as safe as the rest of the park. Thankfully, you're close to a subway station because the hostel isn't near any major attractions.

UPPER WEST SIDE

COMFORT INN AT CENTRAL PARK WEST

31 W. 71st St.
New York, NY 10023
(BETWEEN CENTRAL PARK WEST AND COLUMBUS AVE.)

VALUE ★ ★ ★ ★
CLEANLINESS ★ ★ ★ ★
GUEST SERVICES ★ ★ ★ ★
SECURITY ★ ★ ★ ★
(★POOR - ★★★★★EXCELLENT)

CATEGORY	Limited Services
PHONE	(212) 721-4770 (877) 727-5236 Reservations
FAX	(212) 579-8544
EMAIL	cphw71@aol.com
WEBSITE	www.comfortinn.com/ny209 Slight discount for online bookings
RATES	$99-$325 Discount for AAA and AARP members
GUEST ROOMS	96 rooms on 14 floors, top floors for smokers
ROOM AMENITIES	AC, cable TV with HBO, phone with voice mail and dataport, clock radio, bath products, iron and ironing board, mini-fridge available on request
RESTAURANTS	None
BARS	None
CLIENTELE	Business and leisure travelers
GUEST SERVICES	Continental breakfast, concierge, internet kiosk, small exercise room, business center
PARKING	None
CANCELLATION POLICY	Weekend requires 48 hours, otherwise 24 hours before 3 p.m. check-in
WHEELCHAIR ACCESS	Yes

The strongest selling point of the Comfort Inn is its great location. Throwing distance from the ritzy part of Central Park, the hotel boasts an Upper West Side address that would make most New Yorkers giddy. Landmarks such as Lincoln Square, Tavern on the Green, and the Beacon Theater are within walking distance as are two subway stations, one offering express service to Wall Street, Times Square, and Penn Station.

Location aside, the Comfort Inn is only moderately impressive. Most of the rooms offer double or queen-sized beds, with a few twins. All have a desk and a phone with voice mail and dataport. Closets and bathrooms are perfectly adequate, plus the hotel provides complimentary shampoo and lotions. The cable TV features HBO but no pay-per-view movies.

The third floor was designed especially for business travelers. Larger and nicer, these rooms usually cost about

The Comfort Inn at CPW is ideal for guests who need a West Side address. Credit: Comfort Inn at Central Park West

$40 more and feature an extra phone line, larger work space, and a built-in hair dryer, among other amenities. A business center on lobby level offers fax, copying, and internet access for a charge.

A continental breakfast is available in the Copper Kettle Room, which seats about 30 people. The fare includes fresh fruit, yogurt, and a good selection of breads. Guests can grab a complimentary *USA Today* in the lobby on their way to breakfast. Also, the hotel provides a full-time concierge on staff. During the value months, deluxe rooms can be had for under $150. The rest of the year, the cheapest room costs between $110 and $130.

This is a fine property with a Central Park location and great deals during the off-season and shoulder months. However in peak season, you can probably do better.

COUNTRY INN THE CITY

270 W. 77th St.
New York, NY 10024
(BETWEEN BROADWAY AND WEST END AVE.)

VALUE ★★★★

CLEANLINESS ★★★★★

GUEST SERVICES None

SECURITY ★★★

(★POOR - ★★★★★EXCELLENT)

CATEGORY	Guest House
PHONE	(212) 580-4183
FAX	(212) 874-3981
EMAIL	ctryinn@aol.com
WEBSITE	www.countryinnthecity.com Offers last-minute discounts of 30-50 percent
RATES	$150-$220 Cash and traveler's checks only
GUEST ROOMS	4 studios on 3 floors, all nonsmoking, no elevator
ROOM AMENITIES	AC, cable TV, galley kitchen, safe, phone plus second line (free local calls), answering machine, clock radio, hair dryer, shower, radio

RESTAURANTS	None
BARS	None
CLIENTELE	A mixed crowd
GUEST SERVICES	None
PARKING	None
CANCELLATION POLICY	30 days before check-in
WHEELCHAIR ACCESS	None

Guest rooms in this 1891 townhouse look and feel like studio apartments. And that is co-owner Fergus O'Brien's intention. "Although we're more bed-and-breakfast than hotel," he says, "this is not the kind of place where you

Country Inn The City offers apartment-style lodging in an 1891 townhouse. Credit: Desmond Shaw

will find cutesy décor and interfering hosts. Your self-contained apartment is your own and you are free to come and go as you please."

The large, high-ceilinged rooms are so beautifully decorated they'd make Martha Stewart gnash her teeth with envy. All the rooms feature polished hardwood floors and queen beds (four-posters and one canopy), floral rugs, antiques, and leather couches. Large armoires hide the televisions and serve as closets complete with hangers and shelves; except in one room, which has a walk-in closet. Each apartment has a private line with an answering machine, and all but one provides a second line. Special amenities include extra blankets, books, and a full brandy decanter. The smallest apartment features a covered terrace with table and chairs.

Just like the sleeping areas, the bathrooms offer plenty of space and personal touches. All except one has a tub/shower. Galley kitchens are equally impressive with a full-sized refrigerator, toaster, coffeemaker, stove, and all utensils and dishes. They stock tea, cereal, milk, coffee, and fresh fruit.

Now for the rules. No smoking, pets, or children under age 12. Only cash and traveler's checks are accepted, and guests pay upon arrival. A deposit is required to hold a reservation. The 30-day cancellation policy may seem onerous; but if the owner is able to rebook the space—a common occurrence—you'll just pay a $30 penalty. Usually a three-night minimum stay is required. However, other arrangements can be made on occasion, especially during the off-season.

Did we mention the brandy decanter?

SLEEP CHEAP IN NEW YORK

GERSHWIN 97 HOTEL

258 W. 97th St.
New York, NY 10025
(BETWEEN BROADWAY AND WEST END AVE.)

VALUE ★ ★ ★ ★

CLEANLINESS ★ ★ ★

GUEST SERVICES ★

SECURITY ★ ★ ★ ★ ★

(★POOR - ★ ★ ★ ★ ★EXCELLENT)

CATEGORY	Euro-style
PHONE	(212) 665-7434
FAX	(212) 665-7313
EMAIL	None
WEBSITE	www.gershwin97.com
RATES	Singles shared bath: $240 weekly, $700 monthly Doubles shared bath: $340 weekly, $800 monthly One double with private bath: $400 weekly, $1000 monthly, includes taxes
GUEST ROOMS	32 private rooms, all nonsmoking, all but one with shared bath
ROOM AMENITIES	Bedding and towels
RESTAURANTS	None
BARS	None
CLIENTELE	Visitors who need short-term lodging
GUEST SERVICES	Washers and dryers
PARKING	None
CANCELLATION POLICY	24 hours before check-in
WHEELCHAIR ACCESS	None

The Gershwin Hotel's uptown sibling opened December 2000, and was still at the teething stage at press time. Permanent tenants still occupy half the beds in this apartment building. Stefan Lindfors' signature "flame" sculptures enliven the hallway entrance, but that's the only thing these two siblings have in common.

Guest rooms are renovated, but upstairs hallways and shared baths are in pretty rough condition. Singles come with a twin bed, doubles with full-sized beds and queens. Only one double has a private bathroom. All 32 rooms are nonsmoking with hardwood floors, desks, small dressers and sinks, but no AC. Toilets are tiny cubicles with a towel but no amenities. Radiator heat (in winter) is like Dante's Inferno. Thankfully, security is tight. Everyone gets buzzed in 24 hours a day and guests must sign in before they can go upstairs.

Advantages here are a quiet Upper West Side location near the subway and rock-bottom prices in a secure building. If you are job or apartment hunting, their weekly and monthly rates are unbeatable. Disadvantages are an unrenovated building (at least as of press time) and tenants who share floors and bathrooms with guests. And they have seniority.

HOSTELLING INTERNATIONAL- NEW YORK

891 Amsterdam Ave.
New York, NY 10025
(AT W. 103RD ST.)

VALUE ★ ★ ★ ★

CLEANLINESS ★ ★ ★ ★

GUEST SERVICES ★ ★ ★ ★ ★

SECURITY ★ ★ ★ ★

(★POOR - ★★★★★EXCELLENT)

CATEGORY	Hostel
PHONE	(212) 932-2300
	(800) 909-4776 Reservations
FAX	(212) 932-2574
EMAIL	reserve@hinewyork.org
WEBSITE	www.hinewyork.org
RATES	Dorm beds: $28-$38
	Private room shared bath: $120
	Private room with bath: $135
	Prices include taxes and tariffs
GUEST ROOMS	Accommodations for 624, primarily bunk beds, majority with shared baths, no smoking indoors

ROOM AMENITIES	AC, bedding, towels upon request, small lockers
RESTAURANTS	Cafeteria and coffee bar
BARS	None
CLIENTELE	Budget travelers at least 18 years old, unless accompanied by an adult
GUEST SERVICES	Communal kitchen, concierge, ATM, internet kiosk, vending machines, coin-operated laundry, public phones, gift shop, baggage storage, rec room with TV, video arcade, pool table
PARKING	None
CANCELLATION POLICY	24 hours before check-in
WHEELCHAIR ACCESS	Yes

Are you surprised that New York City boasts the largest hostel in the world?

Dormitory configurations range from four to 12 beds per room, primarily bunk beds. A few private rooms with a bathroom are available and accommodate four people. All the rooms feature small lockers, and padlocks are sold on the main level. Also, guests can rent much larger lockers for $2 to $3 per day. Shared hallway bathrooms are just like those in college dorms. There are two to three per floor, each with multiple showers, sinks, and toilets.

Overall, this is a very self-sufficient hostel offering several amenities and services on site. Everyone has access to a large private garden. For meals, guests can use the self-service kitchen, coffee bar, or cafeteria. Subway and bus cards, phone cards, maps, film, and most essentials are all sold on site. A full-time concierge offers information on all sorts of entertainment options. The hostel provides many free activities as well as discounts on others. It isn't close to most points of interest, but there is a subway station one block away.

A credit card is necessary for reservations. Nonmembers pay $3 over the posted rate. An annual membership to Hostelling International costs $25 for U.S. citizens.

In terms of security, we visited on a busy day and left unimpressed. All the guest rooms use electronic locks. The primary entrance to the dormitories and common areas also requires a key card and is right next to the security desk. But security was frequently pulled away.

With guests rushing in and out, people held the door open for others, including us.

HOTEL BELLECLAIRE

250 W. 77th St.
New York, NY 10024
(BETWEEN BROADWAY AND WEST END AVE.)

VALUE ★ ★ ★ ★
CLEANLINESS ★ ★ ★ ★
GUEST SERVICES ★ ★ ★ ★
SECURITY ★ ★ ★ ★
(★POOR - ★★★★★EXCELLENT)

CATEGORY	Limited Services
PHONE	(212) 362-7700
	(877) 468-3522 Reservations
FAX	(212) 362-1004
EMAIL	Bellerez@aol.com
WEBSITE	www.hotelbelleclaire.com
RATES	Shared bath: $89-$129
	Private bath: $109-$249
GUEST ROOMS	161 rooms on 9 floors, all smoking, some shared baths
ROOM AMENITIES	AC, cable TV with pay movies and Nintendo, clock radio, phone with voice mail and dataport, mini-fridge, hair dryer, iron and ironing board
RESTAURANTS	None
BARS	None
CLIENTELE	Primarily European but growing U.S. market
GUEST SERVICES	Concierge, gift shop, fax and copy services, valet laundry, bellman, room service from Manhattan Diner
PARKING	None
CANCELLATION POLICY	24 hours before check-in
WHEELCHAIR ACCESS	Yes

Smooth, modern lines and bright lighting characterize the Belleclaire's new lobby. Credit: Desmond Shaw

Completely renovated in 2000, the Belleclaire still has some work to do before it achieves its potential. They've got the lobby right. Smooth, modern lines and careful attention to colors and lighting make an excellent first impression. Twin green and yellow parakeets entertain guests in a sitting area near the elevators.

While the lobby is memorable, guest areas aren't. Narrow, winding hallways remind you that this is an older building. Rooms have a spacious, uncluttered look and are decorated with cheery yellow walls, soft gray carpets, and white duvets. Sparse furnishings include a full desk, night stand, and mini-fridge. Larger rooms have shelves or an armoire, and closets are larger than average.

The shared bathrooms are not in the hallway. Rather, two to three bedrooms are grouped together, akin to a large suite, and these units share facilities. Best suited for a small group or family, it's like a large apartment without a kitchen or living room. Each shared-bath accommodation has a sink in the bedroom. All the bathrooms feature a tub/shower, shampoo and conditioner, but no vanity shelf.

The Belleclaire offers a full-time concierge available until 9 p.m. during the week and 8 p.m. Friday and Saturday. Front desk personnel provide fax and copy services for a fee. The gift shop is small, but big enough to supply film, postcards, and other sundries. Several car rental agencies are located within a couple of blocks as well as a few parking garages.

HOTEL NEWTON

2528 Broadway
New York, NY 10025
(BETWEEN W. 94TH AND W. 95TH STREETS)

VALUE ★ ★ ★ ★

CLEANLINESS ★ ★ ★ ★ ★

GUEST SERVICES ★ ★

SECURITY ★ ★ ★ ★

(★POOR - ★★★★★EXCELLENT)

CATEGORY	Limited Services
PHONE	(212) 678-6500
	(800) 643-5553 Reservations
FAX	(212) 678-6758
EMAIL	None
WEBSITE	www.newyorkhotel.com
	Offers seasonal specials
RATES	Singles: $85-$95
	Doubles: $105-$200
	Discounts to AAA and AARP members
GUEST ROOMS	104 rooms on 9 floors, primarily nonsmoking, 10 shared baths
ROOM AMENITIES	AC, cable TV, phone with voice mail, clock radio, iron and ironing board, hair dryer; suites have refrigerators and microwaves
RESTAURANTS	None
BARS	None
CLIENTELE	Primarily European

GUEST SERVICES	Vending machines, internet kiosk, phone card machine, room service from Key West Diner
PARKING	None
CANCELLATION POLICY	24 hours before check-in
WHEELCHAIR ACCESS	None

Despite its boutique size, the Hotel Newton feels like a well-run chain property with attentive, competent staff and reliable accommodations. Standard rooms are just as clean and comfortable as the suites. The décor doesn't wow you, but you don't hide your eyes. Keep in mind Broadway is very busy, so consider booking a room away from the street.

Overall, the guest rooms offer plenty of space. Rollaways or cribs won't need to be shoved in a corner. All the rooms feature at least a full desk and night stand. Good-sized closets provide hangers as well as a luggage rack and extra pillows. Larger rooms also have an armoire or chest of drawers. Suites with fridges and microwaves start at about $120. All the bathrooms offer amenities such as a built-in hair dryer and bath products.

The few shared-bath accommodations use full-sized bathrooms down a hallway. Rates range from $85 to $105. The guest rooms look exactly like the smaller standard rooms, except no facilities.

The Newton has a special arrangement with a diner three doors down to offer room service. Actually, it's just like ordering delivery from any local restaurant except that if something goes wrong, the hotel has some interest in rectifying the problem. In terms of security, all the rooms use electronic key locks. The hotel desk is staffed 24 hours and located right next to the elevators.

As one of the Empire Hotel Group, the Newton can't help being compared to its pricier relatives. Rest assured, travelers here get a good, fair deal.

UPPER WEST SIDE

HOTEL OLCOTT

27 W. 72nd St.
New York, NY 10023
(BETWEEN CENTRAL PARK WEST AND COLUMBUS AVE.)

VALUE ★ ★ ★ ★
CLEANLINESS ★ ★ ★
GUEST SERVICES ★
SECURITY ★ ★ ★
(★POOR - ★★★★★EXCELLENT)

CATEGORY	Limited Services
PHONE	(212) 877-4200
FAX	(212) 580-0511
EMAIL	None
WEBSITE	www.hotelolcott.com Offers seasonal specials
RATES	Studios: $130, $840 weekly Suites: $150, $980 weekly 3-night minimum on weekends
GUEST ROOMS	100 rooms on 16 floors, all allow smoking, guests share building with permanent residents
ROOM AMENITIES	AC, cable TV, phone with voice mail and dataport, kitchenette
RESTAURANTS	Dallas BBQ
BARS	None
CLIENTELE	Leisure travelers
GUEST SERVICES	Internet kiosk, vending machines
PARKING	None
CANCELLATION POLICY	7 days before check-in
WHEELCHAIR ACCESS	Yes

Is this a pretty hotel? No. Does it offer any guest services? Not really. Is this hotel a great deal? Absolutely.

Tired and in dire need of a good sprucing up, the Olcott certainly won't win any design awards. It looks like an older apartment building because it is one. About one-half of the 200-plus units house full-time residents. However, considering the location and general spaciousness of the rooms, we were shocked this hotel is so affordable.

Only a few doors down from the famed Dakota with its celebrity residents, the Olcott is located near one of the most popular entrances to Central Park at 72nd Street. Lincoln Square and the American Museum of Natural History are within a 10-minute walk. You also have easy access to two subway stations, one with express service to Times Square and Penn Station.

Most of the guest rooms have hardwood floors and wood furniture, chosen more for durability than style. Sparsely decorated, both the studios and suites offer an amazing amount of space, more than the average New Yorker enjoys. A suite usually consists of two rooms with two double beds and a couch, while the studio has one bed. Some of the mattresses have a worrisome straw sound and feel to them. All the accommodations provide a chest of drawers, table with chairs, and kitchenette. These cooking units vary in size and offer at least a mini-fridge, toaster, plates, and utensils as well as a hot plate. Bathrooms are average-sized, but closets are larger than normal with hangers and shelves.

The Olcott offers weekly rates: $840 for studios and $980 for suites. Payment in full is required upon arrival. Its location, low prices, large rooms, and super-friendly staff help compensate for its occasional shabbiness.

JAZZ ON THE PARK HOSTEL

36 W. 106th St.
(aka Duke Ellington Blvd.)
New York, NY 10025
(BETWEEN CENTRAL PARK WEST AND MANHATTAN AVE.)

VALUE ★ ★ ★ ★ ★

CLEANLINESS ★ ★ ★ ★ ★

GUEST SERVICES ★ ★ ★ ★ ★

SECURITY ★ ★ ★ ★

(★POOR - ★★★★★EXCELLENT)

CATEGORY	Hostel
PHONE	(212) 932-1600
FAX	(212) 932-1700
EMAIL	info@jazzonthepark.com
WEBSITE	www.jazzonthepark.com

RATES	Dorm beds: $27-$30 Private rooms: $68 Includes taxes and tariffs
GUEST ROOMS	Accommodations for 300 on 5 floors, primarily bunk beds, all shared baths, no smoking, no elevator
ROOM AMENITIES	AC, coin-operated locker, bedding, towels; clock radio, hair dryer and iron available on request
RESTAURANTS	Café sells hot and cold food
BARS	None
CLIENTELE	Budget travelers at least 18 years old, unless accompanied by an adult
GUEST SERVICES	Continental breakfast, internet kiosk, coin-operated laundry, public phones, free entertainment, summer BBQs, passes to talk shows
PARKING	None
CANCELLATION POLICY	24 hours before check-in
WHEELCHAIR ACCESS	One room

No one could remain hostile toward hostels after staying at Jazz on the Park. You feel the vibrant, friendly atmosphere the minute you walk up the steps. The check-in desk and adjacent café are East Village casual. In fact, the leopard-print couch; modern art posters; mix of booths, tables, and bar stools; and a large TV might remind you of your college days. Except that the furniture is in better condition.

Jazz on the Park has been open three years, and the facilities still look new. Rooms can sleep up to 10, primarily in bunk beds. Each floor has one bathroom for each sex with three toilets and three shower stalls. The hostel provides all bedsheets and towels. Overall, it offers perks rarely found in most hostels. The room rate includes a continental breakfast of bread, yogurt, cereal, and fruit. Open from 7 a.m. to 12:30 a.m., the café sells an assortment of hot and cold food. You can borrow an alarm clock, hair dryer, and various board games with a $10 deposit.

Throughout the week, social activities are geared toward getting people together. Saturday is open-mike night and Wednesday features live jazz. The satellite dish is a big hit as are the summer BBQs on the outdoor terraces. One of the most popular perks: free passes to various syndicated talk shows filmed in New York.

Security is tight. A sturdy metal door right next to the check-in area is the only entrance into the dormitories. Front desk is staffed 24 hours. A credit card is required to hold a reservation and payment is expected upon check-in.

The only drawbacks here are price and location. Rates are a bit more than at other city hostels, but you're getting more for your money. Occasionally, discounts are offered during off-peak months. The hostel is only three blocks from a subway station, however you are nowhere near most tourist attractions. Also, 106th Street isn't as safe as 20th Street.

In its favor: Jazz on the Park is the nicest, cleanest hostel we've ever visited.

MALIBU HOTEL

2688 Broadway
New York, NY 10025
(BETWEEN W. 102ND AND W. 103RD STREETS)

VALUE ★ ★ ★

CLEANLINESS ★ ★ ★

GUEST SERVICES ★ ★ ★

SECURITY ★ ★ ★ ★

(★POOR - ★★★★★EXCELLENT)

CATEGORY	Bare Essentials
PHONE	(212) 663-0275 (800) 647-2227 Reservations
FAX	(212) 678-6842
EMAIL	rooms@malibuhotelnyc.com
WEBSITE	www.malibuhotelnyc.com Offers specials on occasion
RATES	Shared bath: $79-$99 Private bath: $129-$169
GUEST ROOMS	138 rooms on 5 floors, some shared baths, all nonsmoking, no elevator
ROOM AMENITIES	AC, TV without cable, phone with dataport, clock radio
RESTAURANTS	None
BARS	None

UPPER WEST SIDE

Quirky design and cheap rates are a part of The Malibu's appeal.
Credit: Malibu Hotel

CLIENTELE	Primarily European
GUEST SERVICES	Continental breakfast, internet kiosk, luggage storage, bellman during the day
PARKING	None
CANCELLATION POLICY	24 hours before check-in
WHEELCHAIR ACCESS	None

The Malibu Hotel isn't exactly a day at the beach. After a hike up two flights of stairs, you enter a semi-lit lobby. Actually, the low lights in the check-in area reflect muted décor and lighting throughout the property. It's as if all the lights in the hotel are on a dimmer. Some of Manhattan's high-end properties take this approach, but it doesn't work here.

All the rooms offer one or two double beds. The sparse black modular furniture is rather 1980s but in decent condition. Beds are adequately firm, but a bit too low to the floor. In most of the rooms, a bar with hangers and an indent in the wall passes for the closet. Some feature a mini-fridge. You can use the dataport phone for your laptop, but there's no voice mail. Bathrooms are passably clean and a decent size. Approximately 30 rooms share hallway facilities, with about three to five per bathroom. They are furnished like the private accommodations, with the addition of a sink.

You can buy snacks and soda from vending machines, but there's no ice. A continental breakfast is served in a small room off the lobby. It includes yogurt and dry cereal. Each room provides a book of menus from neighborhood restaurants that deliver. Guest rooms use keys, rather than electronic cards; however, everyone must be buzzed in from the street by front desk staff. Eager to please and professional, they help compensate for the hotel's flaws.

UPPER WEST SIDE

MILBURN HOTEL

242 W. 76th St.
New York, NY 10023
(BETWEEN BROADWAY AND WEST END AVE.)

VALUE ★ ★ ★ ★ ★

CLEANLINESS ★ ★ ★ ★ ★

GUEST SERVICES ★ ★ ★ ★

SECURITY ★ ★ ★ ★ ★

(★POOR - ★★★★★EXCELLENT)

CATEGORY	Limited Services
PHONE	(212) 362-1006
	(800) 833-9622 Reservations
FAX	(212) 721-5476
EMAIL	milburn@milburnhotel.com
WEBSITE	www.milburnhotel.com
RATES	Studios: $119-$175
	Junior suites: $149-$190
	1-bedroom suites: $159-$205
GUEST ROOMS	115 rooms on 15 floors, all smoking
ROOM AMENITIES	AC, cable TV with VCR, 2-line phone with voice mail and dataport, kitchenette with coffeemaker and microwave, safe, bathrobe, hair dryer, iron and ironing board, Caswell-Massey bath products
RESTAURANTS	None
BARS	None
CLIENTELE	A mix of business and leisure travelers
GUEST SERVICES	Complimentary hot or cold drinks in lobby, small exercise room, $22 passes to health club, free book and video library, discounts at local restaurants
PARKING	None
CANCELLATION POLICY	72 hours before check-in
WHEELCHAIR ACCESS	Yes

Who would have guessed a hotel as affordable and attractive as the Milburn could be found in one of Manhattan's most expensive neighborhoods? Leafy green plants and fresh flowers in the lobby create a serene atmosphere. Cider during the winter and iced tea during the summer are a welcome surprise. Overall, front desk staff exude a professional and friendly attitude.

Brightly decorated guest rooms are equally welcoming. This isn't a stylish hotel, rather it's warm and comfortable. Rooms with mostly king- and queen-sized beds provide plenty of space to stretch out. Even the smallest studio has a desk, chest of drawers, and pantry kitchenette. Suites feature a sofa bed, table with chairs, and a small stereo as well as a bigger kitchen. Bathrooms are larger than average and offer plenty of mirrors. Kitchenettes include a microwave and coffeemaker, plates, utensils, and at least a mini-fridge. Coffee, herbal tea, and cookies are replenished daily.

The Milburn provides an array of guest services. Its Dining Program offers a 10 percent discount or a free dessert at participating restaurants. Children receive a goody bag with toys, crayons, and drawing paper. The complimentary video library also features kid-pleasing video games. Each phone is programmed with 10 toll-free numbers to nearby pharmacies and restaurants, most of which deliver. Guests who want more equipment than the hotel's small exercise room offers can use the Equinox Health Club nearby for $22 per day.

Overall, the Milburn has much to commend and very little to criticize.

ON THE AVE HOTEL

2178 Broadway
New York, NY 10024
(ENTRANCE ON 77TH ST. BETWEEN AMSTERDAM AVE. AND BROADWAY)

VALUE ★ ★ ★ ★

CLEANLINESS ★ ★ ★ ★ ★

GUEST SERVICES ★ ★ ★

SECURITY ★ ★ ★ ★

(★POOR - ★★★★★EXCELLENT)

CATEGORY	Boutique
PHONE	(212) 362-1100
	(800) 497-6028 Reservations
FAX	(212) 787-9521

EMAIL	None
WEBSITE	www.ontheave-nyc.com Occasionally offers specials
RATES	Standard: $125-$265 Superior: $145-$285 Deluxe: $165-$305
GUEST ROOMS	251 rooms on 12 floors, with 2 floors for smokers
ROOM AMENITIES	AC, cable TV, phone with voice mail, clock radio, bathrobe, Gilchrist & Soames bath products, iron and ironing board, *New York Times* delivered weekdays
RESTAURANTS	None
BARS	None
CLIENTELE	Business and leisure travelers
GUEST SERVICES	Morning coffee, room service from Manhattan Diner, valet laundry, fax and copy services, $20 pass to Equinox Health Club
CANCELLATION POLICY	24 hours before check-in
WHEELCHAIR ACCESS	13 rooms

We're not sure how long this new hotel will be affordable, so take advantage of it while you can. Opened in 1999 by Citylife Hotel Group, On the Ave looks like money. From the sleek lobby to the staff's snazzy dark uniforms, everything is chic and urbane. Despite an "aren't we cool" atmosphere, everyone is friendly and helpful. The lobby is so hip, we immediately became suspicious that the rooms would be tiny. In New York, often the smarter the hotel, the smaller the accommodations.

But we were just borrowing trouble. True, the furniture design is minimalist, but the rooms provide enough space. All the beds are king- or queen-sized. Amenities include a bathrobe, bath products, the *New York Times* delivered weekdays, as well as the latest issues of various magazines. Standard bathrooms are tiny. Most have a tub/shower, but there are a few with stall showers so state your preference. Larger rooms offer a vanity shelf. All the accommodations provide voice mail and high-speed internet access, but the majority lack workspace or any sort of desk. You're here to play, not work.

Guests enjoy a striking setting and friendly ambience when they stay On The Ave. Credit: Citylife Hotel Group

On the Ave is close to several car rental agencies and two parking garages. A laundromat is across the street. There's no restaurant on site, but the 24-hour Manhattan Diner on the corner delivers. No workout area either, but daily passes to the Equinox Health Club are available for $20. The Beacon Theater, Lincoln Center, Central Park, and the American Museum of Natural History are all an easy walk away.

During peak season, you can get a better deal elsewhere, but it will be hard to find a more stylish place to stay in this neighborhood.

UPPER WEST SIDE

QUALITY HOTEL ON BROADWAY

215 W. 94th St.
New York, NY 10025
(BETWEEN BROADWAY AND AMSTERDAM AVE.)

VALUE ★ ★ ★ ★
CLEANLINESS ★ ★ ★ ★
GUEST SERVICES ★ ★ ★
SECURITY ★ ★ ★ ★ ★
(★POOR - ★★★★★EXCELLENT)

CATEGORY	Limited Services
PHONE	(212) 866-6400
	(800) 834-2972 Reservations
FAX	(212) 866-1357
EMAIL	qhob94@aol.com
WEBSITE	www.bestnyhotels.com
RATES	$89–$325
GUEST ROOMS	243 rooms on 14 floors, half nonsmoking
ROOM AMENITIES	AC, cable TV, phone with voice mail and dataport, clock radio, coffeemaker, built-in hair dryer, iron and ironing board
RESTAURANTS	Closed for renovation
BARS	None
CLIENTELE	Mix of European tours and U.S. business and group travel
GUEST SERVICES	Concierge, gift shop, valet laundry, workout area, luggage room
PARKING	None
CANCELLATION POLICY	24 hours before check-in
WHEELCHAIR ACCESS	Yes

Despite slightly shabby hallways, this hotel's guest accommodations are attractive and in good shape. A television is hidden in an armoire with drawers, which come in handy since closets are on the small side. Business travelers will appreciate the full-sized desk with a dataport phone and voice mail. Bathrooms offer plenty of space. Most of them have a large shelf for cosmetics and shaving kits, as well as an extra vanity mirror, telephone, and bathroom fan.

As of press time, the restaurant was closed and undergoing a renovation. It isn't operated by the hotel, rather it rents space from the property. But its status is unclear. The hotel is considering adding a continental breakfast, and a business center will be online soon. It's reassuring to see uniformed security guards on duty in the lobby 24 hours and to use an electronic key card to open your door.

Location is one of the hotel's strongest selling points. It's right next to a subway station that offers express service to Wall Street, Penn Station, and Times Square. Central Park is only a couple of blocks away. If you want a taste of real New York, join the hundreds of joggers that circle the park's reservoir every morning and early evening. Just make sure you're moving in the right direction.

During off-season and shoulder periods, this hotel is a good deal. But during peak periods when room rates surpass $200, you can probably do better.

RIVERSIDE TERRACE

350 W. 88th St.
New York, NY 10024
(BETWEEN WEST END AVE. AND RIVERSIDE DR.)

VALUE ★ ★ ★
CLEANLINESS ★ ★ ★ ★
GUEST SERVICES ★ ★ ★
SECURITY ★ ★ ★
(★POOR - ★★★★★EXCELLENT)

CATEGORY	Residence
PHONE	(212) 724-6100
	(888) 468-3558 Reservations
FAX	(212) 873-5808
EMAIL	None
WEBSITE	www.newyorkhotel.com
RATES	$1600-$2400 per month
	$400-$700 per week
	$100-$150 per night, when available
	One–month minimum stay
	All taxes included
GUEST ROOMS	100 rooms on 8 floors, all smoking
ROOM AMENITIES	AC, cable TV, phone ($50 deposit)

RESTAURANTS	None
BARS	None
CLIENTELE	Mixed business and leisure travelers
GUEST SERVICES	Phone card machine, internet kiosk, coin-operated laundry, kitchen on each floor
PARKING	None
CANCELLATION POLICY	24 hours before check-in
WHEELCHAIR ACCESS	Two rooms

Catering to monthly guests, the Riverside Terrace is a better option than sleeping on your friend's couch and dodging questions about your departure date. The hotel finished a complete renovation in early 2001. About 100 units are occupied by guests, and the rest by full-time residents.

Small- to average-sized rooms offer few amenities. All the accommodations have a double bed, phone, full desk and chair, nightstand, and armoire for the television. Beds are new and in good condition. Clothing storage is limited to drawers in the armoire since the rooms don't have closets. Average-sized bathrooms are clean with a tub/shower and small vanity.

This isn't the ideal extended-stay hotel. None of the rooms has a kitchenette or even a mini-fridge. Each floor does offer a small kitchen with a stove and refrigerator but no cooking utensils. Considering the hotel wants to attract business travelers, it should offer voice mail. Also, we were surprised the renovation didn't include the change to an electronic key system.

A phone card machine, change machine, internet kiosk, and coin-operated laundry are all handy services. Its location on a residential, very quiet street close to Riverside Park is a huge asset, and a subway station is less than three blocks away. For monthly and weekly guests, the Riverside Terrace is a pretty good deal, but if you're only in town a few days, it's not a bargain.

RIVERSIDE TOWER HOTEL

80 Riverside Drive
New York, NY 10024
(AT W. 80TH ST.)

VALUE ★ ★
CLEANLINESS ★ ★
GUEST SERVICES ★
SECURITY ★ ★
(★POOR - ★★★★★EXCELLENT)

CATEGORY	Bare Essentials
PHONE	(212) 877-5200
FAX	(212) 873-1400
EMAIL	rivhotel@access1.net
WEBSITE	None
RATES	Singles: $95 Doubles: $100 Suites: $110-$140
GUEST ROOMS	120 rooms on 16 floors, all smoking
ROOM AMENITIES	AC, TV without cable, mini-fridge, phone; hair dryer and iron on request
RESTAURANTS	None
BARS	None
CLIENTELE	Low-maintenance travelers
GUEST SERVICES	Coin-operated laundry
PARKING	None
CANCELLATION POLICY	24 hours before check-in
WHEELCHAIR ACCESS	None

What is a hotel like this doing in such a high-end neighborhood? Considering the painful housing crunch in New York, we don't understand why the building's owners didn't convert this depressing hotel into overpriced apartments during the economic boom. The hotel is located on a beautiful residential street on the edge of Riverside Park. Taller than the surrounding buildings, it offers postcard views of the Hudson River and a good portion of Manhattan's Upper West Side.

A tiny, rickety elevator is scary as well as claustrophobic. Extremely narrow, the building has only six to eight small units on each floor. Doors are less than sturdy, and rooms don't have deadbolt locks. With the thin walls, you can hear the wind whipping around the building as well as your neighbor's blaring television. The hotel doesn't provide voice mail. A brochure advertised kitchenettes in all the rooms, but we couldn't find anything more than a mini-fridge.

The smallest room was only a bit larger than an office cubicle. The suite was simply two rooms sharing a bathroom. The outer room offered a table and chairs as well as a bed that folds up to transform it into a living room. All the rooms have old televisions, dressers, and small closets with wire hangers. Most of the tiny bathrooms barely have room for a sink and toilet and use shower stalls rather than tubs. Full payment is required upon check-in.

This lodging reminded us uncomfortably of the Pioneer Hotel downtown, except that the Riverside Tower can brag all its rooms have private bathrooms and phones.

WEST END STUDIOS

850 West End Ave.
New York, NY 10025
(BETWEEN W. 101ST AND W. 102ND STREETS)

VALUE ★ ★ ★ ★

CLEANLINESS ★ ★ ★ ★

GUEST SERVICES ★ ★ ★

SECURITY ★ ★ ★

(★POOR - ★★★★★EXCELLENT)

CATEGORY	Euro-style
PHONE	(212) 749-7104
FAX	(212) 865-5130
EMAIL	westendstudios@aol.com
WEBSITE	www.westendstudios.com
RATES	Singles: $49–$79 Doubles: $69–$119
GUEST ROOMS	80 rooms on 6 floors, all shared baths, about one-half smoking

ROOM AMENITIES	AC, cable TV , mini-fridge, clock radio; microwave available on request
RESTAURANTS	None
BARS	None
CLIENTELE	Leisure travelers
GUEST SERVICES	Internet kiosk, public phones, fax and dataport machine, phone cards, valet and coin-operated laundries, newspapers in lobby
PARKING	None
CANCELLATION POLICY	24 hours before check-in
WHEELCHAIR ACCESS	None

This property blends perfectly with the attractive apartment buildings and townhouses around it, and nothing identifies it as a hotel. Visitors must be alert to its street number. The pretty lobby looks like the parlor of a B&B, where daily newspapers are available for all guests. Off the lobby there is a dataport machine and internet kiosk as well as public phones. None of the rooms has a phone.

Once we left the lobby, it became clear the hotel is tired and a bit shabby. The property is not in poor condition, it just needs sprucing up. All the rooms are decorated a little differently, yet sparsely and with few amenities. But they are clean and offer plenty of space. All have a sink and a small closet with hangers. Room configurations range from two twin beds to two double beds, along with a few bunk beds. There are three to four bathrooms per floor. Each has a tub/shower and paper towel dispenser but few offer a vanity shelf. All were clean and in fair condition.

This is a quiet, residential area so you shouldn't be bothered by street noise. A subway station is only two blocks away and Riverside Park is just around the corner. West End Studios is not as nice as The Larchmont, an all-shared bath property in Greenwich Village, but it may be a little cheaper. It's a reasonable option for those who want to stay near Columbia University or "way up west."

UPPER WEST SIDE

WEST SIDE INN

237 W. 107th St.
New York, NY 10025
(BETWEEN AMSTERDAM AVE. AND BROADWAY)

VALUE ★ ★ ★

CLEANLINESS ★ ★ ★

GUEST SERVICES ★ ★

SECURITY ★ ★

(★POOR - ★★★★★EXCELLENT)

CATEGORY	Bare Essentials
PHONE	(212) 866-0061
FAX	(212) 866-0062
EMAIL	info@westsideinn.com
WEBSITE	www.westsideinn.com
RATES	Singles: $49-$79 Doubles: $69-$119 Cash and traveler's checks only
GUEST ROOMS	75 rooms on 6 floors, all shared baths, about one-half smoking
ROOM AMENITIES	AC, TV without cable, mini-fridge, clock radio
RESTAURANTS	None
BARS	None
CLIENTELE	Leisure travelers
GUEST SERVICES	Internet kiosk, public phones, fax and dataport machine, phone cards, bike rental
PARKING	None
CANCELLATION POLICY	24 hours before check-in
WHEELCHAIR ACCESS	None

West Side Inn is a poor relation of West End Studios, both owned by Robert Beda. Dilapidated is too strong a word so we'll choose shabby. The musty smell in the lobby certainly doesn't help. When the desk clerk is called away, no one takes his place, so anyone can walk in and gain access to the guest areas.

Rooms are sparsely decorated and offer few amenities. Some of the doors close oddly, probably because the wood is warped. Some rooms have a bar for a closet while others offer a real closet with a full-length mirror. Most of the accommodations provide a television, but channels are limited. There are sinks but no phones. Shared bathrooms are cleaner and in better condition than we expected.

Full payment is required upon check-in with either cash or traveler's checks. You may use a credit card to guarantee your reservation. While guest services clearly are not a priority, the hotel has a special arrangement with a nearby bike shop. Guests can rent a bike for $8 per hour or $25 per day.

Considering both properties offer the same rates and similar rooms, you're better off at West End Studios.

WEST SIDE YMCA

5 W. 63rd St.
New York, NY 10023
(BETWEEN CENTRAL PARK WEST AND BROADWAY)

VALUE ★ ★ ★ ★

CLEANLINESS ★ ★ ★ ★

GUEST SERVICES ★ ★ ★ ★ ★

SECURITY ★ ★ ★

(★POOR - ★★★★★EXCELLENT)

CATEGORY	YMCA
PHONE	(212) 875-4100
	(800) 348-9622 Reservations
FAX	(212) 875-1334
EMAIL	wsguestrooms@ymcanyc.org
WEBSITE	www.ymca.nyc.org
RATES	Shared bath: $70-$95
	Private bath: $110-$150
GUEST ROOMS	530 private rooms on 13 floors, primarily shared bath, no smoking
ROOM AMENITIES	AC, TV, towels
RESTAURANTS	International Café, open daily 6 a.m. to 1 a.m., serves hot and cold food
BARS	None
CLIENTELE	Mixed

GUEST SERVICES	Concierge, self-service laundry, internet kiosks, maid service, phone cards, luggage storage, health club
PARKING	None
CANCELLATION POLICY	3 days before check-in
WHEELCHAIR ACCESS	Yes

You know you're on Manhattan's Upper West Side when the YMCA café delivers and the menu includes a salmon sandwich with dill sauce. The lobby is nicer than many of the budget hotels we visited. A full-time concierge helps with airport transportation and tours. Off the lobby, guests can play the grand piano or relax in the café, which seats about 70.

We were amazed by the health club, which is larger than most gyms in the city and free to guests. The club features two swimming pools, steam rooms, sauna, basketball court, indoor running track, weights, and cardiovascular machines. Any classes are extra.

While common areas are attractive, guest areas are bland and look just like college dorms. All the rooms are private and sleep one to two people, usually in springy bunk beds. The floors are tiled rather than carpeted. Closets serve their purpose but aren't roomy. The YMCA provides daily maid service, linens, towels, soap, and plastic cups. Shared bathrooms are large hallway facilities with three shower stalls, three sinks, and two toilets. For security purposes, the women's bathroom requires a code to enter.

We were surprised by the lax security in the lobby. Uniformed guards are stationed at the entrance, but during the day people don't have to show any ID or proof of residence. Anyone can easily gain access to the guest areas upstairs. There are security cameras in the elevators, but nothing in the dorms. Guest accommodations use electronic locks.

Maximum stay is 25 days, and payment in full is required upon arrival. This YMCA is located in a safe neighborhood, close to Lincoln Center and Central Park. But make sure you use the health club to get your money's worth; otherwise you may be overpaying for the private bathrooms.

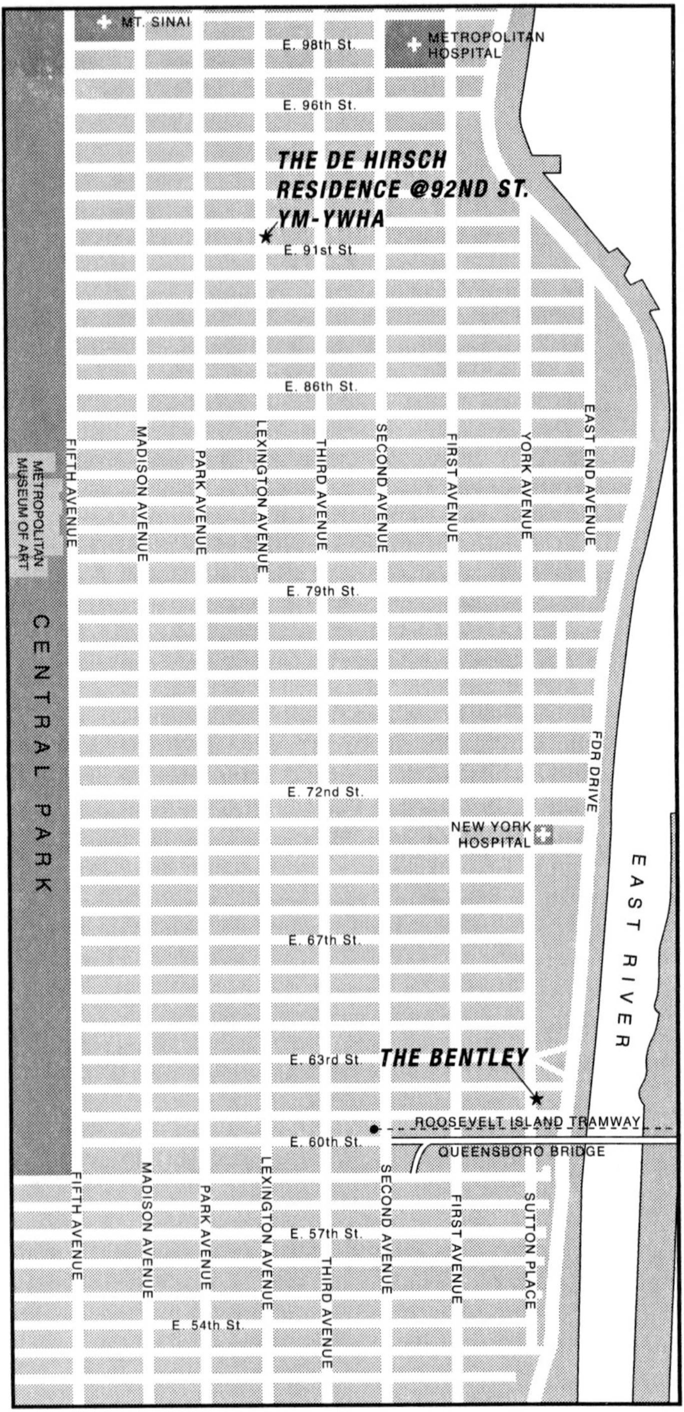
MT. SINAI
METROPOLITAN HOSPITAL
E. 98th St.
E. 96th St.
THE DE HIRSCH RESIDENCE @92ND ST. YM-YWHA
E. 91st St.
E. 86th St.
METROPOLITAN MUSEUM OF ART
FIFTH AVENUE
MADISON AVENUE
PARK AVENUE
LEXINGTON AVENUE
THIRD AVENUE
SECOND AVENUE
FIRST AVENUE
YORK AVENUE
EAST END AVENUE
E. 79th St.
CENTRAL PARK
FDR DRIVE
E. 72nd St.
NEW YORK HOSPITAL
EAST RIVER
E. 67th St.
E. 63rd St.
THE BENTLEY
ROOSEVELT ISLAND TRAMWAY
E. 60th St.
QUEENSBORO BRIDGE
SUTTON PLACE
E. 57th St.
E. 54th St.

UPPER EAST SIDE

> *"On a clear Sunday afternoon in July, David and his aunt set out together toward the Third Avenue Elevated. They were going to the Metropolitan Museum.... At 86th St. they got off and after further inquiry walked west toward Fifth Avenue. The farther they got from Third Avenue, the more aloof grew the houses, the more silent the streets. David began to feel uneasy at his aunt's loud voice and Yiddish speech, both of which seemed out of place here. "Hmm!" she marveled in resounding accents. "Not a single child in the street. Children, I see, are not in style in this portion of America."*
> —*Henry Roth*

Roth got it right in his 1934 autobiographical novel *Call It Sleep*. The Upper East Side is worlds apart from the tenements of the Lower East Side. Known for art museums, galleries, upscale boutiques, and private schools, it's the city's most prestigious residential neighborhood. That portion of Fifth Avenue called "Museum Mile" claims at least six major museums with the Whitney, Asia Society, and Frick Collection close by. Madison Avenue boasts its own collection of designer clothing stores, like Giorgio Armani and Calvin Klein. While other neighborhoods exude bohemianism, commerce, or nightlife, the Upper East Side exudes wealth.

THE BENTLEY

500 E. 62nd St.
New York, NY 10021
(AT YORK AVE.)

VALUE ★ ★ ★ ★ ★

CLEANLINESS ★ ★ ★ ★ ★

GUEST SERVICES ★ ★ ★ ★

SECURITY ★ ★ ★ ★ ★

(★POOR - ★★★★★EXCELLENT)

CATEGORY	Boutique
PHONE	(212) 644-6000 (888) 66-HOTEL Reservations
FAX	(212) 207-4800 (212) 751-7868 Reservations
EMAIL	None
WEBSITE	www.nychotels.com
RATES	$115-$425
GUEST ROOMS	197 rooms on 19 floors, mostly nonsmoking
ROOM AMENITIES	AC, TV with pay movies and games, phone with voice mail and dataport, hair dryer, iron and ironing board, mini-fridge available on request
RESTAURANTS	Dinner 5 p.m.-10 p.m.
BARS	Open 3 p.m.-midnight
CLIENTELE	A mix of business and leisure travelers
GUEST SERVICES	Continental breakfast, library, $15 pass to health club, limited room service, valet laundry, business services, complimentary coffee and tea
PARKING	None
CANCELLATION POLICY	24 hours before check-in
WHEELCHAIR ACCESS	None

Tall and sleek, the Bentley looks like just another office building along York Avenue. But fortunately for us, it's one of New York's great new hotels. In 1998, Amsterdam Hospitality Group transformed the interior space by

The Bentley boasts custom-designed furniture, original art, and panoramic views. Credit: Amsterdam Hospitality Group

doubling the height of the lobby ceiling and emphasizing glass exposure to maximize city and river views. The result is a joy to behold, especially when you consider their rates.

The serene lobby is a harmonious blend of brown and taupe leather sofas, silk draperies, floating silver-leaf lights, and original art. A mahogany-panelled library off the lobby provides a 24-hour cappuccino bar and rack of magazines.

Guest rooms and junior suites feature the same cream-brown-black color scheme and contemporary décor. A standard double/double is huge with a large working desk, tall standing mirror, small walk-in closet, and TV with pay movies and games. The small bathroom in beige marble is fully equipped. Junior suites look the same, except they have two TVs and a separate bedroom with a queen bed. All the rooms have great views of the city facing west or the East River facing east. If you want to overlook the river and Queensboro Bridge, ask for an east corner room. There are two on each floor.

The restaurant and bar on the 21st floor really takes advantage of this building's panoramic views. Two-tiered and glass-enclosed, it's an invigorating way to begin your day over bagels, fruit, and coffee, compliments of the house. You can grab a cocktail at the bar here from 3 p.m. to midnight and order dinner from 5 p.m. to 10 p.m. The restaurant is worth a visit even if you're not a hotel guest.

Expansive views; clean, comfortable rooms; a highly rated restaurant/bar; and great value: it's all part of the welcome package in this carefully designed boutique hotel. Judging by the gracious, eager-to-please staff, it must also be a great place to work.

THE DE HIRSCH RESIDENCE AT THE 92ND STREET YM-YWHA

1395 Lexington Ave.
New York, NY 10128
(BETWEEN 91ST AND 92ND STREETS)

VALUE ★ ★ ★ ★
CLEANLINESS ★ ★ ★
GUEST SERVICES ★ ★ ★ ★
SECURITY ★ ★ ★ ★

(★POOR - ★★★★★EXCELLENT)

CATEGORY	Residence
PHONE	(212) 415-5650 (888) NY-YOUTH Reservations
FAX	(212) 415-5578
EMAIL	dehirsch@92ndsty.org
WEBSITE	www.92ndsty.org
RATES	Singles: $1045 monthly Doubles: $725-$845 monthly per person. 1-month minimum stay
GUEST ROOMS	225 rooms in 2 buildings, all smoking (with roommate's permission), all shared bath. Separate men's and women's floors
ROOM AMENITIES	Bedding, AC
RESTAURANTS	None
BARS	None

CLIENTELE	Men and women 18 and older, who are working and/or studying
GUEST SERVICES	Maid service, health club membership at discounted rates, coin-operated laundry, kitchens on each floor, TV lounge, library
PARKING	None
CANCELLATION POLICY	2 weeks before arrival for long-term stays; full payment for one-month stays is not refundable
WHEELCHAIR ACCESS	Yes

The 92nd Street Y is justly famous for its cultural programs, classes, library, and health club. But it also offers low-cost, long-term housing to men and women in school or pursuing careers.

The facilities resemble a college dorm, and rooms are slightly larger in the newer building. A huge advantage here in summer months is air-conditioning. Other residences ask you to buy and install your own AC, for which you'll pay a monthly charge.

Singles have walk-in closets, a twin bed, a small dresser and desk, shelves, and linoleum floors. Doubles are twice as large with two twins and the same furniture. A fully equipped kitchen on each floor allows you to prepare your own meals and save your cash for serious pleasures. Each floor also offers washers, dryers, an in-house phone, and pay phones. Shared bathrooms, one to a floor, have five stall showers and four toilets. Visitors who sign in are allowed into guest rooms, and those who want to stay overnight pay $10 if they get prior approval from the front office.

If an institutional setting doesn't depress you and an East Side address is a priority, this may be a suitable choice. But other residences with comparable rates include two meals.

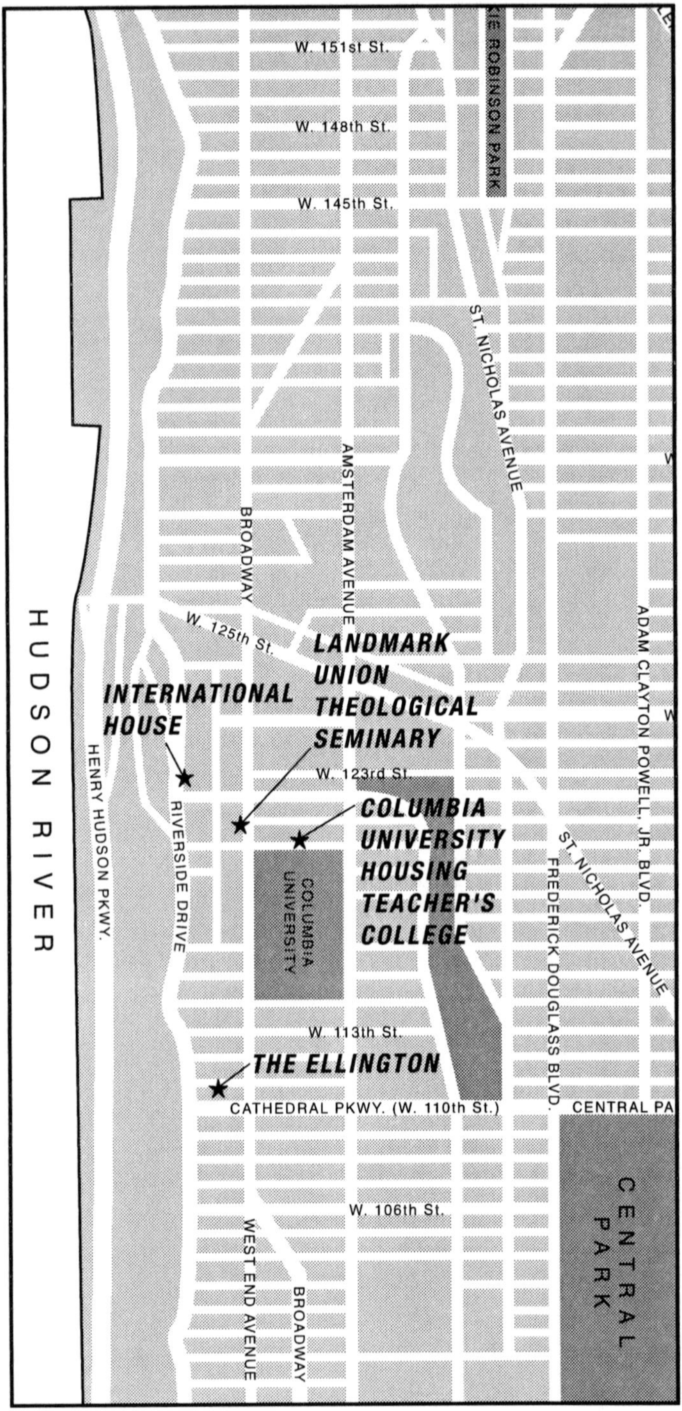
W. 151st St.
W. 148th St.
W. 145th St.
ROBINSON PARK
ST. NICHOLAS AVENUE
AMSTERDAM AVENUE
BROADWAY
W. 125th St.
LANDMARK
UNION
THEOLOGICAL
SEMINARY
INTERNATIONAL
HOUSE
HUDSON RIVER
HENRY HUDSON PKWY.
RIVERSIDE DRIVE
W. 123rd St.
COLUMBIA
UNIVERSITY
HOUSING
TEACHER'S
COLLEGE
COLUMBIA UNIVERSITY
ADAM CLAYTON POWELL, JR. BLVD.
ST. NICHOLAS AVENUE
FREDERICK DOUGLASS BLVD.
W. 113th St.
THE ELLINGTON
CATHEDRAL PKWY. (W. 110th St.)
CENTRAL PA
W. 106th St.
WEST END AVENUE
BROADWAY
CENTRAL PARK

MORNINGSIDE HEIGHTS

> *"The West End was one of those nondescript places, before the era of white walls and potted ferns and imitation Tiffany lamps, that for some reason always made the best hangouts."*
> —Joyce Johnson, "Minor Characters"

The West End, as the cavernous restaurant and bar at 2911 Broadway is known today, still draws Columbia University coeds and neighborhood barflies. But in the late '40s, it was the favored watering hole of writers Jack Kerouac, Allen Ginsberg, and William Burroughs. They met on campus and channeled their mutual love of literature and hatred of social conformity into what later was called, by an enterprising journalist, the Beat Movement. Like the Cedar Tavern near New York University, the West End is a literary landmark. Not much has changed here in 50 years, except the price of burgers and brew.

Vibrant with academic life, this neighborhood encompasses Riverside Church, the Cathedral of St. John the Divine, and Grant's Tomb, as well as Columbia. Morningside Park, stretching from 110th to 123rd streets, was landscaped in 1887 by Frederick Law Olmsted. Pretty by day, it's best avoided after dark.

COLUMBIA UNIVERSITY HOUSING TEACHER'S COLLEGE

525 W. 120th St.
Box 312
New York, NY 10027
(ENTRANCE ON AMSTERDAM AVE.)

VALUE ★ ★ ★ ★
CLEANLINESS ★ ★ ★
GUEST SERVICES ★ ★
SECURITY ★ ★ ★ ★
(★POOR - ★★★★★EXCELLENT)

CATEGORY	University
PHONE	(212) 678-3235
FAX	(212) 678-3222
EMAIL	boyd@exchange.pc.columbia.edu
WEBSITE	www.tc.columbia.edu
RATES	Summer-only dorms: $30-$45 Year-round studios: $45-$90
GUEST ROOMS	Combination of dorm singles (smoking) and small apartments (nonsmoking); the majority are shared bath
ROOM AMENITIES	Apartments have AC, TV, phone, desk, wardrobe, mini-fridge, bed linens, towels and kitchenette in half the units. Dorms have phone, wardrobe, desk, bed linens, mini-fridge and microwave
RESTAURANTS	None
BARS	None
CLIENTELE	Primarily students, but no student or faculty affiliation is required
GUEST SERVICES	Coin-operated laundry, vending machines
PHONE POLICY	Free local calls
PARKING	None
CANCELLATION POLICY	48 hours before check-in, nonrefundable $50 application fee for summer dorms
WHEELCHAIR ACCESS	Yes

If you're tired of hostels but can't quite afford a hotel, consider the Teacher's College at Columbia University. All the rooms are in Whittier Hall on Amsterdam Avenue near 120th Street. Two types are available: summer housing in dorm singles and small studio apartments offered year-round. All the rooms are private and tend to be cheaper than a single at a Manhattan hostel.

Available from mid-May through mid-August, the summer dorm rooms are small and lack air conditioning, but feature a phone, wardrobe, desk, mini-fridge, and microwave. On each floor there is a public kitchen with a full stove and refrigerator as well as hallway bathrooms. Bed linens but not towels are provided. Those interested must complete an application with a non-refundable $50 fee. Once a reservation is confirmed, one-half of the total payment is required and the remaining portion must be settled upon check-in.

No application is necessary for the year-round housing, comprised of 10 small studio apartments. About one-half have private bathrooms and a kitchenette; all have a TV and air conditioning. Room configurations include one and two double beds. The university provides linens and towels. The maximum stay is seven days. Also, if any part of the reservation falls on a weekend, the guest must pay for all three nights. Reservations are held with a credit card, and payment in full is required upon arrival.

A guard is on duty 24 hours in the lobby, and everyone is buzzed in. To access the guest areas, you must show a room key. Summer dorm rooms are scooped up by conference attendees, so apply as early as possible. The year-round guest housing is just as popular during peak season.

THE ELLINGTON

610 W. 111th St.
New York, NY 10025
(BETWEEN BROADWAY AND RIVERSIDE DR.)

VALUE ★ ★ ★ ★
CLEANLINESS ★ ★ ★ ★
GUEST SERVICES ★ ★ ★
SECURITY ★ ★ ★
(★POOR - ★★★★★EXCELLENT)

CATEGORY	Boutique
PHONE	(212) 864-7500
FAX	(212) 749-5852
EMAIL	None
WEBSITE	www.nychotels.com
RATES	$85-$165
GUEST ROOMS	85 rooms on 6 floors, mostly smoking
ROOM AMENITIES	AC, TV without cable, phone with dataport, clock radio, hair dryer
RESTAURANTS	None
BARS	None
CLIENTELE	Mixed, with a lot of Columbia University-related business
GUEST SERVICES	Continental breakfast, free coffee all day, valet laundry
PARKING	None
CANCELLATION POLICY	24 hours before check-in
WHEELCHAIR ACCESS	None

You can't imagine anyone raising his voice or behaving badly in the lobby of The Ellington. With its black-and-white tile floor, fresh flowers, and softly playing classical melodies, it is the essence of refinement. In early 2001, the hotel finished a refurbishment of all furniture and fabrics. Retaining the Art Deco motif, the rooms are decorated primarily in black and cream. If they don't quite live up to the lobby, they are comfortable and attractive.

Overall, the accommodations are small- to medium-sized. Some of the closets are much too small, but all have hangers with shelves and extra blankets. Unfortunately, the

Intimate guest rooms feature walnut and maple cabinets and contemporary décor. Credit: Amsterdam Hospitality Group

rooms don't have voice mail or electronic locks. Bathrooms are of average size and weren't included in the recent refurbishment. All feature a built-in hair dryer, tub/shower, and bath products. Some have a vanity shelf.

A basic continental breakfast is served in a room just off the lobby. Daily newspapers are available as well. Only four blocks from Columbia University, the Ellington is popular with visiting faculty and parents. Rates tend to be higher on weekends. A subway station is only one block away. The hotel is five minutes from both Riverside and Morningside parks. St. John the Divine, the famous Gothic cathedral, is just down the street.

INTERNATIONAL HOUSE

500 Riverside Drive
New York, NY 10027-3916
(AT 123RD ST.)

VALUE ★ ★ ★ ★ ★

CLEANLINESS ★ ★ ★

GUEST SERVICES ★ ★ ★ ★ ★

SECURITY ★ ★ ★ ★

(★POOR - ★★★★★EXCELLENT)

CATEGORY	University
PHONE	(212) 316-8436
FAX	(212) 316-1827
EMAIL	admissions@ihouse-nyc.org
WEBSITE	www.ihouse-nyc.org
RATES	Singles with shared bath: $600-$750 per month. Apartments: $800-$1600. Summer only: One-month minimum stay and $500 security deposit. Overnight: $115-$135, 8-10 suites available to non-students
GUEST ROOMS	Over 700 rooms and apartments. I. House South has furnished singles with shared bath; I. House North has studios, one-bedroom, and 3-, 4-, 5-bedroom apartments with private bath and kitchens. I. House South has designated coed, all-male, all-female, and nonsmoking floors
ROOM AMENITIES	Single rooms: desk, sink, book shelves, phone, bedding and towels. Apartments: desk, 2 walk-in closets, dressers, bookshelves, phone, bedding and towels, kitchen with full-sized refrigerator. Central heat, no AC. Overnight guest suites have AC, maid service, private bath, phone, cable TV
RESTAURANTS	Cafeteria, daily dining charge of $2.50
BARS	Pub
CLIENTELE	One-third Americans, two-thirds international students

GUEST SERVICES	Coin-operated laundry, gym, music practice rooms, piano, pool table in TV lounge, store, study rooms, full schedule of social activities
PARKING	None
CANCELLATION POLICY	$40 nonrefundable application fee
WHEELCHAIR ACCESS	Yes

Founded in 1924 to create a "global community" for graduate students, interns, and visiting scholars, International House offers rooms and apartments for a minimum stay of one month. There are also a few suites open to the public at a daily rate.

Singles with shared bath in I. House South are older, dormitory-style rooms with linoleum floors. Several floors are being renovated. A second building, I. House North, houses studios, one-bedrooms, and 3-, 4-, and 5-bedroom apartments. Kitchenware isn't provided. All accommodations are larger than the average hotel room. Studios have two twin beds, two walk-in closets; one-bedrooms have a separate living room. Rates vary with location. Overnight guest suites supply AC, maid service, private bath, phone, and cable TV. Security is tight; everyone must show ID to get buzzed in.

Although guest quarters are older and dorm-style, the public areas at International House are magnificent. Its services include a cafeteria and pub, gym, and self-service laundry. Daily free activities like ballroom dancing, films, and lectures are all quite popular.

Some overnight accommodations are available, but this is truly a community of scholars with a location convenient for those studying at Columbia and the Manhattan School of Music. Scholarships from $1,000 to $3,000 are offered.

LANDMARK UNION THEOLOGICAL SEMINARY

3041 Broadway
New York, NY 10027
(AT W. 121ST ST.)

VALUE ★ ★ ★

CLEANLINESS ★ ★ ★

GUEST SERVICES ★ ★

SECURITY ★ ★ ★

(★POOR - ★★★★★EXCELLENT)

CATEGORY	University
PHONE	(212) 280-1313
FAX	(212) 280-1488
EMAIL	None
WEBSITE	landmark@uts.columbia.edu
RATES	Singles: $130 Doubles: $160 Triples: $180 Rates are for guests affiliated with an educational, religious, or nonprofit organization, otherwise cost is $20 more
GUEST ROOMS	24 rooms, primarily on first floor, all have private baths
ROOM AMENITIES	AC, cable TV, phone with dataport, mini-fridge, iron and ironing board, linens, towels
RESTAURANTS	Cafeteria serves breakfast and lunch
BARS	None
CLIENTELE	Primarily business from Columbia University
GUEST SERVICES	Continental breakfast, microwave
PARKING	None
CANCELLATION POLICY	48 hours before check-in
WHEELCHAIR ACCESS	One room

On the doorstep of Columbia University, the Landmark Union Theological Seminary is a spot to consider for anyone doing business with the school. Its rates don't really vary by season, so these prices are very competitive for Manhattan at peak times of the year. However, during slow months—January, February, July, and August—many Upper West Side hotels will offer cheaper rates.

In comparison to Columbia Teacher's College, the Landmark is more expensive. However, it has more rooms, all private bathrooms, and includes a continental breakfast. Guest rooms look like your basic motel accommodation. The décor could be updated but it isn't really depressing. Many of the rooms include small efficiencies, and all have a mini-refrigerator. The cafeteria offers a full continental breakfast of pastries, donuts, cold cereal, and juices. It also serves lunch, but this is not included in the room rate.

Many hotels offer discounts for guests associated with educational, religious, and nonprofit organizations. But the Landmark specifically caters to people serving their communities.

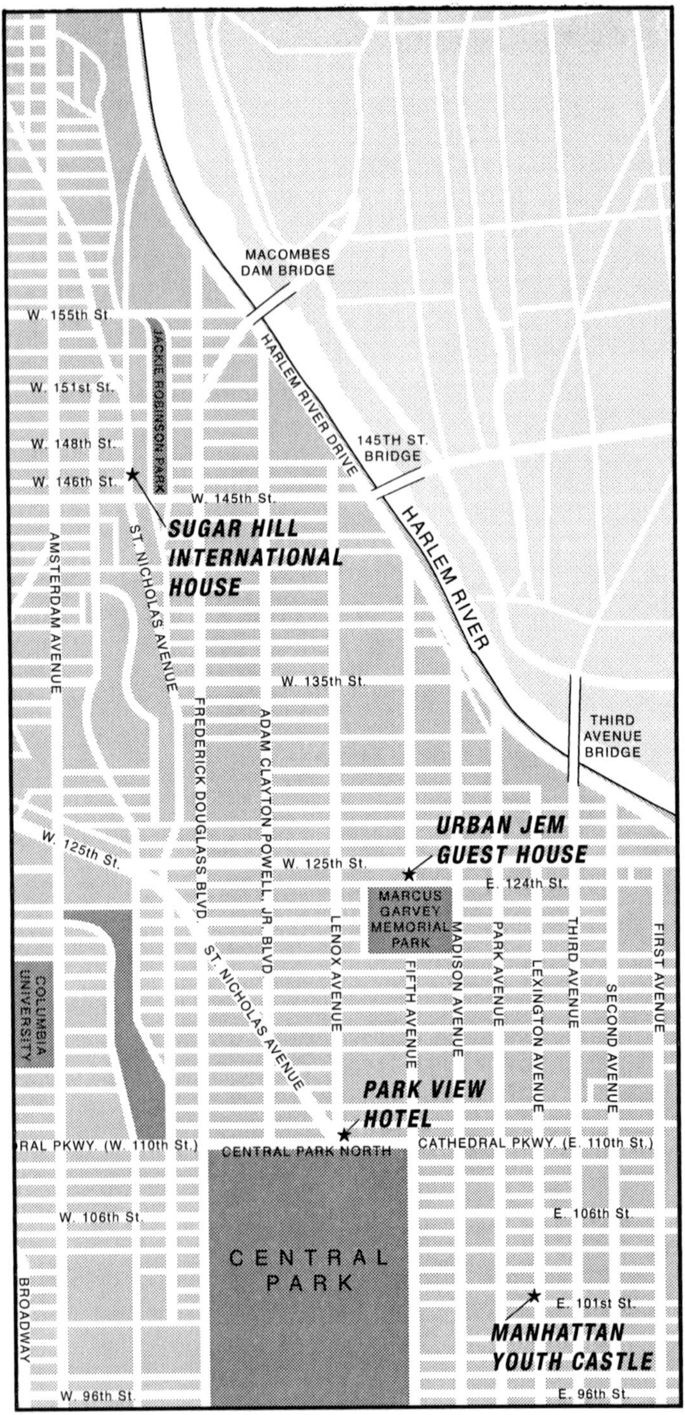
MACOMBES
DAM BRIDGE
W. 155th St.
JACKIE ROBINSON PARK
HARLEM RIVER DRIVE
W. 151st St.
W. 148th St.
145TH ST.
BRIDGE
W. 146th St.
W. 145th St.
HARLEM RIVER
SUGAR HILL
INTERNATIONAL
HOUSE
ST. NICHOLAS AVENUE
AMSTERDAM AVENUE
W. 135th St.
FREDERICK DOUGLASS BLVD.
ADAM CLAYTON POWELL, JR. BLVD.
THIRD
AVENUE
BRIDGE
URBAN JEM
GUEST HOUSE
W. 125th St.
W. 125th St.
E. 124th St.
MARCUS
GARVEY
MEMORIAL
PARK
LENOX AVENUE
FIFTH AVENUE
MADISON AVENUE
PARK AVENUE
LEXINGTON AVENUE
THIRD AVENUE
SECOND AVENUE
FIRST AVENUE
COLUMBIA
UNIVERSITY
ST. NICHOLAS AVENUE
PARK VIEW
HOTEL
RAL PKWY. (W. 110th St.)
CENTRAL PARK NORTH
CATHEDRAL PKWY. (E. 110th St.)
W. 106th St.
E. 106th St.
CENTRAL
PARK
BROADWAY
E. 101st St.
MANHATTAN
YOUTH CASTLE
W. 96th St.
E. 96th St.

HARLEM

> *"O, sweep of stars over Harlem Streets,
> O, little breath of oblivion that is night."*
> —Langston Hughes

Harlem is the most famous African-American community in America, and the cultural pre-school for generations of musicians, writers, and performers. Harlem's architectural history is equally rich and, thanks to urban renewal and economic redevelopment, its 19th-century brownstones are worth a tour. Most popular with tourists, however, are the neighborhood's jazz clubs on Saturday nights and church gospel choirs, who tune up on Sunday mornings. Landmarks to visit include the Apollo Theater, Sylvia's (soul food) restaurant, Wells bar and jazz joint, the Schomburg Center for Research in Black Culture, and the Abyssinian Baptist Church.

Spanish Harlem, known as El Barrio, runs along the east side of Manhattan from 96th Street to 125th Street. Its population is almost entirely Latino, and Spanish is more commonly spoken than English. Landmarks to visit here include El Museo del Barrio, at 104th Street and Fifth Avenue, and La Marqueta, the city's oldest public market, between 112th and 116th streets.

MANHATTAN YOUTH CASTLE

1596 Lexington Ave.
New York, NY 10029
(BETWEEN 101ST AND 102ND STREETS)

VALUE ★ ★

CLEANLINESS ★ ★

GUEST SERVICES ★ ★ ★

SECURITY ★ ★ ★

(★POOR - ★ ★ ★ ★ ★ EXCELLENT)

CATEGORY	Hostel
PHONE	(212) 831-4440
FAX	(212) 722-5746
EMAIL	info@1291.com
WEBSITE	www.1291.com
RATES	Dorm beds: $25-$33 Student discount May-Nov: $30; $150-$198 weekly, includes taxes
GUEST ROOMS	5 dorm rooms sleep from 6 to 10 people
ROOM AMENITIES	AC, bedding, towels
RESTAURANTS	None
BARS	None
CLIENTELE	Mostly Europeans, ages 18-35
GUEST SERVICES	Small TV room with refrigerator and microwave, free access to the internet, VCR, coin-operated laundry, pay phone, lockers, safe at front desk
PARKING	None
CANCELLATION POLICY	48 hours before check-in
WHEELCHAIR ACCESS	None

A castle it's not; in fact this hostel, in the area of Spanish Harlem known as "El Barrio," looks like a crash pad. The building was originally a dry cleaners, and 1291 International Company decided to make the dry cleaning equipment part of the *mise-en-scène*—along with posters of cultural icons Keith Haring, the Beatles, and The Who.

Rooms on two levels have their own bathrooms with stall showers and toilets. One dorm room is reserved for women.

Every guest gets a key to a second private entrance; there is no curfew. The front office closes at 8 p.m., but staff sleeps across the street, which is handy if you misplace your key. Ask for their promotional literature, which answers just about any question you can imagine.

Our question is: why would you stay here when other uptown hostels—such as the Park View, Jazz on the Park, or Hostelling International—offer better accommodations at the same rates? Perhaps the 20-year-olds who choose to bunk here consider the cramped quarters and Bohemian whimsy an adventure.

PARK VIEW HOTEL

55 Central Park North
New York, NY 10026
(AT LENOX AVE.)

VALUE ★★★

CLEANLINESS ★★★

GUEST SERVICES ★★★

SECURITY ★★★

(★POOR - ★★★★★EXCELLENT)

CATEGORY	Hostel
PHONE	(212) 369-3340
FAX	(212) 369-3046
EMAIL	parkviewnyc@aol.com
WEBSITE	www.NewYorkCityHostels.com
RATES	Dorm beds: $20-$45 Private rooms: $50-$75
GUEST ROOMS	260 dorm beds plus 90 private rooms on 6 floors, all shared baths, some smoking rooms
ROOM AMENITIES	Linens, towels
RESTAURANTS	No, but a snack bar is open during peak season
BARS	None
CLIENTELE	Budget travelers at least 18 years old, unless accompanied by an adult

GUEST SERVICES	Dataphone, internet kiosks, phonecards, public phones, vending machines, TV lounge, communal kitchens, pay lockers, coin-operated laundry
PARKING	None
CANCELLATION POLICY	24 hours before check-in
WHEELCHAIR ACCESS	None

The sign outside may say hotel, but the Park View is 100 percent hostel. At press time, management was completing a much-needed renovation, replacing furniture and remodeling the communal kitchens.

Most of the rooms are dorm units with bunk beds, usually six beds to a room. All the accommodations have a little armoire and shelves. A private double is two twin beds or bunk beds. The larger family rooms offer one double bed with two to four bunk beds. Lockers are available in the lobby instead of in each unit. Small hallway bathrooms are private in that only one person can use them at a time.

Communal kitchens are located on each floor and feature a refrigerator, stove, and microwave. During busy season, the coffee bar sells sandwiches, yogurt, and other carry-out items. Also, the deli attached to the hostel is open until 11 p.m. There is a 24-hour deli across the street as well as a laundromat.

Guests are invited to hang out in the basement and watch a large-screen TV. A nearby bike shop offers hostelers a special rental rate. A subway station with express service to Times Square, Penn Station, and Wall Street is just around the corner.

Cash-paying guests must pay upon arrival. The front desk is staffed 24 hours, but there isn't a security door separating guest rooms from public areas. Officially, there are security personnel, but we didn't see any when we visited. If someone gets by the lobby, they have clear and easy access to guest accommodations.

HARLEM

SUGAR HILL INTERNATIONAL HOUSE

722 St. Nicholas Ave.
New York, NY 10031
(BETWEEN W. 146TH AND W. 147TH STREETS)

VALUE ★★

CLEANLINESS ★★

GUEST SERVICES ★★

SECURITY ★★★

(★POOR - ★★★★★EXCELLENT)

CATEGORY	Hostel
PHONE	(212) 926-7030
FAX	(212) 283-0108
EMAIL	infohostel@aol.com
WEBSITE	www.sugarhillhostel.com
RATES	Dorm beds: $25 Private rooms: $30 Cash only, includes taxes and tariffs Two-week maximum stay
GUEST ROOMS	Accommodations for 30 in bunk beds, all shared baths, no smoking
ROOM AMENITIES	Fans, bed linens
RESTAURANTS	None
BARS	None
CLIENTELE	Budget travelers at least 18 years old, unless accompanied by an adult
GUEST SERVICES	Communal kitchen, internet access in front office
PARKING	None
CANCELLATION POLICY	Must confirm day before arrival to keep reservation
WHEELCHAIR ACCESS	None

Sugar Hill is being renovated: that's the good news. The bad news is that it scores dead last on our short list of lodgings in this neighborhood. Boy, does it need work. Bathrooms should be gutted, staircases reinforced, and the kitchen updated. Also, the bunk bed mattresses should be replaced, but on the owner's long list of improvements, this is probably at the bottom.

One dormitory room is reserved for up to six women, who have their own sink and toilet. All the other dorms are coed with six to eight bunk beds per room. There aren't any lockers in the rooms, but guests can store small packages in the front office. A small communal kitchen offers a hot plate, toaster, stove, and refrigerator. Don't forget to bring your own towels.

A passport is required of all guests plus payment in cash upon arrival. You'll also pay a $10 key deposit. Neither house provides an official desk staffed 24 hours. Each guest receives a key for the room and a security code to open the front door. Guests may check email during office hours. Staff here are friendly and knowledgeable about the area; they just can't make up for the accommodations.

A laundromat is just up the block as well as a grocery store. Across the street, a subway station offers express service to Rockefeller Center, Herald Square, and Washington Square Park.

Until their renovation is done, consider skipping a few cups of latte or a few pints of Ben & Jerry's for a private room that may cost more but offers greater value. If you prefer a dorm bed in Harlem, the Park View gives bigger bang for the same bucks.

HARLEM

URBAN JEM GUEST HOUSE
2005 Fifth Ave.
New York, NY 10035
(BETWEEN E. 124TH AND E. 125TH STREETS)

VALUE ★ ★ ★ ★ ★

CLEANLINESS ★ ★ ★ ★

GUEST SERVICES ★ ★ ★

SECURITY ★ ★ ★ ★

(★POOR - ★★★★★EXCELLENT)

CATEGORY	Bed & Breakfast
PHONE	(212) 831-6029
FAX	(212) 831-6940
EMAIL	JMendel760@aol.com
WEBSITE	www.urbanjem.com
RATES	Shared bath: $90-$125 Private bath: $105-$140
GUEST ROOMS	4 rooms on 3 floors, 2 with shared baths, no smoking
ROOM AMENITIES	AC, cable TV, phone (free local calls), CD/clock radio, kitchenette, VCR, hair dryer, iron, full-length mirror
RESTAURANTS	None
BARS	None
CLIENTELE	Leisure travelers
GUEST SERVICES	Continental breakfast, self-service laundry, Sunday jazz series
PARKING	None
CANCELLATION POLICY	Nonrefundable 1-night deposit unless rescheduled within reasonable time
WHEELCHAIR ACCESS	None

Looking for an affordable, comfortable berth to watch the New York City Marathon? The Urban Jem is a good spot during the race as well as year-round. Opened in 1998, this Harlem B&B has watched approvingly as buildings around it have arisen from the dead. The Body Shop and a Starbuck's Coffee now draw customers where once boarded-up stores only attracted stray animals. It is close to a subway station with express service to Times Square and Penn Station.

Decorated in warm, rich tones and surprisingly roomy, all the accommodations have hardwood floors and large area rugs. Kitchenettes feature a refrigerator, stove, microwave, plates, and utensils. Two of the four rooms have private bathrooms. One room has two double futons and the others have queen beds. Closets are larger than expected. Most of the rooms have a small desk, but no voice mail or answering machines. Of average size, the bathrooms are fresh and clean.

Their continental breakfast includes biscuits, instant hot cereals, and frozen waffles; in warm weather, you can eat it outdoors on the deck. There is a rambling cat in residence, but he usually stays downstairs. During the evenings, the owners occasionally plan author readings and just kicked off a Sunday jazz series. Events are free and open to the public, but donations are requested.

This B&B requires a minimum two-night stay on weekends and holidays. Payment in full is expected upon arrival. Daily maid service is $7.50 per day, otherwise rooms are cleaned once a week. Of course, they are cleaned between guests. Laundry is $3 per day, self service. Guests can send and receive faxes for a nominal fee.

The Urban Jem Guest House is easy to find, thanks to white lights around the main door and along the stoop. And it's easy to remember for all the right reasons.

HARLEM

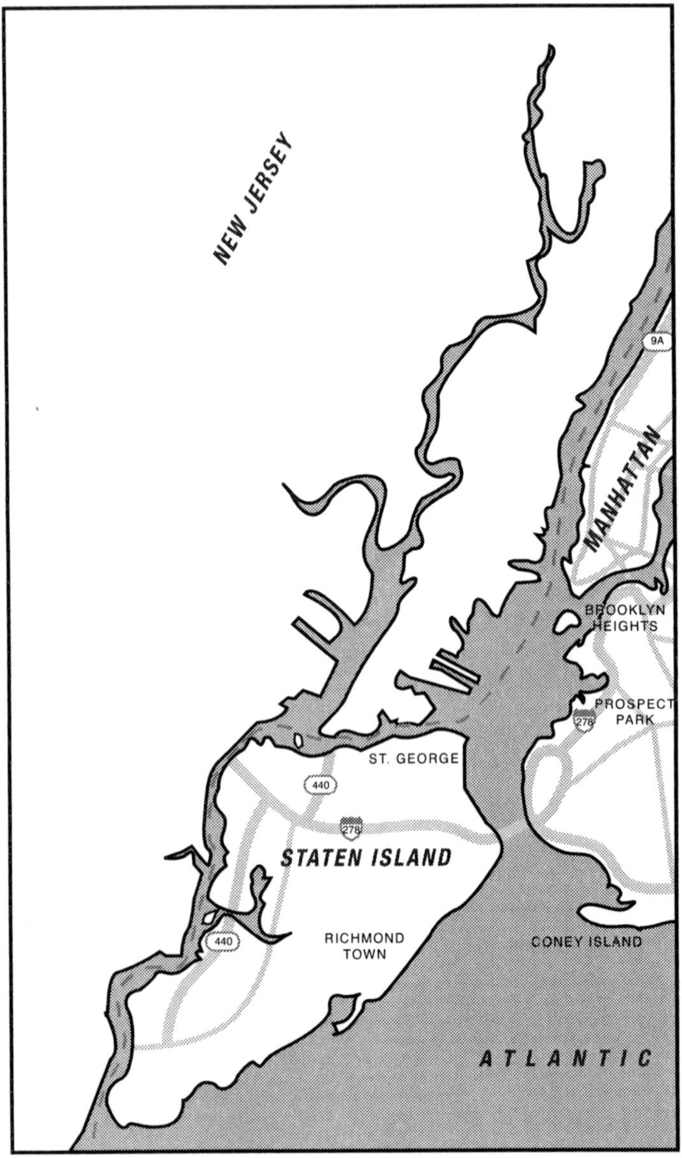
NEW JERSEY
9A
MANHATTAN
BROOKLYN HEIGHTS
PROSPECT PARK
278
ST. GEORGE
440
278
STATEN ISLAND
RICHMOND TOWN
440
CONEY ISLAND
ATLANTIC

THE OUTER BOROUGHS

THE BRONX

New York's northernmost borough had a notorious reputation before urban redevelopment made it safer and more pleasant to visit its world-class attractions. For sports fans, that attraction is probably Yankee Stadium. But most spectators don't realize that they can tour the field, clubhouse, and dugout any time the baseball team is out of town. The Bronx Zoo is considered by many to be America's greatest zoo. One of the reasons is its success in creating simulated natural habitats—like the Wild Asia exhibit, where tigers and elephants roam freely on 40 acres, or the Himalayan Highlands exhibit, a refuge for rare species like the red panda and snow leopard. A children's playground and park make the zoo a popular family daytrip.

Across from the Bronx Zoo is the New York Botanical Garden, where you can experience a variety of ecosystems in the conservatory and wander among floral splendor outside. City Island, off the eastern shore in Long Island Sound, was originally a fishing community. Today a short causeway from the mainland brings seafood-hungry tourists.

LE REFUGE INN BED AND BREAKFAST

620 City Island Ave.
Bronx, NY 10464

VALUE ★ ★ ★ ★ ★
CLEANLINESS ★ ★ ★ ★ ★
GUEST SERVICES ★ ★
SECURITY ★ ★ ★

(★POOR - ★★★★★EXCELLENT)

CATEGORY	Bed and Breakfast
PHONE	(718) 885-2478
FAX	(718) 885-1519
EMAIL	lerefugeinn@lerefugeinn.com
WEBSITE	www.lerefugeinn.com
RATES	Singles: $74 Doubles: $96 Suite: $160 Cottage: $160 Offers weekend packages Rates include taxes
GUEST ROOMS	6 rooms share baths, the suite and cottage have private baths
ROOM AMENITIES	AC, cable TV, CD player, phone in cottage, fridge available
RESTAURANTS	Sunday for brunch and lunch, Wed.-Sun. for dinner, French cuisine with a $45 prix-fixe, three-course dinner
BARS	Restaurant has a liquor license
CLIENTELE	A mix of business and leisure American and foreign visitors
GUEST SERVICES	Continental breakfast, Sunday concerts
PARKING	Yes
CANCELLATION POLICY	7 days before arrival or 1 month prior for a stay of more than 2 weeks
WHEELCHAIR ACCESS	None

Innkeeper and chef Pierre Saint-Denis owns this former sea captain's house on tiny City Island. Diners who have enjoyed his Manhattan restaurant of the same name can also enjoy the flavors of his French cuisine in this relaxing setting. In spirit, the inn is far removed from Gotham's merry-go-round, but you can stand on the shore of Long Island Sound and still see the skyscrapers of the Financial District.

Saint-Denis chose his colors and themes to recreate an inn in his native Normandy. Rooms feature toile-patterned wallpaper and curtains, rustic antiques, and throw rugs over hardwood floors. Guests can share a glass of wine with the innkeeper/chef in his walk-through kitchen and admire the terra-cotta floor, painted ceramic tiles and pottery, bleached wood cabinets, and brick oven. Meals and a continental breakfast are served in a dining room on the main floor. This *auberge* is a refuge from urban toil, and City Island's other attractions make it well worth a trip.

This former sea captain's house makes a great weekend getaway.
Credit: Le Refuge Inn Bed and Breakfast

BROOKLYN

A Tree Grows in Brooklyn, Last Exit to Brooklyn, "Crossing Brooklyn Ferry"—our literature is rich in portraits of Brooklynites, as is our popular culture courtesy of famed sons and daughters like Woody Allen, Beverly Sills, and Barbra Streisand. If Brooklyn were a separate city, it would be the fourth largest in America, with 2.3 million residents and 93 distinct ethnic groups. Like Manhattan, it's a collection of colorful neighborhoods, each with its own identity. Brooklyn Heights, on the northern rim, has its "old-money" mansions and panoramic views of the New York skyline. Williamsburg's converted lofts are warrens for transplanted East Village artists. Carroll Gardens has its Italian-American community, Brighton Beach its Russian emigrés. Crown Heights embraces both West Indians and Hasidic Jews, though not without some racial tension. Park Slope has its brownstones and the pastoral beauty of Prospect Park. Near the park stand the Brooklyn Museum of Art, Brooklyn Children's Museum, and Brooklyn Botanic Gardens, all worth a leisurely visit.

AKWAABA MANSION BED AND BREAKFAST

347 MacDonough St.
Brooklyn, NY 11233
(BETWEEN STUYVESANT AND LEWIS AVENUES)

VALUE ★ ★ ★ ★ ★
CLEANLINESS ★ ★ ★ ★ ★
GUEST SERVICES ★ ★ ★
SECURITY ★ ★ ★ ★
(★POOR - ★★★★★EXCELLENT)

CATEGORY	Bed and Breakfast
PHONE	(718) 455-5958
FAX	(718) 774-1744
EMAIL	akwaabainn@aol.com
WEBSITE	www.akwaaba.com
RATES	Weekdays: $120-$135 Weekends: $135-$150
GUEST ROOMS	4 suites with private baths, 2 with Jacuzzi baths
ROOM AMENITIES	Clock radio, AC
RESTAURANTS	Akwaaba Café serves Southern American, African, and Caribbean dinners on weekends
BARS	None
CLIENTELE	American tourists
GUEST SERVICES	Full breakfast, TV room, library, sitting parlor with working fireplace, portable phone, iron on request
PARKING	None
CANCELLATION POLICY	Two weeks before arrival
WHEELCHAIR ACCESS	None

The name means "welcome" in Ghana, and that's what innkeepers Monique Greenwood and Glenn Pogue do with a flourish in their 1860 Italianate villa.

Afrocentric décor and collectibles distinguish four suites, each with a large bedroom and sitting room, each named for a cultural theme. The Jumping the Broom Suite, for example, is aglow in shades of white with a

Jacuzzi for two, mood-setting lights on dimmers, candles, and a canopy bed. The Ashante, Regal Retreat, and Black Memorabilia suites are equally luxurious, as are the common rooms. In winter, the parlor fireplace beckons, in summer it's the sunporch or shady garden.

Tea is served at 4 p.m., cookies at bedtime, and a full Southern-style breakfast in the a.m. For your evening meal, you can head down the street, where the same owners run the Akwaaba Café. At press time, the café was open only on weekends. There's jazz on Friday nights and a Sunday brunch for $11.95. An ethnic menu features Southern, African, Caribbean, and Mediterranean dishes.

The Brooklyn neighborhood called "Bed-Stuy" isn't the handiest overnight for those who want to sightsee in Manhattan. But it's delightful for honeymooners or any couple who wants to reignite the spark of romance and craves pampering and privacy. This memorable lodging sits on a quiet, tree-lined street, and the subway to Manhattan is just two blocks away.

BAISLEY HOUSE

294 Hoyt St.
Brooklyn, NY 11231
(BETWEEN UNION AND SACKETT STREETS)

VALUE ★ ★ ★ ★

CLEANLINESS ★ ★ ★ ★

GUEST SERVICES ★ ★

SECURITY ★ ★ ★ ★

(★POOR - ★★★★★EXCELLENT)

CATEGORY	Bed and breakfast
PHONE	(718) 935-1959
FAX	(718) 935-1959
EMAIL	BaisleyHouseNYC@aol.com
WEBSITE	www.Brooklynx.org/Tourism/BaisleyHouse
RATES	$95-$150 2-night minimum, 50 percent deposit required. Ask about spa packages
GUEST ROOMS	3 share one bath, all are nonsmoking

ROOM AMENITIES	AC, cable TV with VCR, phone with free local calls (need a phone card for long-distance calls)
RESTAURANTS	None
BARS	None
CLIENTELE	60 percent Europeans
GUEST SERVICES	A generous hot and cold breakfast. The chef will try to accommodate dietary requests. Spa services
PARKING	None
CANCELLATION POLICY	2 weeks before arrival with a $25 fee. Deposit is nonrefundable if cancellation is less than 2 weeks
WHEELCHAIR ACCESS	None

This Victorian brownstone in the residential Carroll Gardens neighborhood has been lovingly restored by interior decorator/owner Harry Paul. Sitting in the burgundy-and-gold drawing room is like entering a time portal. You can almost imagine Charles Baisley, who built the row house in 1853, gazing at himself in the ornate mirror that hangs above the white marble mantlepiece. Certainly he would approve of Paul's collection of 18th- and 19th-century oil paintings and Greek statues. Paul serves breakfast in a small dining room or, weather permitting, a small garden overflowing with English roses and white garden furniture.

The largest double has a queen-sized, four-poster bed; paisley wallpaper; heavy draperies; a silk brocaded sofa; oriental carpets; and a walk-in closet. The next largest has a full-sized French quarter bed, and the smallest a twin sleigh bed. One small bathroom serves all three rooms, but it's got everything you'll ever need. Guests get room and front door keys, and there's no curfew. One room is devoted to holistic spa treatments.

Carroll Gardens is lively with plenty of interesting restaurants, especially on Smith Street. When you've exhausted the sights in Brooklyn, the F train will take you to midtown Manhattan in 20 minutes.

BROOKLYN

BED AND BREAKFAST ON THE PARK

113 Prospect Park West
Brooklyn, NY 11215
(BETWEEN SIXTH AND SEVENTH STREETS)

VALUE ★ ★ ★ ★

CLEANLINESS ★ ★ ★ ★ ★

GUEST SERVICES ★ ★ ★

SECURITY ★ ★ ★ ★

(★POOR - ★★★★★EXCELLENT)

CATEGORY	Bed and Breakfast
PHONE	(718) 499-6115
FAX	(718) 499-1385
EMAIL	liana@bbnyc.com
WEBSITE	www.bbnyc.com
RATES	$125-$300 Plus taxes and a 10 percent staff tip. 1-night stays accepted day before only. Minimum 2-night stay, 3 nights on some weekends
GUEST ROOMS	8 rooms, 6 with private baths, 3 with fireplaces, all nonsmoking
ROOM AMENITIES	AC, cable TV, phone with voice mail and dataport, hair dryer, candy and cookies, iron and ironing board
RESTAURANTS	None
BARS	None
CLIENTELE	American and international vacationers
GUEST SERVICES	Full breakfast, communal kitchen
PARKING	None
CANCELLATION POLICY	Deposit is returned up to 10 days before arrival minus a $25 charge
WHEELCHAIR ACCESS	None

You're never very far from the Big Apple in this four-story Victorian townhouse. (In warm weather the Manhattan skyline is within sight from the rooftop garden.) But you're far enough to ensure tranquillity and to explore the woodsy charm of Prospect Park, directly across the street. Be prepared to catch your breath when you enter the lavishly decorated parlor; it's full of museum-quality paintings and antiques. Some of the period furnishings and features to note throughout this B&B include oriental carpets, Rococo armoires, gas-burning fireplaces, stained-glass windows, and intricately carved moldings of oak, African mahogany, and bird's-eye maple.

Breakfast is equally lavish and might include fruit crepes, pancakes, and sticky buns served in silver baskets and on fine china in the formal dining room. Two guest rooms share a bath, all are good-sized. The least expensive is the French Cottage, the most expensive is the Grand Victorian Suite, which boasts feather pillows, bird's-eye maple bay windows topped with stained glass, an antique tub, a working fireplace, a huge canopy bed draped with French lace, and a second room with a single bed. The Lady Liberty Room on the fourth floor has access to a rooftop garden and views of the torch-waving Lady as well as the Financial District.

Only two of these rooms meet our budget parameters, but staying here is an experience you'll want to reserve for a special occasion when counting pennies isn't a priority. The setting is memorable, the Brooklyn Museum and Botanic Gardens are 12 blocks away, and Manhattan is a 30-minute subway ride.

BROOKLYN

NEW YORK MARRIOTT BROOKLYN

333 Adams St.
Brooklyn, NY 11201
(BETWEEN TILLARY AND WILLOUGHBY STREETS)

VALUE ★ ★ ★ ★ (WEEKENDS ONLY)
CLEANLINESS ★ ★ ★ ★
GUEST SERVICES ★ ★ ★ ★
SECURITY ★ ★ ★ ★

(★POOR - ★★★★★EXCELLENT)

CATEGORY	Full Services
PHONE	(718) 246-7000 (800) 228-9290 Reservations
FAX	(718) 246-0563
EMAIL	None
WEBSITE	www.nycmarriott.com. Occasionally offers promotional packages
RATES	$139-$279 Weekend rates are lowest Discount to AAA members
GUEST ROOMS	376 rooms on 7 floors include 21 suites, 80 percent nonsmoking
ROOM AMENITIES	AC, cable TV with pay movies and games, 2 two-line phones with voice mail and dataport, high-speed internet access, iron, safe, coffeemaker, mini-bar
RESTAURANTS	Archives is open 6 a.m.-10 p.m.
BARS	Yes
CLIENTELE	Mostly corporate guests on weekdays, leisure guests on weekends
GUEST SERVICES	Room service 6 a.m.-midnight, fitness center, concierge, valet laundry, business center, gift shop, meeting space, lap pool and excercise equipment
PARKING	$15 a day
CANCELLATION POLICY	Before 4 p.m. day of arrival
WHEELCHAIR ACCESS	19 rooms

No one can claim this Marriott, new in 1998 and still the borough's only full-services hotel, wasn't designed with flair. The entrance to the second-floor lobby is a forest of greenery: palms and banana trees in marble planters and a trompe l'oeil dome above that mimics the conservatory dome at the Brooklyn Botanic Gardens. It's also designed to showcase Brooklyn's rich cultural history, lest you forget where you're staying. Behind the front desk is a mural of the Brooklyn Bridge, and Archives restaurant takes its name from memorabilia—like photos of the Dodgers baseball team—displayed in glass cases. Even the locally brewed ale on tap at the bar shouts "Brooklyn" with pride.

From the lobby—with its gleaming marble floors, recessed lighting, and expensive-looking carpets—you ascend with a dull thud to your guest room. The décor is standard Marriott, but hallways and rooms are spacious. Standard doubles with either a king- or two full-sized beds are clean and fresh-smelling, though they show some wear. An armoire holds a TV, mini-bar, drawers, and a safe that's the perfect size for your laptop. There's a desk, high-speed internet access for a fee, phones with dataports, climate control, a large walk-in closet with iron and ironing board, and a roomy bathroom that's fully equipped.

Rooms on Concierge Level provide extra pampering for extra bucks: terry-cloth robes, continental breakfast, and turn-down service. Inside rooms are the quietest, but even rooms on Adams Street aren't noisy. The fitness center, run by Eastern Athletics Club, boasts a lap pool, whirlpool, lockers, and every type of exercise machine. This hotel is popular with business guests because it offers extensive services, but it has advantages for tourists as well. They'll get a great weekend rate and still be only minutes away from Manhattan by subway.

New arrivals ascend to the Marriott's second-floor lobby under a trompe l'oeil dome. Credit: New York Marriott Brooklyn

QUEENS

Most people who visit Queens never get farther than its two airports, La Guardia and John F. Kennedy International. Not surprisingly, that is where major hotels are located. It's New York's largest borough, with a diverse ethnic population, but lacks any central focal point. Sports fans will recognize names like Shea Stadium and Flushing Meadows, home to the U.S. Open tennis tournament. The Astoria neighborhood has recently been rediscovered by the film industry, and you can visit the American Museum of the Moving Image in the old Paramount Studios. Astoria also claims the largest Greek community outside Greece itself. Jackson Heights boasts "Little India," with a concentration of aromatic restaurants, as well as a thriving South American population. Long Island City has the Isamu Noguchi Garden Museum, Socrates Sculpture Park, and PS 1 Contemporary Art Center. Like other Queens neighborhoods, it's an affordable alternative to Manhattan's pricey real estate.

QUEENS

AIRWAY MOTOR INN AT LA GUARDIA

82-20 Astoria Blvd.
E. Elmhurst, NY 11370
(BETWEEN 82ND AND 83RD STREETS)

VALUE ★★★
CLEANLINESS ★★★
GUEST SERVICES ★
SECURITY ★★★

(★POOR - ★★★★★EXCELLENT)

CATEGORY	Motel
PHONE	(718) 565-5100
	(800) 356-0250 Reservations
FAX	(718) 565-5194
EMAIL	None
WEBSITE	None
RATES	$111-$129
GUEST ROOMS	58 rooms on 4 floors in 2 buildings; some are nonsmoking
ROOM AMENITIES	AC, cable TV, hair dryer, mini-fridge, phone with voice mail and dataport
RESTAURANTS	None
BARS	None
CLIENTELE	Airline passengers and business travelers
GUEST SERVICES	Video rentals, valet laundry, free airport shuttle
PARKING	Yes, small lot
CANCELLATION POLICY	Before 6 p.m. day of arrival
WHEELCHAIR ACCESS	One

This motel might better be called the Motorway. The constant roar of traffic on Astoria Boulevard makes you feel like you're in a box seat right near the track at the Indy 500.

Rooms in the older, lobby building are preferable to rooms in the newer building, which can be rented for four hours or more. Those rooms are badly beaten up. Doubles in the older building feature either a king- or two full-sized beds. Four units have an extra sofa bed. Carpet and furniture look new, mattresses are firm, wall mirrors are handy, there's adequate lighting and new closets. A large armoire houses a TV and mini-fridge as well as drawer space. The bathroom with a tub/shower combo provides plenty of space.

This is the least desirable choice of the hotels we visited near La Guardia, but it will do if the others are booked. Pack earplugs, and bring your own videotapes. A rental costs $6.

BEST WESTERN CARLTON HOUSE JFK AIRPORT

138-10 135th Ave.
Jamaica, NY 11436
(AT N. CONDUIT AVE.)

VALUE ★ ★ ★ ★ ★

CLEANLINESS ★ ★ ★ ★

GUEST SERVICES ★ ★ ★ ★ ★

SECURITY ★ ★ ★ ★ ★

(★POOR - ★★★★★EXCELLENT)

CATEGORY	Full Services
PHONE	(718) 322-8700 (877) 535-4683 Reservations
FAX	(718) 529-0749
EMAIL	On the website
WEBSITE	www.bestwestern.com/carlton house
RATES	$129-$199 Discounts to AAA and AARP members. Children under 12 stay free
GUEST ROOMS	330 rooms on 9 floors, some are nonsmoking
ROOM AMENITIES	AC, cable TV with pay movies, coffeemaker, iron, hair dryer, 2-line phone with voice mail and dataport, mini-bar, safe
RESTAURANTS	Café Manhattan serves breakfast, lunch, and dinner

BARS	The Oyster Bar
CLIENTELE	Corporate and airline personnel, primarily
GUEST SERVICES	Room service till 11:30 p.m., fitness center, meeting rooms, business services, gift shop, valet laundry, free shuttle to and from airport, TV lounge
PARKING	Yes
CANCELLATION POLICY	Before 4 p.m. day of arrival
WHEELCHAIR ACCESS	Yes, nonsmoking rooms

Forget what you know about the Best Western; this hotel is a different breed. It benefits from an older building's generous space, in both public and private quarters, and graceful features it inherited from its former incarnation as a Hilton. The lobby is awesome. You could land a 747 here, but that would break the aura of quiet refinement created by classical music, fresh floral bouquets, richly patterned carpets, glass chandeliers, and blonde wall paneling. The Concorde Lounge, just off the lobby, is an elegant oasis with floor-to-ceiling windows. It's the perfect place to catnap or catch up on the day's news.

Park yourself here for a touch of elegance at reasonable rates.
Credit: Best Western Carlton House JFK

All guest rooms are clean and nicely appointed with mint green carpets and matching floral bedspreads. A massive armoire holds the TV and mini-bar plus it offers several drawers to store your clothes. You might need that space because the walk-in closet is teensy. There is ample work space and central heat and air; no thermostats. Small bathrooms are unimpressive. All rooms, except the suites, are identical in size and décor. Services here are too lengthy to list, but they include a "doctor on call" and foreign currency exchange. Needless to say, the Café Manhattan's international menu and stocked wine cellar isn't standard Best Western either.

The hotel's $195 Park and Fly program, a one-night stay and parking for up to a week, is outmatched by other hotels. Nothing has changed here since BW took over from Hilton except the outside logo, stationery, and room rates. You'll benefit from those lower rates and get a lot of value in a plush setting.

BEST WESTERN CITY VIEW INN

33-17 Greenpoint Ave.
Long Island City, NY 11101
(BETWEEN BRADLEY AND GALE AVENUES)

VALUE ★ ★ ★ ★

CLEANLINESS ★ ★ ★ ★ ★

GUEST SERVICES ★ ★ ★ ★

SECURITY ★ ★ ★ ★ ★

(★POOR - ★★★★★EXCELLENT)

CATEGORY	Limited Services
PHONE	(718) 392-8400
	(800) 248-9843 Reservations
FAX	(718) 392-2110
EMAIL	None
WEBSITE	www.bestwestern.com
	Offers promotional packages
RATES	$120-$150
	Children under 12 stay free,
	10 percent discount to seniors,
	military personnel, and members
	of AAA and AARP

QUEENS

GUEST ROOMS	71 rooms on 5 floors, most are nonsmoking
ROOM AMENITIES	AC, cable TV with VCR, coffeemaker, iron, hair dryer, phone, some Jacuzzis, *USA Today*, clock radio
RESTAURANTS	None
BARS	None
CLIENTELE	A mix
GUEST SERVICES	Exercise bikes in 55 rooms, continental breakfast, free shuttle to local restaurants and La Guardia Airport, valet laundry, 24-hour coffee and muffins, meeting room, video rentals
PARKING	Yes
CANCELLATION POLICY	24 hours before check-in
WHEELCHAIR ACCESS	None

This Best Western occupies a 1890 school building in a semi-residential neighborhood. That means the area is fairly quiet and, as a bonus, a free shuttle will take you to La Guardia in 10 minutes or to the #7 subway into Manhattan in the same time.

Guest rooms won't win any decorating awards, but they are presentable, spacious, newly furnished, and most of them have exercise bikes (for you fitness fanatics). There are built-in armoires with lots of clothes storage space and a thermostat to control heat and air. Small bathrooms have tub/showers, hair dryers, and toiletries. If you've always dreamed of waking up in a canopy bed, this is your chance. On the other hand, you might prefer one of the eight rooms with Jacuzzi tubs. They cost $150 a night.

Among a host of amenities and guest services is a complimentary *USA Today*, a mini-fridge, a clock radio, continental breakfast, and free coffee, tea, and muffins any time you feel like a snack. If you want more than a snack, the shuttle van will take you to a local restaurant.

The hotel is just minutes away from Shea Stadium and U.S. Open tennis, and only two miles from midtown Manhattan. Its best rooms do have "city views" of the Empire State Building and Chrysler Building. If you're tempted to test your "little town" shoes, you can sign up for a tour of the Big Apple at the front desk. The tour company provides door-to-door service.

SLEEP CHEAP IN NEW YORK

BEST WESTERN EDEN PARK HOTEL

113-10 Corona Ave.
Flushing, NY 11368
(AT 108TH ST.)

VALUE ★ ★ ★ ★
CLEANLINESS ★ ★ ★ ★ ★
GUEST SERVICES ★ ★ ★ ★
SECURITY ★ ★ ★ ★ ★

(★POOR - ★★★★★EXCELLENT)

CATEGORY	Limited Services
PHONE	(718) 699-4400 (800) 521-0099 Reservations
FAX	(718) 760-3916
EMAIL	None
WEBSITE	www.bestwestern.com/edenparkhotel
RATES	$99-$259 Discounts to AAA and AARP members Children under 17 stay free
GUEST ROOMS	74 rooms on 5 floors, most are nonsmoking
ROOM AMENITIES	AC, cable TV with VCR, iron, hair dryer, phone with voice mail and dataport, coffeemaker, mini-fridge available on request
RESTAURANTS	Yes, open for breakfast and dinner
BARS	Yes
CLIENTELE	A mix of business and leisure travelers
GUEST SERVICES	Fitness room, meeting room, valet laundry, free shuttle to JFK and La Guardia, room service
PARKING	Yes
CANCELLATION POLICY	24 hours before check-in
WHEELCHAIR ACCESS	One room

As of press time, this hotel was completing a total renovation. Doubles are roomy and standard in size. They are decorated with bright floral spreads, mahogany-stained furniture, and sea-green carpets. Full-length mirrors cover one wall, which adds the illusion of even more space.

There's a 25-inch TV with VCR, phone with voice mail and dataport, firm mattresses, desk, climate control, rack with clothes hangers, and small bathroom with a tub/shower, hair dryer, and toiletries. Some doubles sleep up to four in a queen bed and sofa bed. Ask for an inside room unless you want a view of 10 lanes of speeding traffic.

But there's more to this neighborhood than the exhaust fumes of the Long Island Expressway and Grand Central Parkway. A park nearby is safe for runners to jog in during the day. The U.S. Open tennis at Flushing Meadows, Shea Stadium, and the New York Hall of Science are all within walking distance. A hotel van will shuttle you to both airports and to the #7 train into Manhattan.

This attractive property has already improved its facilities, and the owner has even bigger plans. Its restaurant and bar, fitness room, and friendly front desk staff offer convenience and comfort at a reasonable price.

FLUSHING YMCA

138-46 Northern Blvd.
Flushing, NY 11354
(BETWEEN UNION AND BOWNE STREETS)

VALUE ★ ★ ★ ★

CLEANLINESS ★ ★ ★ ★

GUEST SERVICES ★ ★ ★

SECURITY ★ ★ ★ ★

(★POOR - ★★★★★EXCELLENT)

CATEGORY	YMCA
PHONE	(718) 961-6880
FAX	(718) 445-8392
EMAIL	flushingguestrooms@ymcanyc.org
WEBSITE	www.ymcanyc.org
RATES	Singles: $50 Doubles: $70 Triples: $80
GUEST ROOMS	127 private rooms with shared bathrooms, some are nonsmoking
ROOM AMENITIES	AC, cable TV
RESTAURANTS	None

BARS	None
CLIENTELE	Low-maintenance travelers
GUEST SERVICES	Breakfast voucher, maid service, luggage room, fitness center with two pools
PARKING	Yes
CANCELLATION POLICY	Before 6 p.m. day of arrival
WHEELCHAIR ACCESS	None

Whether you're a "distressed passenger" or just cruising the sights in downtown Flushing, this Y offers an affordable alternative to the higher-priced properties surrounding La Guardia Airport. You'll sleep in a carpeted, small, clean room with AC and cable TV. Shared bathrooms with five or six stall showers and toilets are located in the hallways as are public phones. Two floors are reserved for male guests, one floor for both sexes, and two floors are occupied by a fitness center. The extensive gym and two swimming pools, all included in your room rate, are a great perk. There's a voucher for breakfast at a local diner.

This part of Northern Boulevard is relatively safe and lined with lots of stores and restaurants worth exploring. The YMCA is two blocks from the #7 train into Manhattan's Grand Central Station and 10 minutes to La Guardia or 15 minutes to JFK by bus. Reserve your room several months ahead for summer; at least a week ahead at other times of the year. A photo ID is required at check-in.

QUEENS

LA GUARDIA COURTYARD BY MARRIOTT

90-10 Grand Central Parkway
E. Elmhurst, NY 11369
(AT 94TH ST.)

VALUE ★ ★ ★ ★ ★ (WEEKENDS ONLY)
CLEANLINESS ★ ★ ★ ★ ★
GUEST SERVICES ★ ★ ★ ★ ★
SECURITY ★ ★ ★ ★ ★
(★POOR - ★★★★★EXCELLENT)

CATEGORY	Limited Services
PHONE	(718) 446-4800
	(800) 321-2211 Reservations
FAX	(718) 446-5733
EMAIL	None
WEBSITE	www.courtyard.com/lgaca
RATES	$99-$259
	Lowest rates apply on weekends
	Discounts to AAA and AARP members
GUEST ROOMS	288 rooms on 5 floors include 7 suites, most are nonsmoking
ROOM AMENITIES	AC, cable TV with pay movies, coffeemaker, iron, hair dryer, 2 phones with voice mail, high-speed internet access, *USA Today* (weekdays), *New York Times* (weekends)
RESTAURANTS	Courtyard Café serves breakfast, lunch, and dinner
BARS	Courtyard Lounge
CLIENTELE	20 percent airline crews, 80 percent business and tourists
GUEST SERVICES	Fitness center, outdoor pool, meeting rooms, business center, valet laundry, free shuttle to La Guardia leaves every 15 minutes, gift shop, room service 5 p.m.-11:30 p.m.
PARKING	Yes
CANCELLATION POLICY	Before 4 p.m. day of arrival
WHEELCHAIR ACCESS	Yes

"Courtyards" are Marriott's answer to a business traveler's special needs. This one offers more guest services than most, but isn't full services like the nearby La Guardia Marriott. What its low-ceilinged lobby lacks in style it makes up for in acreage: you could accommodate a small city here. There's a restaurant, bar, and lounge on lobby level with the TV tuned to CNBC, so you can see how your stocks are trading. Room service is only available for dinner, though the restaurant is open for breakfast, lunch, and dinner.

Guest rooms are standard Marriott: no surprises. Doubles offer either a king- or two full-sized beds and are identical in size and décor. You can really spread out your work on the desk and take advantage of the high-speed modem to connect to the internet. When you want to relax, there's a soft lounge chair (the mattresses, alas, are equally soft). No overhead lights, but there are walk-in closets with an iron and ironing board. Large bathrooms are fully equipped with hair dryers and a handrail on the tub (for us seniors). Two-room suites feature similar amenities plus a mini-fridge and microwave. Double-paned windows and sound-proofed walls ensure quiet sleep.

In addition to soundproofing, this Marriott boasts an outdoor pool, whirlpool, fully equipped fitness center, business center, and meeting space. Except during the U.S. Open tennis championship, when you'll pay top dollar, rooms here are a bargain on weekends.

LA GUARDIA MARRIOTT

102-05 Ditmars Blvd.
E. Elmhurst, NY 11369
(AT 102ND STREET)

VALUE ★ ★ ★ ★ ★ (WEEKENDS ONLY)

CLEANLINESS ★ ★ ★ ★ ★

GUEST SERVICES ★ ★ ★ ★ ★

SECURITY ★ ★ ★ ★ ★

(★ POOR - ★ ★ ★ ★ ★ EXCELLENT)

CATEGORY	Full Services
PHONE	(718) 565-8900
	(800) 228-9290 Reservations

FAX	(718) 898-4955
	(718) 533-3001 Reservations
EMAIL	None
WEBSITE	www.marriott.com
RATES	$109-$259
	Ask about discounts and weekend rates
GUEST ROOMS	432 rooms on 9 floors, 2 floors are nonsmoking
ROOM AMENITIES	AC, cable TV with pay movies, coffeemaker, iron, hair dryer, heat lamp, 2 two-line phones with voice mail and dataport
RESTAURANTS	JW's serves breakfast, lunch, and dinner
BARS	Empire Lounge
CLIENTELE	About 30 percent groups; the rest are tourists and business travelers
GUEST SERVICES	Fitness center, indoor pool, meeting rooms, business center, valet laundry, free shuttle to La Guardia every 15 minutes, concierge, gift shop, room service until 1 a.m.
PARKING	$10 a day; $15 a day long term
CANCELLATION POLICY	Before 6 p.m. day of arrival
WHEELCHAIR ACCESS	9 rooms

This Marriott is much larger and more glamorous than the Courtyard By Marriott nearby, but if crowds bother you, the Courtyard may be a better choice. The tradeoff is extras like room service and a concierge level vs. the need to compete with 200 SONY sales reps.

About half of their guest rooms had been "refreshed" by press time. The new rooms feature floral-patterned comforters, wall art, and marble-top sinks in the bathrooms. They are brighter and livelier than the older rooms, but all rooms have two phones with voice mail and dataports, work desks with swivel chairs, closets, climate control, and average-sized bathrooms with hair dryers and Neutrogena bath products. Weekend rates offer the best value, but if you're staying during the week, you might consider paying $20 more to upgrade to Concierge Level. You'll enjoy extras perks like happy hour, a continental breakfast, and, of course, the concierge.

Gleaming marble and plush carpets cover floors in the public areas. A fitness center is staffed during the day and locked when no attendant is present. JW Restaurant is an attractive space designed with large picture windows and elegant furnishings. You can stay tuned to sports on one of six TVs in the sports bar and to airline departures and arrivals on a monitor in the lobby. If you want to unwind, there's a 50-foot indoor pool with skylights and a sliding glass door to a patio that's ideal for sunbathing if you can tolerate the roar of jet engines. Take advantage of the whirlpool, sauna, steam room, and lockers, if you have time.

This Marriott makes a perfect headquarters if you are staying several days. You'll never have to venture out on Ditmars Boulevard for a chicken sandwich or the daily newspapers.

PAN AMERICAN HOTEL

7900 Queens Blvd.
Flushing, NY 11373
(AT 51ST AVE.)

VALUE ★ ★ ★ ★

CLEANLINESS ★ ★ ★ ★

GUEST SERVICES ★ ★ ★

SECURITY ★ ★ ★ ★

(★POOR - ★★★★★EXCELLENT)

CATEGORY	Full Services
PHONE	(718) 446-7676
	(800) 937-7374 Reservations
FAX	(718) 446-7991
EMAIL	reservations@panamhotel.com
WEBSITE	www.panamhotel.com
RATES	$99-$169
	Ask about discounts
GUEST ROOMS	216 rooms on 6 floors, most are nonsmoking
ROOM AMENITIES	AC, cable TV, hair dryer, phone with voice mail and dataport, mini-fridge
RESTAURANTS	Duke's Steak House

BARS	Yes
CLIENTELE	A mix
GUEST SERVICES	Free pass to Bally's fitness center, internet kiosk, meeting room, business services for a fee, valet laundry, free shuttle to JFK and La Guardia runs about every 2 hours, room service
PARKING	Yes
CANCELLATION POLICY	24 hours before check-in
WHEELCHAIR ACCESS	None

Lobby and guest rooms here are furnished in 1950s motel-style. The suites break rank: they are designed with more care and expense. Singles and doubles are spacious and clean with very basic furniture, central heat and air, a small desk, two large mirrors, a three-drawer dresser, an armoire with a few clothes hangers, and double-paned windows. Rooms overlooking 51st Avenue are preferable to ones overlooking clamorous Queens Boulevard. Small bathrooms are equipped with tub/showers and hair dryers. Families can rent an oversized double with a sofa bed.

Suites feature a pleasing traditional décor, a king or two queen-sized bed, sofa bed, and small armoire. There is a sitting area but no second room. The one we visited smelled of cigarettes though a sign warned against smoking. There are ice and vending machines on each floor and three elevators to whisk you there quickly.

This hotel is a fair deal for the price with an assortment of bars, restaurants, and stores within walking distance along the boulevard. Take the R train or the Q60 bus into Manhattan and a free shuttle to either JFK or La Guardia. But remember that the shuttle isn't on call. It runs on a set schedule, so plan accordingly.

RADISSON HOTEL JFK AIRPORT

135-30 140th St.
Jamaica, NY 11436
(AT 140TH ST.)

VALUE ★ ★ ★

CLEANLINESS ★ ★ ★

GUEST SERVICES ★ ★ ★ ★ ★

SECURITY ★ ★ ★ ★

(★POOR - ★★★★★EXCELLENT)

CATEGORY	Full Services
PHONE	(718) 322-2300 (800) 333-3333 Reservations
FAX	(718) 322-6894
EMAIL	rhi_jfka@radisson.com
WEBSITE	www.radisson.com
RATES	$139-$239 Discounts for seniors and AARP and AAA members
GUEST ROOMS	386 rooms on 12 floors include 21 junior suites
ROOM AMENITIES	AC, cable TV with pay movies and games, coffeemaker, iron, hair dryer, 2-line phone with voice mail and dataport, high-speed internet access
RESTAURANTS	The Big Apple Market serves breakfast, lunch, and dinner
BARS	Aviator's Lounge serves a free hot buffet at happy hour
CLIENTELE	Corporate and vacation travelers, airline personnel
GUEST SERVICES	Fitness center, meeting rooms, business center, room service, gift shop, valet laundry, free shuttle to JFK and the Green Acres Mall (is that an oxymoron or what?)
PARKING	Yes, indoor and outdoor
CANCELLATION POLICY	Before 4 p.m. day of arrival
WHEELCHAIR ACCESS	14 rooms

In 1998, Radisson invested $23 million in this hotel's renovation, but it still looks and feels like a budget hotel. The lobby isn't elegant like the Sheraton JFK or even warm and welcoming. Radio rock music was blaring when we visited, and lobby furniture and carpets were shabby and well worn. A bar off the lobby serves a hot buffet at happy hour. If you need food at any hour, the restaurant will serve you at a table or in your room.

Guest rooms are both cleaner and more comfortable than the lobby. The double/double room we saw was huge and well equipped for business travelers with two phones, high-speed internet access, and a large work desk. The double with king-sized bed is smaller, but it, too, offers individual climate control, cable TV with pay-movies and Nintendo, a coffeemaker, iron, and a hair dryer. Mini-fridges are available for a fee. As expected, mattresses are firm, bathrooms well provisioned. Groups can book the corner, connecting suites.

This hotel offers room service from 6 a.m. till 11 p.m. Another of its outstanding features is a large, well-equipped fitness center with views of the airport through picture windows. For security reasons, the center is accessible only to guests. Other handy services include an ATM, a flight monitor, and business center with a fax, internet kiosk, copier, printer, and computer.

This is an acceptable lodging choice, but we won't pretend the location is serene. Anything on the Belt Parkway and a half-mile from incoming planes is bound to be noisy.

SLEEP CHEAP IN NEW YORK

RAMADA INN ADRIA

220-33 Northern Blvd.
Bayside, NY 11361
(BETWEEN 221 AND 222 STREETS)

VALUE ★ ★ ★
CLEANLINESS ★ ★ ★ ★
GUEST SERVICES ★ ★ ★ ★
SECURITY ★ ★ ★ ★
(★POOR - ★★★★★EXCELLENT)

CATEGORY	Full Services
PHONE	(718) 631-5900
	(800) 272-3742 Reservations
FAX	(718) 279-9080 ADRIA
	(718) 631-7501 RAMADA
EMAIL	None
WEBSITE	www.adriahotelny.com
RATES	$125-$149
	Ask about discounts
GUEST ROOMS	105 rooms on 4 floors, 70 percent are nonsmoking
ROOM AMENITIES	AC, cable TV, iron, hair dryer, phone with voice mail and dataport
RESTAURANTS	Marbella features Spanish cuisine
BARS	Yes, in the restaurant
CLIENTELE	Mix of families, corporate clients, and airline crews
GUEST SERVICES	Continental breakfast (Adria only), valet laundry, free use of nearby health club, conference center, coffee machine in lobby, room service 7 a.m.-midnight
PARKING	Yes
CANCELLATION POLICY	Before 4 p.m. day of arrival
WHEELCHAIR ACCESS	One room

Two separate, but adjoining, buildings offer a different set of services. The Ramada Inn has a restaurant, which serves breakfast, lunch, and dinner; the Adria serves a free, bountiful continental breakfast. But guest rooms at both facilities are standard-issue for chain hotels: dark blue carpets and floral spreads. Overall, clean but nothing fancy. Both sleeping areas and bathrooms are medium-sized. Sinks are outside the bathrooms at the Ramada Inn. The Adria's windows are double-paned, which cuts down on some of the traffic noise from busy Northern Boulevard.

Price-wise, you can do better than the limited comforts and services available here. But if you need to be in Bayside, this may be your best bet.

RAMADA PLAZA JFK AIRPORT

JFK Airport, Van Wyck Expressway
Jamaica, NY 11430
(AT N. CONDUIT AVE.)

VALUE ★ ★ ★

CLEANLINESS ★ ★ ★

GUEST SERVICES ★ ★ ★ ★ ★

SECURITY ★ ★ ★ ★ ★

(★POOR - ★★★★★EXCELLENT)

CATEGORY	Full Services
PHONE	(718) 995-9000
	(800) 272-6232 Reservations
FAX	(718) 995-9075
	(718) 244-8962 Reservations
EMAIL	reservations@ramadajfk.com
WEBSITE	www.ramadajfk.com
RATES	$129-$259
	Ask about discounts
GUEST ROOMS	478 rooms on 5 floors include 5 suites, some are nonsmoking
ROOM AMENITIES	AC, cable TV, coffeemaker, iron, hair dryer, phone with voice mail and dataport, some rooms with mini-fridge
RESTAURANTS	Leonardo's, the Millennium Café
BARS	Connections Lounge
CLIENTELE	A mix

GUEST SERVICES	Exercise room, meeting rooms, business center, gift shop, valet laundry, free shuttle to JFK, room service from 6:30 a.m.-10:30 p.m.
PARKING	Yes
CANCELLATION POLICY	Before 4 p.m. day of arrival
WHEELCHAIR ACCESS	6 rooms

Because this hotel is directly under the flight path of incoming planes, daytime noise can be deafening. According to the manager, the noise at night only bothers light sleepers. Unfortunately, the noise level inside can be deafening, too. A spacious lobby with salmon-colored marble floors and dusky pink walls leads into a small café, Leonardo's restaurant, Connections lounge, an entertainment area with video games and a pool table, then into the Grand Ballroom, and a separate entrance. Low ceilings tend to magnify the sound and don't do much for the hotel's aesthetics.

This is the oldest hotel in the area, but Ramada invested $1 million to upgrade guest rooms in 2000. They are acceptably clean, decorated in soft pastels, and average-sized. Ask for one with a mini-fridge at no extra cost. Bathrooms are small with a tub/shower combo, hair dryer, and toiletries. There are racks to hang your clothes on, no walk-in closets. Bedding choices include kings, queens, and double/doubles. Mattresses were too soft for our taste. Suites offer lots of stretching space: a large bedroom, living room, two TVs, two phones, and two marble bathrooms.

There's a convenient business center; a good-sized, secure exercise room; and huge meeting spaces, in case you're planning a conference. Most guests tend to gather on weekday evenings at Connections lounge during happy hour, where the hot buffet is free with the price of any alcoholic drink. For nondrinkers, the buffet costs $7.50.

This hotel's Park and Fly is worth considering if you need to park your car for up to 10 days. The $219 cost includes a one-night stay. Manhattan transit is available from the airport or you can hop on the Q10 bus outside the hotel and transfer to the E or F train. For $1.50, it's the cheapest way to go.

QUEENS

SHERATON JFK AIRPORT HOTEL

151-20 Baisley Blvd.
Jamaica, NY 11434
(AT N. CONDUIT AVE.)

VALUE ★ ★ ★ ★
CLEANLINESS ★ ★ ★
GUEST SERVICES ★ ★ ★ ★ ★
SECURITY ★ ★ ★ ★

(★POOR - ★★★★★EXCELLENT)

CATEGORY	Full Services
PHONE	(718) 489-1000
	(800) 325-3535 Reservations
FAX	(718) 489-1004
EMAIL	On the website
WEBSITE	www.sheraton.com
RATES	$150-$249
	Discounts for AARP and AAA members
GUEST ROOMS	184 rooms include 15 suites on 5 floors, 1 floor reserved for smokers
ROOM AMENITIES	AC, cable TV with pay movies and games, coffeemaker, iron, hair dryer, 3 phones per room with voice mail and dataport, *USA Today* (weekdays)
RESTAURANTS	The Birchwoods serves breakfast, lunch, and dinner
BARS	Fitzgerald's Lounge and Cigar Bar
CLIENTELE	Corporate and vacation travelers, airline personnel
GUEST SERVICES	Fitness center, meeting rooms, ATM, business services for a fee, gift shop, room service, express check-out, valet laundry, free shuttle to JFK
PARKING	Yes
CANCELLATION POLICY	Before 6 p.m. day of arrival
WHEELCHAIR ACCESS	8 rooms

Remodeled in 1999 by Starwood Resorts, this European-style hotel has an invitingly upscale lobby. You can lounge on leather couches surrounded by carefully chosen antiques, floral bouquets, glass chandeliers, and a grand piano. Warm tones of cream, pink, and black marble intermingle on floors and banquettes as sunlight streams through broad windows. The bellman is eager to dispense with your bags, front desk staff eager to greet you. When we visited we weren't stampeded by tour groups, as in other chain hotels; we were aware of pleased customers getting first-class service.

Hallways are also brightly lit and colorfully decorated. Guest rooms, though fully equipped, aren't nearly as impressive as the public areas. The single room we inspected showed signs of cheap renovation and décor chosen for economy rather than style. Singles, doubles, and suites are all roomy with large bathrooms and walk-in closets. Water pressure is strong, mattresses firm, and the working desk and three phones with dataports are designed to assist business travelers. The Junior Suite sleeps up to four in two rooms and offers a huge, cream-tiled bathroom with two sinks and a good-sized closet. At $189, it's a deal.

A grand staircase from lobby level leads to meeting rooms, Fitzgerald's Lounge, the Birchwoods restaurant, an outside patio and a tiny, unlocked fitness center, which is more for show than use. After the Best Western Carlton House, we found this to be the most appealing of all JFK Airport lodging choices.

STATEN ISLAND

Some people think the best thing about Staten Island is the free ferry ride. But there's plenty to see and do when the ferry docks at St. George Station in what may be New York's least-known borough. Did you know, for example, that Staten Island has the world's largest landfill? It may not be high on your list, but the Snug Harbor Cultural Center, an arts complex of 28 buildings spread across 80 acres, should be. It includes a maritime museum, art lab, music hall, botanical garden, art gallery, and children's museum. Want another surprise? Then visit the Jacques Marchais Museum of Tibetan Art housed in a Buddhist temple on Lighthouse Hill. You'll also get a great view of the Staten Island Lighthouse high on the hill.

The Greenbelt is a group of six contiguous parks and nature preserves that encompasses 2,800 acres in the center of the island. There are public beaches that stretch along its eastern shore. Finally, before you reboard the ferry don't miss the chance to discover the work of pioneering photographer Alice Austen in her cottage "Clear Comfort" on lush grounds that face the water, the Verrazano Bridge, and Brooklyn.

SLEEP CHEAP IN NEW YORK

HARBOR HOUSE INN BED AND BREAKFAST

1 Hylan Blvd.
Staten Island, NY 10305
(AT EDGEWATER ST.)

VALUE ★ ★ ★ ★
CLEANLINESS ★ ★ ★ ★
GUEST SERVICES ★
SECURITY ★ ★ ★ ★

(★POOR - ★★★★★EXCELLENT)

CATEGORY	Bed & Breakfast
PHONE	(718) 876-0056 (800) 626-8096
FAX	(718) 983-7768
EMAIL	skyline@erols.com
WEBSITE	www.nyharborhouse.com
RATES	$69-$150
GUEST ROOMS	11 rooms, 3 suites, all nonsmoking, 5 with private baths
ROOM AMENITIES	AC, TV; hair dryer and iron available
RESTAURANTS	None
BARS	None
CLIENTELE	Mostly Europeans
GUEST SERVICES	Continental breakfast
PARKING	Streetside
CANCELLATION POLICY	50 percent deposit returned 10 days before arrival, minus a $20 fee
WHEELCHAIR ACCESS	None

Of the few lodging choices in Staten Island, this B&B has the advantage of a waterfront setting and a charming host, Mervyn Rampaul. You can relax in a rocker on the porch and watch container ships pass by on The Narrows, and even spot the QE2 sailing into port. Though this Victorian B&B was built in 1890, it has the look and laid-back feeling of a beach house.

Rooms are spacious, each with a unique name and décor, and offer either a queen or full-sized bed. The largest, most expensive is the Staten Suite with a king-sized bed, two fireplaces, a Victorian tub, and kitchen. On the second floor, the Verrazano Suite boasts views of the New York skyline, Statue of Liberty, and the Verrazano Bridge. It can sleep up to four comfortably. Some rooms feature canopy beds, some private baths. Shared bathrooms have a tub/shower and shampoo. Ask for a hair dryer and iron if you need one. Young children are welcomed, pets are not.

The Harbor House Inn is 5 minutes by taxi or the S51 bus from the Staten Island ferry terminal. Take time to visit the Alice Austen Museum and Park next door. It showcases the works of that early photographer in her 18th-century cottage. If you want a comfortable berth at affordable rates that's easily accessible to Manhattan, this is a good choice.

Harbor House guests enjoy views of the water and New York skyline. Credit: Harbor House Inn Bed & Breakfast

STANBROOK I

396 Van Duzer St.
Staten Island, NY 10306
(BETWEEN BEACH AND WRIGHT STREETS)

VALUE ★ ★ ★ ★
CLEANLINESS ★ ★ ★ ★
GUEST SERVICES ★
SECURITY ★ ★ ★ ★

(★POOR - ★★★★★EXCELLENT)

CATEGORY	Bed and Breakfast
PHONE	(718) 273-7365 (888) 727-8585
FAX	(718) 390-0710
EMAIL	ke396@aol.com
WEBSITE	www.nycbnb.com
RATES	Private bath: $75; shared-bath: $65
GUEST ROOMS	4 rooms with private bath, 4 rooms with shared bath, all nonsmoking
ROOM AMENITIES	AC and ceiling fans; hair dryer and iron available
RESTAURANTS	No
BARS	No
CLIENTELE	Mostly Europeans and Canadians
GUEST SERVICES	Full breakfast, valet laundry
PARKING	Yes
CANCELLATION POLICY	$75 nonrefundable security deposit
WHEELCHAIR ACCESS	None

Karen Stanbrook inherited her hospitality genes from her father, who has hosted guests at his B&Bs in England and Spain for 30 years. Her two inns are within a half-mile of each other at the northeastern tip of Staten Island, near the Ferry Terminal. This 1899 Victorian manor has an imposing red brick façade, but its interior space is modestly furnished with a mix of period antiques and reproductions, all of which are for sale. There is a spacious drawing room and opposite it a dining room, where manager Handom Khamis serves breakfast from 8 a.m. to 10 a.m.

Guest rooms aren't aesthetically impressive, but they are priced right for budget travelers. Some offer king-sized beds, some full-sized, and there are no phones or TVs. Bathrooms are pretty primitive and some have only a stall shower. Both properties are pet-friendly, so fair warning if you suffer from allergies.

STANBROOK II

126 Vanderbilt Ave.
Staten Island, NY 10304
(BETWEEN TOMPKINS AND TALBOT STREETS)

VALUE ★ ★ ★ ★

CLEANLINESS ★ ★ ★ ★

GUEST SERVICES ★ ★

SECURITY ★ ★ ★ ★

(★POOR - ★★★★★EXCELLENT)

CATEGORY	Bed and Breakfast
PHONE	(718) 556-5535
	(888) 727-8585
FAX	(718) 556-4775
EMAIL	ke396@aol.com
WEBSITE	www.nycbnb.com
RATES	$65
GUEST ROOMS	4 nonsmoking rooms, all share bathrooms
ROOM AMENITIES	AC, ceiling fans, TV
RESTAURANTS	No
BARS	No
CLIENTELE	Mostly Europeans and Canadians
GUEST SERVICES	Will pick up guests at the airport for a fee; free local calls, use of backyard
PARKING	Yes
CANCELLATION POLICY	$65 nonrefundable security deposit
WHEELCHAIR ACCESS	No

Vanderbilt Avenue is named for railroad tycoon and native son Cornelius, who built this white-and-green Gothic Tudor house in 1899 for his guests. We can assume his furnishings were a bit more lavish than the modern décor that graces the present public areas. Large, Victorian-style guest rooms feature four-poster beds, lace curtains, statuary, mahogany furniture, and oriental rugs. Roomy bathrooms feature a tub and shower but no amenities. Guests can use the house phone and local calls are free. There's a TV in the living room as well as in guest rooms. A resident manager serves breakfast in a small room off the kitchen, and guests are welcome to use the backyard for relaxing or sunbathing in warm weather.

This is a quiet, residential neighborhood with a bus and subway one block away. A taxi ride to the ferry to Manhattan takes less than five minutes.

STATEN ISLAND HOTEL

1415 Richmond Ave.
Staten Island, NY 10314
(OFF I-278 EXPRESSWAY)

VALUE ★ ★ ★

CLEANLINESS ★ ★ ★ ★ ★

GUEST SERVICES ★ ★ ★ ★

SECURITY ★ ★ ★ ★

(★POOR - ★★★★★EXCELLENT)

CATEGORY	Full Services
PHONE	(718) 698-5000
	(800) 532-3532 Reservations
FAX	(718) 354-7071
EMAIL	On the website
WEBSITE	www.statenislandhotel.com
RATES	$134-$159
	Ask about discounts
GUEST ROOMS	187 rooms on 9 floors, 2 suites, some nonsmoking
ROOM AMENITIES	AC, cable TV with pay movies and games, 2-line phones with voice mail and dataport, coffeemaker, hair dryer, iron and ironing board, *USA Today*

RESTAURANTS	Stanley's Place serves all day
BARS	Yes
CLIENTELE	Group business is about 40 percent: meetings, weddings, reunions
GUEST SERVICES	Room service 7 a.m.-10 p.m., banquet and meeting rooms, valet laundry, free pass to Bally's Fitness Club, internet kiosk and business services for a fee
PARKING	Yes
CANCELLATION POLICY	Before 6 p.m. day of arrival
WHEELCHAIR ACCESS	2 rooms

As a Holiday Inn, this property went to seed. But new owners are proud of its refreshed look and reinvigorated clientele. The hotel is not a good choice for tourists who want quick access to the ferry and a scenic location. It is a good choice, however, for parents of students at Staten Island's three colleges—St. Johns, Wagner, and the College of Staten Island—as well as motorists seeking a layover off the I-278 expressway.

A clean, unremarkable lobby leads to Stanley's Place, a full-service restaurant named for the effusive general manager Stanley Friedman. On Friday and Saturday nights a DJ entertains in the lounge.

Doubles are spacious and spotless with a large desk (handy for business travelers), a 2-line phone with voice mail and dataport, climate control, and all manner of amenities, including *USA Today* delivery. Roomy bathrooms are well-stocked. Some rooms feature balconies with views of the Staten Island Expressway.

In sum, this hotel provides acceptable lodging, especially to business travelers. The Hilton Garden Inn, opened in November 2001, may give it stiff competition.

SLEEP CHEAP IN NEW YORK

B&B AND APARTMENT AGENCIES

...AAAH! BED & BREAKFAST AND APARTMENT REGISTRY P.O. Box 2093, NY, NY 10108. (212) 246-4000, fax: (212) 765-4229, www.nybnb.com, email: info@nybnb.com. Manager Will Salisbury can find you a hosted B&B or unhosted apartment in Manhattan. B&Bs start at $80 for a single, $100 for a double, which includes 8.25 percent sales tax and breakfast. Apartments start at $125 for a studio, $160 for a one-bedroom, $300 for a two-bedroom. Two-night minimum for apartment stays.

ABODE P.O. Box 20022, NY, NY 10021. (212) 472-2000 or (800) 835-8880, www.abodenyc.com. Furnished, unhosted apartments begin at $135 for a studio. Apartments are required to meet certain standards of cleanliness, attractiveness, and hospitality. The price drops the longer you book, and there's a minimum four-night stay.

AFFORDABLE NEW YORK CITY 21 E. 10th St., Apt. WPH, NY, NY 10003. (212) 533-4001, fax: (212) 387-8732, email:information@affordablenewyorkcity.com. Owner Susan Freschel represents more than 120 lodgings in Manhattan and requires a three-night minimum stay. B&Bs with shared baths run $85-$120, with private bath $100-$145, depending on location and amenities. Studio apartments start at $140, one-bedrooms at $165.

ALL AROUND THE TOWN 150 Fifth Ave., Suite 837, NY, NY 10011. (212) 675-5600, fax: (212) 675-6366, email: aroundtown@worldnet.att.net. Furnished, unhosted apartments begin at $130 for a studio, $150 for a one-bedroom. Three-night minimum stay.

ANCO STUDIOS 1202 Lexington Ave., NY, NY 10028. (212) 717-7500, fax: (212) 472-6827, email: bbnycusa@aol.com. Furnished, unhosted apartments on the Upper East Side start at $125.

AT HOME IN NEW YORK P.O. Box 407, NY, NY 10185. (212) 956-3125 or (800) 692-4262, fax: (212) 247-3294, email: athomeny@erols.com. Unhosted studio apartments start at $125, B&Bs start at $75 for one person, $90 for two. Most accommodations are in Manhattan, but a few are outside. There is a two-night minimum stay.

BED & BREAKFAST (& BOOKS) 35 W. 92nd St., Apt. 2C, NY, NY 10025. Phone and fax: (212) 865-8740, email: bedbreakfastbook@aol.com. B&Bs start at $100. Unhosted studio apartments start at $120, one-bedrooms at $160, and two-bedrooms at $200. Two- to three-night minimum stay.

BED-AND-BREAKFAST IN MANHATTAN P.O. Box 533, NY, NY 10150. (212) 472-2528, fax: (212) 988-9818. B&Bs start at $90, unhosted apartments at $130.

BED-AND-BREAKFAST NETWORK OF NEW YORK 130 Barrow St., Suite 508, NY, NY 10014. (212) 645-8134 or (800) 900-8134. Leslie Goldberg offers both B&Bs and unhosted apartments in and around Manhattan. B&Bs for one person start at $80, two persons at $110. Unhosted apartments start at $130. Cash only. 25 percent deposit. Two-night minimum stay.

CITY LIGHTS BED AND BREAKFAST P.O. Box 20355, Cherokee Station, NY, NY 10021. (212) 737-7049, fax: (212) 535-2755, email: reservations@citylightsbandb.com. Yedida Nielsen can match you with the ideal B&B or short-term apartment from among 400 properties in Manhattan and Brooklyn. B&Bs start at $85, unhosted apartments at $135. 25 percent deposit. Two-night minimum stay.

CITY SONNET Village Station, P.O. Box 347, NY, NY 10014-0347. (212) 614 3034, fax; (425) 920-2384, email: mail@citysonnet.com, www.citysonnet.com. B&Bs start at $90, unhosted studio apartments at $130, and larger apartments at $175. Most accommodations are in downtown Manhattan.

A HOSPITALITY COMPANY 247 W. 35th St., New York, NY 10001. (212) 965-1102, fax: (212) 965-1149, www.hospitalitycompany.com, email: info@hospice.com. Unhosted studio apartments begin at $99, one-bedrooms at $125, and two-bedrooms at $175. They are available nightly, weekly, and monthly. The nightly rate includes continental breakfast.

NEW WORLD See All Around the Town.

URBAN VENTURES 38 W. 32nd. St., Suite 1412, NY, NY 10001. (212) 594-5650, fax: (212) 947-9320, www.nyurbanventures.com, email: jennifer@urbanventures.com. Mary McAuley started this service in 1979, making her a pioneer in opening the city's apartments to out-of-towners. B&Bs start at $70 for one person, $80 for two. Studio apartments start at $100, one-bedrooms at $125, two-bedrooms at $220. Two-night minimum stay.

HOTEL RESERVATION SERVICES

These services usually work as consolidators, buying a block of rooms at a discount and selling them to customers at a profit. You can often get 20 percent to 30 percent off the rate the hotel will quote you for the same day. But never rely on just one reservation service; check around to see which offers the best rate. Also, check with the hotel's reservations desk to see what rates they are quoting and its website to see if they are offering any "internet-only" specials. Only then will you know how much you are truly saving.

CENTRAL RESERVATION SERVICE
(www.reservation-services.com, 800-555-7555) has a limited selection of New York hotels with limited descriptions, some of which are outdated. Its star rating system isn't explained, but it does offer photos of hotels, maps, and directions.

CITYSEARCH
(www.newyork.citysearch.com, 212-647-5700) is owned by the Ticketmaster ticketing service and has access to over 100 New York hotels. This attractive site is easy to use and allows you to select hotels by neighborhood or price. You can also read and submit customer reviews. Provides a link to a hotel's website and gives maps and directions.

EXPEDIA
(www.expedia.com, 800-397-3342) offers detailed information on hotels, although that information is provided by the hotels. Its star ratings are based on type of lodging, not on site inspections nor on customer feedback. You can't select hotels by price, which limits search efficiency. Offers photos and maps.

HOTEL RESERVATIONS NETWORK
(www.hoteldiscount.com, 800-715-7666) allows you to select from over 160 hotels by name, price, or rating, but its star rating system is based on type of lodging (ie., economy, first-class, etc.) not on a hotel inspection nor on customer feedback. Photos, maps, free newsletter.

PRICELINE.COM
(www.priceline.com, 866-925-5373) allows you to name your own rate for a room at over 6,000 hotels in 1,500 North American cities. Bidders are promised a "yes" or "no" within 15 minutes.

QUIKBOOK
(www.quikbook.com, 800-789-9887 or 212-779-7666) has its own Q rating system and a very user-friendly site. It features detailed hotel profiles, customer feedback ("What Our Customers Say..."), photos, seasonal promotions, and maps. An excellent resource with none of those annoying ads.

RMC TRAVEL
(www.travelnow.com, 800-782-7666) does not allow you to limit your search by price or neighborhood. Its star ratings are based on type of lodging, not evaluations. Descriptions are hotel-provided and it includes New Jersey properties as "New York hotels."

TRAVELSCAPE
(www.travelscape.com, 888-335-0101) guarantees the lowest room rate available at the time of booking or it will refund the difference. Generally, its rates are very competitive, but you can't select by price or neighborhood. Hotel descriptions are hotel-provided, and there's no rating system. It offers air/hotel packages, a newsletter, seasonal promotions, and excellent maps.

INDEXES

ALPHABETICAL INDEX

Airway Motor Inn at La Guardia	267
Akwaaba Mansion Bed and Breakfast	258
Aladdin Hotel	110
American Dream Hostel (1)	48
American Dream Hostel (2)	92
Americana Inn	111
Ameritania Hotel	112
Amsterdam Court Hotel	115
Amsterdam Inn	190
Arlington Hotel	68
Astor on the Park	191
Baisley House	259
Bed and Breakfast on the Park	261
Belvedere Hotel	117
Bentley	228
Best Western Ambassador	119
Best Western Carlton House JFK Airport	268
Best Western City View Inn	270
Best Western Eden Park Hotel	272
Best Western Manhattan	121
Best Western President	123
Best Western Woodward	125
Big Apple Hostel	127
Broadway Inn	128
Carlton Arms Hotel	49
Central Park Hostel	193
Chelsea Brownstone	69
Chelsea Inn	71
Chelsea International Hostel	72
Chelsea Pines Inn	74
Chelsea Savoy Hotel	76
Chelsea Star Hotel	78
Clarion Hotel Park Avenue	93
Colonial House Inn	80
Columbia University Housing Teacher's College	234
Comfort Inn at Central Park West	195
Comfort Inn Manhattan	130
Comfort Inn Midtown	132
Cosmopolitan Hotel-Tribeca	14
Country Inn the City	197
Days Hotel	134
De Hirsch Residence at the 92nd Street YM-YWHA	230
East Village Bed & Coffee	26
Edison Hotel	135
Ellington	236

INDEXES

Flushing YMCA	273
414 Inn	138
Gershwin Hotel	51
Gershwin 97 Hotel	200
Grand Union Hotel	95
Habitat Hotel	182
Hampshire Hotel and Suites	139
Harbor House Inn Bed and Breakfast	288
Herald Square Hotel	141
Hostelling International-New York	201
Hotel 17	54
Hotel 31	97
Hotel Belleclaire	203
Hotel Broadway Plaza	82
Hotel Deauville	96
Hotel Metro	143
Hotel Newton	205
Hotel Olcott	207
Hotel Pennsylvania	145
Hotel Stanford	147
Hotel Wolcott	148
Howard Johnson Plaza Hotel	150
Incentra Village House	35
International House	238
Jazz on the Park Hostel	208
La Guardia Courtyard by Marriott	275
La Guardia Marriott	276
La Semana Hotel	84
Landmark Union Theological Seminary	240
Larchmont Hotel	37
Le Refuge Inn Bed and Breakfast	255
Leo House	85
Madison Hotel	55
Malibu Hotel	210
Manhattan Inn	87
Manhattan Seaport Suites	15
Manhattan Youth Castle	244
Marcel	56
Markle Evangeline Residence	39
Mayfair New York	152
Menno House	59
Milburn Hotel	213
Milford Plaza	153
Moderne	155
Murray Hill Inn	99
New York Inn	157
New York Marriott Brooklyn	263
New York University Summer Housing	28

New Yorker-Ramada Plaza	158
Off SoHo Suites	17
On the Ave Hotel	214
Pan American Hotel	278
Park Savoy	161
Park View Hotel	245
Parkside Evangeline Residence	60
Penington Friends House	62
Pickwick Arms Hotel	183
Pioneer Hotel	19
Portland Square	162
Quality Hotel and Suites Midtown	164
Quality Hotel East Side	100
Quality Hotel on Broadway	217
Radio City Apartments	166
Radisson Hotel JFK Airport	280
Ramada Inn Adria	282
Ramada Plaza JFK Airport	283
Red Roof Inn	167
Riverside Terrace	218
Riverside Tower Hotel	220
Rooms to Let B & B	40
Seafarers and International House	64
Second Home on Second Avenue	32
Senton Hotel	88
Sheraton JFK Airport Hotel	285
Skyline Hotel	169
Sleeping Deal	172
SoHo Bed & Breakfast	21
Soldiers', Sailors', Marines', and Airmen's Club	102
St. Mark's Hotel	30
Stanbrook I	290
Stanbrook II	291
Staten Island Hotel	292
Sugar Hill International House	247
Ten Eyck-Troughton Residence for Business Women	104
ThirtyThirty	106
Travel Inn	173
Union Square Inn	33
Urban Jem Guest House	249
Vanderbilt YMCA	186
Washington Square Hotel	42
Washington-Jefferson Hotel	175
West End Studios	221
West Side Inn	223
West Side YMCA	224
Westpark Hotel	176
Wyndham	178

INDEXES

INDEX BY TYPE OF LODGING AND VALUE RATING

Lodging categories are defined in the Introduction. Value ratings are based on (1) room prices, (2) guest services, (3) cleanliness and appearance, (4) in-room amenities, and (5) security, after two visits to each property.
(★ poor - ★★★★★ excellent)

FULL SERVICES HOTELS

BEST WESTERN CARLTON HOUSE JFK AIRPORT ★★★★★	268
LA GUARDIA MARRIOTT ★★★★★ (WEEKENDS ONLY)	276
MILFORD PLAZA ★★★★	153
NEW YORK MARRIOTT BROOKLYN ★★★★★ (WEEKENDS ONLY)	263
NEW YORKER-RAMADA PLAZA ★★★★★	158
PAN AMERICAN HOTEL ★★★★	278
RADISSON HOTEL JFK AIRPORT ★★★★	280
RAMADA INN ADRIA ★★★	282
RAMADA PLAZA JFK AIRPORT ★★★★	283
SHERATON JFK AIRPORT HOTEL ★★★★	285
SKYLINE HOTEL ★★★★★	169
STATEN ISLAND HOTEL ★★★	292
TRAVEL INN ★★★★	173

LIMITED SERVICES HOTELS

BELVEDERE HOTEL ★★★★★	117
BEST WESTERN AMBASSADOR ★★★	119
BEST WESTERN CITY VIEW INN ★★★★	270
BEST WESTERN EDEN PARK HOTEL ★★★★	272
BEST WESTERN MANHATTAN ★★★★	121
BEST WESTERN PRESIDENT ★★★★★	123
BEST WESTERN WOODWARD ★★★	125

SLEEP CHEAP IN NEW YORK

CHELSEA SAVOY HOTEL ★★★★	76
CLARION HOTEL PARK AVENUE ★★★★★	93
COMFORT INN AT CENTRAL PARK WEST ★★★★	195
COMFORT INN MANHATTAN ★★★	130
COMFORT INN MIDTOWN ★★★★★	132
COSMOPOLITAN HOTEL-TRIBECA ★★★★	14
DAYS HOTEL ★★★★	134
EDISON HOTEL ★★★★	135
GRAND UNION HOTEL ★★★★★	95
HOTEL BELLECLAIRE ★★★★	203
HOTEL NEWTON ★★★★	205
HOTEL OLCOTT ★★★★	207
HOTEL PENNSYLVANIA ★★★★	145
HOTEL STANFORD ★★★★	147
HOTEL WOLCOTT ★★★★★	148
HOWARD JOHNSON PLAZA HOTEL ★★★★	150
LA GUARDIA COURTYARD BY MARRIOTT ★★★★★ (WEEKENDS ONLY)	275
MANHATTAN SEAPORT SUITES ★★★★ (WEEKENDS ONLY)	15
MILBURN HOTEL ★★★★★	213
QUALITY HOTEL AND SUITES MIDTOWN ★★★★	164
QUALITY HOTEL EAST SIDE ★★★★★	100
QUALITY HOTEL ON BROADWAY ★★★★	217
RADIO CITY APARTMENTS ★★★★	166
RED ROOF INN ★★★★★	167
THIRTYTHIRTY ★★★★	106
WASHINGTON SQUARE HOTEL ★★★★	42
WASHINGTON-JEFFERSON HOTEL ★★★	175

WESTPARK HOTEL ★★★★ — 176

WYNDHAM ★★★★★ — 178

MOTELS

AIRWAY MOTOR INN AT LA GUARDIA ★★★ — 267

EURO-STYLE HOTELS

CHELSEA INN ★★★ — 71

CHELSEA STAR HOTEL ★★★★ — 78

414 INN ★★★★ — 138

GERSHWIN 97 HOTEL ★★★★ — 200

HABITAT HOTEL ★★★★ — 182

HOTEL 17 ★★★★ — 54

HOTEL 31 ★★★★ — 97

HOTEL DEAUVILLE ★★★ — 96

LA SEMANA HOTEL ★★★ — 84

LARCHMONT HOTEL ★★★★★ — 37

MURRAY HILL INN ★★★★ — 99

OFF SOHO SUITES ★★★ — 17

PARK SAVOY ★★★ — 161

PICKWICK ARMS HOTEL ★★★★★ — 183

SLEEPING DEAL ★★★ — 172

UNION SQUARE INN ★★★ — 33

WEST END STUDIOS ★★★★ — 221

BOUTIQUE HOTELS

AMERITANIA HOTEL ★★★★ — 112

AMSTERDAM COURT HOTEL ★★★★ — 115

ASTOR ON THE PARK ★★★★ — 191

BENTLEY ★★★★★ — 228

ELLINGTON ★★★★	236
GERSHWIN HOTEL ★★★★	51
HAMPSHIRE HOTEL AND SUITES ★★★★★	139
HOTEL BROADWAY PLAZA ★★★★	82
HOTEL METRO ★★★★★	143
MARCEL ★★★★★	56
MAYFAIR NEW YORK ★★★★★	152
MODERNE ★★★★	155
ON THE AVE HOTEL ★★★★	214

BED AND BREAKFAST INNS

AKWAABA MANSION BED AND BREAKFAST ★★★★★	258
BAISLEY HOUSE ★★★★	259
BED AND BREAKFAST ON THE PARK ★★★★	261
BROADWAY INN ★★★★★	128
CHELSEA PINES INN ★★★★	74
COLONIAL HOUSE INN ★★★★	80
HARBOR HOUSE INN BED AND BREAKFAST ★★★★	288
LE REFUGE INN BED AND BREAKFAST ★★★★★	255
ROOMS TO LET B&B ★★★	40
SOHO BED AND BREAKFAST ★★★★★	21
STANBROOK I ★★★★	290
STANBROOK II ★★★★	291
URBAN JEM GUEST HOUSE ★★★★★	249

GUEST HOUSES

CHELSEA BROWNSTONE ★★★★	69
COUNTRY INN THE CITY ★★★★	197
EAST VILLAGE BED & COFFEE ★★★★	26

INCENTRA VILLAGE HOUSE ★★★★ — 35

LEO HOUSE ★★★★★ — 85

SECOND HOME ON SECOND AVENUE ★★★★ — 32

BARE ESSENTIALS

AMERICANA INN ★★★ — 111

AMSTERDAM INN ★★★ — 190

ARLINGTON HOTEL ★★★ — 68

CARLTON ARMS HOTEL ★★★ — 49

HERALD SQUARE HOTEL ★★★ — 141

MADISON HOTEL ★★ — 55

MALIBU HOTEL ★★★ — 210

MANHATTAN INN ★★★★ — 87

NEW YORK INN ★★ — 157

PIONEER HOTEL ★★★ — 19

PORTLAND SQUARE ★★ — 162

RIVERSIDE TOWER HOTEL ★★ — 220

SENTON HOTEL ★ — 88

SOLDIERS', SAILORS', MARINES', AND AIRMEN'S CLUB ★★★★ — 102

ST. MARK'S HOTEL ★★★ — 30

WEST SIDE INN ★★★ — 223

HOSTELS

ALADDIN HOTEL ★★ — 110

AMERICAN DREAM HOSTEL (1) ★★★ — 48

AMERICAN DREAM HOSTEL (2) ★★★★ — 92

BIG APPLE HOSTEL ★★★ — 127

CENTRAL PARK HOSTEL ★★★★ — 193

CHELSEA INTERNATIONAL HOSTEL ★★★★ — 72

HOSTELLING INTERNATIONAL-NEW YORK ★★★★	201
JAZZ ON THE PARK HOSTEL ★★★★★	208
MANHATTAN YOUTH CASTLE ★★	244
PARK VIEW HOTEL ★★★	245
SUGAR HILL INTERNATIONAL HOUSE ★★	247

RESIDENCES

DE HIRSCH RESIDENCE AT THE 92ND STREET YM-YWHA ★★★★	230
MARKLE EVANGELINE RESIDENCE ★★★★★	39
MENNO HOUSE ★★★★	59
PARKSIDE EVANGELINE RESIDENCE ★★★★★	60
PENINGTON FRIENDS HOUSE ★★★★	62
RIVERSIDE TERRACE ★★★	218
TEN EYCK-TROUGHTON RESIDENCE FOR BUSINESS WOMEN ★★★★★	104

UNIVERSITY HOUSING

COLUMBIA UNIVERSITY HOUSING, TEACHER'S COLLEGE ★★★★	234
INTERNATIONAL HOUSE ★★★★★	238
LANDMARK UNION THEOLOGICAL SEMINARY ★★★	240
NEW YORK UNIVERSITY SUMMER HOUSING ★★★★	28

YMCA

FLUSHING YMCA ★★★★	273
VANDERBILT YMCA ★★★★	186
WEST SIDE YMCA ★★★★	224

INDEXES